DIETER HASSENPFLUG
THE URBAN CODE OF CHINA

Birkhäuser
Basel

市

ACKNOWLEDGEMENTS

— This book, first published in the German language in 2008, is the result of seven years of research from 2002 to 2008, conducted during visits to China and invitations to various universities across the country. These travels led me to many big cities, most of all in the east and north of the country; to Beijing, Shanghai, Harbin, Changchun, Jilin, Shenyang, Dalian, Qingdao, Zengzhou, Xi'an, Ningbo, Changsha, Shenzhen, Hong Kong, Macao, Zhongshan, Guangzhou, and many more. The most important destinations were, however, the guest professorships of six weeks per year within a total of four years at the School of Architecture and Urban Planning at the Harbin Institute of Technology (HIT) as well as one month in 2005 and another seven months in 2007 at the College of Architecture and Urban Planning (CAUP) at Tongji University, Shanghai. I share a particular bond with Tongji University as a result of the creation of the twin diploma study program 'Integrated International Urban Studies' (IIUS) for the Institute of European Urban Studies, which I co-founded at the Bauhaus University Weimar. The creation of this study program resulted in further projects, research endeavors, and conferences as well as numerous related visits to Shanghai.

— First, I would like to thank the German Academic Exchange Service (DAAD) and the German Research Foundation (DFG). Their financial support made travel and numerous visits for lectureships, lecture series, and coordination visits possible, for projects and programs such as IIUS or the International Doctorate Study Program 'European Urban Studies' (IPP-EU). I would like to extend my gratitude to Birkhäuser Publishers for their commitment to publish this book in English following its initial German publication. My appreciation also goes to the Goethe Institute in Munich and the Main Research Area 'Urban Systems' at University Duisburg-Essen, and in particular to their chairpersons Jens Gurr and Alexander Schmidt for their generous funding for this translation. My cordial thanks also go to Mark Kammerbauer for his translation, which in my view fully meets the quality of the German original, in both terminology and style. Thanks also to Julia Dawson for proof reading.

— My sincere appreciation goes to my former students Lu Xin and Liu Chong, who mark the beginning of my China experience. They convinced me to visit their home country and thus established friendships that endure to this day. I would like to extend my gratitude to my colleague Zhang Lingling at HIT (today the Dean of the Architecture Faculty at Shenyang Jianzhu University) for a continuing, trusting cooperation which enabled me to make numerous exciting trips to the interior of the country and provided me with deep insight into the country's society and culture; and also the many friends and colleagues in Harbin whose heartfelt hospitality turned me into a real "Sinophile". My colleagues Wei Chunyu and Liu Su from the honorable Wuhan University in Changsha contributed to this by providing me with valuable understanding of Chinese urban history. I should include the former Dean of CAUP, Wu Zhiqiang (Siegfried), for many years of constructive cooperation in the field of developing study programs as well as research and planning projects. This led me to many Chinese provinces and cities, giving me the opportunity to gain closer knowledge of planning practice in China. Numerous colleagues at CAUP should be included here as well, Jongjie Cai, Zhang Guanzeng, Li Zhenyu, Tong Ming, Li Jingsheng, and others who furthered my knowledge of Chinese cities with dedicated collegiality.

— Thanks also to my former doctorate student Ma Hang from HIT-Shenzhen; her project of a 'gentle restructuring' of 'villages' in Shenzhen offers urban planning an innovative solution beyond demolition and informal continuation. Cordial thanks for enriching my experience of the Chinese capital city also to Che Fei from Beijing, architect, artist, and curator of the Architecture Biennale in Beijing. I should mention many individuals, colleagues, officials of planning authorities, students, and doctorate students from all across China here as well; however, this would go beyond the limits of these acknowledgements.

— The original German edition has received much attention from professionals but also through general public interest in China's urban development, and has attracted overwhelmingly positive praise. In particular, reviews have been published in the topical publication *disp* of the ETH Zurich, the architecture journals *Bauwelt* and *Architectural Review,* the daily newspapers *Frankfurter Allgemeine Zeitung* (FAZ), *Neue Zürcher Zeitung* (NZZ), *Süddeutsche Zeitung* (SZ), *Die Welt*, and *tageszeitung* (taz), and in the online-magazine of the German-Chinese Culture Network. *Frankfurter Rundschau* (FR) and the economy platform *AsiaBridge* requested original excerpts as contributions. Further, I would like to extend my special appreciation to Thomas Sieverts, Klaus Kunzmann, Robert Kaltenbrunner, Layla Dawson, and Sabine Kühnast for their enthusiastic reactions to the book.

— I would also like to thank Peter Neitzke and Birkhäuser Verlag once more for the constructive cooperation in editing and publishing the German manuscript, basis for this translation, in the renowned series 'Bauwelt Fundamente'. Numerous classics of urbanism by authors such as Le Corbusier, Jane Jacobs, Kevin Lynch, Robert Venturi, and Thomas Sieverts were published here. I am indebted, wholeheartedly, to my long-time partner in life, Gabriele Jahnke, who shaped my perceptions, thoughts, and writings in a lasting way that influences this book as well. My deep gratitude finally goes out to my wife Chen Fang and her parents Sun Zhi Fen and Chen Yong Kang, who have supported me with their love and encouragement in every phase of working on this book.

INTRODUCTION

— When you look at China, you see a world power in ascendance. Here, everything is important; for instance, the production of urban space, its 'language', its 'grammar', and its 'syntax'. The most significant aspect of China's contemporary spatial urban development is the speed and depth with which the old, poor, backward China is quite literally demolished, discarded, and replaced by a new, glittering China. In this forward-looking China, taking shape before our eyes in time-lapse speed, a nation's aspirations are reflected; a nation that is rediscovering itself and rising anew to former greatness after almost two centuries of revolutions, trials, and tribulations.

— What influences this newness? Is it the import of ideas and concepts, of copies or imitations – in the absence of homegrown concepts? Or are we dealing with something specific, something authentically Chinese? Does the new include the old as well, without which, according to Ernst Bloch's maxim, something really new actually can't develop?

— The opening of China, initiated roughly thirty-two years ago by legendary reformer Deng Xiao Ping, exposes the former 'middle kingdom' to a tremendous, limitless flood of influences from within, from China's own history, in part to be discovered and interpreted anew, but also from the outside. Through the nearly uncontrollable portals of the Internet, through the open window of television and film, and in tow of goods and services flooding the country through international trade, an influx of foreign ideas, symbols, images, styles, concepts, techniques and customs takes place. Originating most of all in the USA, in the past the destination of many immigrants of Chinese origin whose descendents are today a part of American society, in Europe, and also in developed Asian neighbors farther towards the east, influences seep into the metropolises of the eastern coastal region, the north, and by now, the western Hinterland as well.

— The global sphere of communications also influences the use of language. Today, the signs and signage systems in the 'public space' of China's cities can't be imagined without English words and sentences, in contrast to comparatively introverted Germany. Be it public notice, street sign, or signage for direction or advertisement, foreign guests can generally rely on an English translation.

— The USA provides Windows, Google, iPod, and fast food restaurants. New shopping malls can hardly do without a typical franchise restaurant such as KFC, Starbucks, Pizza Hut, Burger King, McDonald's, and so forth – and as a result, create an almost overwhelming presence of corresponding brand signs in urban space. The 'McDonaldization' of Chinese food culture with its exceptional diversity seems almost unstoppable. With enthusiasm, the originally American and now global 'fast food culture' is applied to Chinese cuisine: McNoodle says hi!

— France delivers red wine, perfume, and TGV; the fiction of the villa in Tuscany, Armani, and elegant men's suits and shoes come from Italy; images of the Premier League and inspirations for China pop originate in England – and of course, water treatment plants, process control, machines of all kinds – and not to forget, the automobile as consumer product par excellence, stems from Germany, the world champion of the 'backstage economy' of engineering, invisible to the consumer. Certainly, this list is only a caricature. It however represents a growing number of so-called Western imports to the 'open' China of today.[1]

— Architectural styles and fashions, in addition to applied urban planning and design paradigms, seem of Western origin as well. Slab housing construction, propagated by early twentieth-century Modernist architects and dogmatically formulated within the Charter of Athens (1933) has been triumphant in China ever since its Soviet-dominated early communist phase. We can hardly imagine Chinese cities without it. The new residential compounds of the ascending middle and upper classes, equipped with walls, fences, and gated entrances, are reminiscent of American 'gated communities'. Inspired by the example of the United States, every self-confident Chinese mega-city today wants to plan and build a new 'Central Business District'. These CBDs are filled with skyscrapers in the International Style, and every now and then loosened up a little by flagship architecture of Postmodern or even Deconstructivist origin. For some time now, the metropolises of Beijing and Shanghai have been competing against each other for the most striking buildings designed by internationally renowned architects such as Rem Koolhaas, Arata Isozaki, Norman Foster, Richard Rogers, Jacques Herzog & Pierre de Meuron, Paul Andreu, von Gerkan, Marg & Partner, Gunter Henn, Albert Speer, Zaha Hadid, and many more. Most provincial capital cities have, in the meantime, enthusiastically joined the run for architectural brands. Also, the practice of functional differentiation (zoning), created in the West, has become wildly popular and been put in the service of increasing both local and regional Gross Domestic Product (GDP).

— We are therefore not surprised when we read and are told repeatedly that Western influence on Chinese development is big, yes, even far-reaching. Some people might, with a Sinophilic tinge of regret, assume that China is becoming Westernized – which means nothing other than that a country is surrendering its identity, if only to a certain degree.[2] Shanghai, former colonial metropolis and today world city, is considered the vanguard of this surrender of Chinese identity. This observation is, by the way, reinforced by numerous Chinese experts as well. When asked about this assumed Westernization, they often answer that China, for the sake of its future development, doesn't have any other choice than to emulate the West. And especially the United States, a global power, are seen as successful – thus, to be successful as well, the Chinese think they are obliged to follow the American example.

— But is China really following Western examples? To which extent does it follow them, and how far is it actually capable of following them? We have to be cautious when speaking of the Westernization of China, and this fact can be illustrated by two basic examples of everyday life.

— The fast food franchises KFC and Pizza Hut are wildly successful in China. Their restaurants are more or less omnipresent in the metropolises of the East. However, when we take a look at their menus, we can see that they are significantly different to their Western counterparts. Differences reach from seasoning mix to genuinely Chinese dishes.

— The success of these franchises is obviously not only based on the curiosity of Chinese customers seeking new culinary sensations, but also their willingness to adapt to customer preferences. Success is guaranteed, at least to a certain degree, by a franchise management's intercultural competence. Where China opens itself to Western influences, these franchises obviously successfully open themselves to the country's culinary preferences – without surrendering their brand identity. The results of these adaptations are North American-Chinese fast food hybrids. So the question is: What does 'Westernization' actually mean here?

— We can make similar observations when looking at the automobile as Western product. Just like the Koreans, the Chinese love big cars. Reasons for this are based on the extremely hierarchic structure of society, in which status is demonstrated through accentuated symbolism. In the past this was expressed by clothing and residence, or to be more exact, by headdress and roof construction. Today, the automobile quite literally 'drives' this bonfire of the vanities. Until recently, affording a car was mostly limited to those who were, at the same time, capable of hiring a driver as well. Cars needed to be big and provide plenty of room. Car owners would sit in the back of the car, where they desired ample legroom. As a result, for instance, cars produced by Volkswagen under the brand name Passat, as well as Audi, were redesigned to be about 10 cm longer than the original German models. Maybe we can describe the cultural creative force behind this as 'rickshaw-mentality'…!

— In the meantime, many things have changed. Affordable cars are now available on the market, income has increased, and lifestyles have changed. Many of those who previously could afford a driver no longer desire to do so. And yet others still can't afford a driver today but now have the means and the will to buy a car. What has remained, however, is the love for big cars. A remarkable paradox, considering the high density of Chinese cities!

— Our claim is that China actually isn't Westernizing at all. Instead, it extensively consumes Western products – and thoroughly 'digests' them, using them to build a new world; new, but still Chinese. The great, hungry Chinese 'stomach' obviously makes use of cultural creative energies ('cultural enzymes', so to speak) that result in the more or less effective Sinicization[3] of material imported from all over the world. China, to use the words of Daniel Bell, not only adopts these materials, but also adapts them to its needs. (Bell 2008)

— This observation equally applies to current Chinese urban development paradigms. What at first glance seems to be the result of so-called Westernization reveals itself, under increased scrutiny, as rooted deeply within Chinese traditions. A particularly good and popular example for this is slab housing construction with southern orientation originated in Europe. In its application, however, this building type is informed by Chinese tradition. If one compares the satellite cities and slabtopias created in Europe after World War II to the Fordist Wohnsiedlungen or housing estates of communist and post-socialist China, it becomes apparent here that southern orientation has been and is enforced much more stringently. The reason lies not only in the climate-related preference for buildings facing the south, but also within the social capital or status it guarantees. We will return to this subject matter later.

— When we look at what happens to products and ideas after they are imported to China, we should not forget that in the creation of the new China, the old China – most of all of the Imperial era, but also of the republican era, as well as the Mao era – is updated endogenously. And it is precisely Chinese history with its deeply rooted traditions developed over the course of millennia where we find the mystery of these creative forces mentioned above.[4] We must therefore keep both in mind: the Chinese project of re-establishing itself through both internal and external influences.

— Our study of China's urban code begins on two interrelated levels. The first is descriptive-analytical: the actual 'reading' of Chinese urban space. The second is explanatory; it offers the terminology and theoretical framework for a discursive classification of empirical findings. The first level places readers in the front row, facing the stage, where they experience both stage set (the Chinese city) and performance (reading the city). The second level is akin to leading them behind and beneath the stage, to rehearsals, stage infrastructure, and stage technology.

— We begin with discussing the question of how to actually decipher or read urban space. Here, two aspects come to mind: on the one hand, the semiotics of the built environment, i.e. the science of dealing with landscapes, villages, towns, cities, urban spaces, and architecture as signs, or rather as fabric of spatial signs; on the other hand, the knowledge of historic and current Chinese practices of appropriation and production of space. Both space and tradition are tightly and deeply interwoven. This interaction leads to the conclusion that production of space not only bears witness to fashions of short-term validity and transient ideologies, but always of deeply rooted cultural practices as well. In this regard, the semiotics of the built environment has always been a science of spatial signs of cultural origin. This is where the fields of (historic) Sinology and cultural geography merge.

— Readers who feel that Chapters 1 and 8, which are dedicated to the methods and theories of reading the city as well as the language[5] of the city, are theory-laden detours and prefer to skip them, may do so without any difficulty: people who like yoghurt don't need to know the yoghurt cup's value chain in order to enjoy the taste of its content.

— In the chapter titled 'Pajamas and Clotheslines', we begin the actual reading of the city within a context that, more than any other, is aimed at the heart of Chinese spatial culture – the relationship between 'open' and 'public' space. Our observations and interpretations of scenes of everyday life in the street are followed by an identification of important types of open urban places and an attempt to understand their social 'message' (Chapter 2). It becomes clear that particular urban spaces are identified all too quickly, in a simplifying way, and from a Western viewpoint, as public. But these spaces are actually open urban space, the dark horse of socio-cultural spatial appropriation. We can experience this any time and everywhere, in sizes both small and large, from the microcosm of any sidewalk scene to the macrocosm of street networks. The importance of 'empty' or 'open space' informs this study significantly, in a way that is similar to a basic melody, improvised upon in the individual chapters, topically adapted and interpreted. Because it is so important, the subject of open urban space receives the pole position within our study.

— The chapter to follow includes observations on the development of the functionalist agenda of modern residential housing construction after its migration from Europe to China (Chapter 3). We recognize that Chinese urbanism has adopted the legacy of Fordist residential housing construction in ways both uniquely unconventional and also independent. It transcends this legacy by developing it further into 'swinging lines and dancing dots', as the chapter title suggests.

— The importance of the subject of dwelling in this book reflects its general importance for current urban development. The reason is that the new Chinese city is, to this day, largely the city of socialist residential housing construction in an advanced form. But it is also the city of closed neighborhoods, of introverted neighborhood courtyards, of vertical form, of roof and light sculptures, and, last but not least, of neighborhoods as lifestyle product equipped with a brand identity[6] (Chapter 4). Within the new gated neighborhoods the old and the new China merge in a distinct and creative way.

— Describing the interaction of the old China with the new China in terms of dwelling gives us the opportunity to include an analysis on spatial-cultural hybrids. These hybrids are the product of the direct encounter of Orient and Occident. Exciting examples of this are housing estates in Shanghai named lilong,[7] which initially appeared in the 1860s, followed by the jingyu blocks, born from a combination of Russian and Chinese-Manchurian influences and located in the city center of Harbin (Daowai district).

— In the new China, juxtaposed to the closed city, we find the open city – open indeed, but not yet actually public. The embodiments of this open city – from perimeter block retail via neighborhood center to community center – are the main subject of Chapter 5. But before we analyze these structures more closely, we first take a look at the concept of centrality in the Chinese metropolis. Here, we discover efforts to reactivate the concept of linear centrality historically defunct until now. As sign, this form once reflected a hierarchical social structure. What does it mean to reanimate this spatial form? As the 'Golden Corridor' in Shenyang demonstrates, this reanimation is very successful! Obviously, Chinese society is still capable of recognizing itself without difficulty within the hierarchically organized spatial succession of large-scale, axial urban structures.

— To this day, the European city gains its flair from medieval and early modern bourgeois society's enthusiasm for extroverted urban stage settings, for the dramatization of public spaces through decorated building facades. In terms of this passion for dramatization, the Chinese don't have to hide behind the Europeans. Actually, while the joy of the theatrical or decorative in Europe has suffered under the influence of Modernist rules and dogmas, it celebrates its joyful resurrection in the blooming Postmodern China of today.

— However, there is a decisive difference. In China, the passion for urban spatial theatrics is not articulated in facade ornamentation, but instead in an enthusiasm for glitter, neon lights, illuminated objects and colorful spotlights, in symbols, drawings, logos, pictograms, and many other items – which is, on occasion, almost delirious and confidently ignores Western aesthetic paradigms. The sculpting of color and light generates a completely new image of the open city, the image of media space and its media facades. Towards the end of Chapter 5, we conclude that China is, in fact, the hyperactive laboratory for the media city of the future. Its impressive results are already visible today.

— The chapter on open urban space closes with an exemplary analysis of the conceptual conglomerate and eclecticism of the model for a new government district in Harbin, an urban design perceived as ideal type. This shows how imported stylistic elements are introduced into the overall spatial structure of China and thus become Sinicized. We consider China's media-related way of dealing with the cultural heritage of the Western, especially the European city, as a topically related process. Therefore, the analysis of the media city is followed by the chapter on 'urban fictions' (Chapter 6). In the past twenty years an enormously diverse landscape of theatrical urban dramatizations has emerged in China, so rich in variation that a typological differentiation becomes appropriate. We begin this chapter with observations on three themed satellite cities of Shanghai's 'One City, Nine Villages' plan,[8] i.e. Anting, Taiwushi, and Luodian, already largely completed when this book was first published in 2008. This is followed by an analysis of an urban copy of prominent Dutch buildings in Shenyang ('Holland Village') and a popular theme park equipped with urban set pieces located in the southern Chinese city of Shenzhen.

— Anting, the so-called German town, indeed features characteristics of the German or rather European city within its open basic structure – and thus clashes heavily with the Chinese dualism of closed and open cities. Irresolvable contradictions seem inevitable! Taiwushi, also known as Thames Town, is the so-called English city in this chorus line of new towns. In truth, it is actually a purely Chinese city, an open urban theater stage, furnished with copies of English buildings. Taiwushi is the English travesty[9] of a Chinese new town. The same applies to the Swedish satellite city Luodian. In Holland Village in Shenyang, we finally encounter an actually tragicomical example of a European parody[10] of the Chinese city. This huge compound was bulldozed in 2009, thus becoming the Titanic of Chinese theme towns.

— These observations are complemented by an integrative interpretation of the Chinese city, its size, its density, its type of growth, and its form – for not only the idea of a German city, in fact, exists (it wasn't a mistake on Albert Speer's part to assume this), but by now, the idea of the modern Chinese city exists as well. Its syntax has developed in the past thirty years. We describe how the basic structure of this new Chinese city is dominated by the rhythm of 'great street' and 'vertical block' (Chapter 7).

— Within this spatial basic melody of the city there are still other sounds and noises that loudly demand to be heard. The 'villages' in Shenzhen are the most curious of these, as these 'villages' comprise urban spaces with some of the highest densities in the world. Their inhabitants are the same families that had once lived together in agrarian village collectives before rapidly growing cities swept away their rice fields in a tsunami of urbanization. Instead of harvesting rice, they now 'harvest' labor migrants. This takes place under the supervision of a partly informally operating urban administration at neighborhood level that has evolved from communist-era village collectives. A further interesting note in the Chinese urban melody is the practice of 'river jumping', which has become sort of a fashion in urban planning and design ever since the successful jump of Shanghai from Puxi to Pudong (Chapter 7).

— The task of Chapter 8 finally is to integrate the particular signified meanings and contents we have researched into a consistent text on the Chinese city. In order to accomplish this, we resort to structural hermeneutics, the alpha and omega of which is the 'binary code' of community and society (Gemeinschaft and Gesellschaft, spatially: of rural life and urban life). Based on this, a system of terminology is unfolded that provides the deciphered codes with scientific stability. In China today, this much becomes clear, the constitutive forces of society, especially the economic ones, are pervaded by institutions of community. This reciprocal reflection also informs urban space, which as a result reveals itself as a cityscape of urbanized villages. In the process of modernization, China seems to hold onto the heritage of community life with its rural connotation in a more decisive way than the West. This fact usually results in characterizing China's developmental model as 'Confucian'.

— The book closes with a brief summary of the most important results of our reading of the city. Clarity is our goal. Thus, we support the facts described and analyzed with corresponding illustrations (about one hundred photos, tables, and charts). In addition, we complement select English terms with their German counterparts, in order to strengthen the comprehensibility of a text that stems from a German original, written in a language renowned for its strong tendency towards preferably using nouns and combining individual words, sometimes creating true word giants. Due to its numerous scientific terms, however, not only the translation of the German reference book into (American) English appears a remarkable challenge, but also the translation of a text which is strongly affiliated with those discourses of the German cultural realm of language that are rooted in the structuralistic and dialectical concepts of 'continental philosophy'.

— It is clear that when Westerners read the Chinese city, it is as if they were looking into a mirror. This mirror improves their way of recognizing themselves and the environment they inhabit. If we now claim that a book on China's urban code also deals with the code of Western cities, it is by no means an expression of immodesty. Within the other, we recognize ourselves.

CHAPTERS

1
2
3
4
5
6
7
8

HOW TO READ A CITY?

1

— This book's title refers to the assumption that the built environment is a socio-cultural text that we can read and interpret.[11] Human beings produce spaces for living (in) – and by doing so, they inscribe the forms of their desired, aspired, and actual coexistence in space. Their habitats assume the shape of spatial 'essays' that, if one can read them, tell tales of the life, thoughts, and conflicts of their planners, builders, inhabitants and users.

— This is, however, exactly where the problem begins. We may be capable of using and planning urban space – but capable of reading it? How do we read a text that consists not of letters, syllables, and words, but of images, contours, facades, and volumes, of buildings, streets, plazas, parks – and within these, the most diverse assembly of people: poor and rich, young and old, locals and foreigners, men and women, all inhabiting this space in endlessly different ways?

— As method, the semiotics of urban space (or urban semiotics) might be a helpful instrument.[12] According to this research method, prominently represented by scientists such as Roland Barthes, Henri Lefèbvre, Umberto Eco, and Mark Gottdiener, not only street and traffic signs, light signals, advertisement, facade decoration, etc., but also elements of the built urban environment, such as buildings, places, streets, dwellings, city centers, etc., can be interpreted as signs – and thus compared with the medium of language. By doing so, the functional and aesthetic understanding of space is complemented by a further dimension, the semiotic, which seeks to understand spatial phenomena as signs and thus as carriers of meaning or sense. These three dimensions merge, overlap, and influence each other reciprocally.

— The fact that, for instance, architectural or urban functions are reflected in aesthetic form is an architectural commonplace within the discourse of Modernist architecture. And the fact that the aesthetics of Bauhaus architecture feature signifying aspects as well by transmitting messages is easy to understand when considering the ideological ambitions of the Modernist movement and its terminology: 'scientific rationality', 'social equality', or 'healthy living environment'. Within the paradigmatic urban design concepts of prominent pioneers of architectural Modernism such as Le Corbusier, Gropius, Mies van der Rohe, and Hilberseimer, the functional, aesthetic, and semiotic have completely merged within the utopia of egalitarian, park-like machine cities.

— Based on a classification system by renowned American epistemologist Charles S. Peirce, three types of signs can be generally identified. First, iconic signs, if the relationship between sign and meaning is based on similarity; second, indicative signs, if the relationship between sign and meaning is obvious; and third, symbolic signs, if the relationship between sign and meaning seems arbitrary (Peirce 1931/1991). We assert that this typology is relevant for signs within an urban context as well.

— From the viewpoint of semiotics, elements of urban space become carriers of meaning or sense (signifiers) that refer to meaning or sense (signified). In his semiotics of architecture, Umberto Eco points out that spatial facts most of all transmit iconic messages[13] (Eco 1972/1994). The semiotic analysis of the Chinese city, however, teaches us that especially for complex urban elements such as urban spatial configurations, residential blocks, streetscapes, city centers, etc., not only all three modes of transmission play a role, but also an overlapping of iconic, indicative, and symbolic messages takes place. In Chapter 6, we encounter a memorable case of such overlapping modes of transmission in the example of retrofitted neighborhood gates.

— In reference to Roland Barthes (1976) and in regard to the architectural signifiers he researched, Eco differentiates between denotative and connotative messages. Primary functions or meanings are denoted, and secondary (subordinate) functions or meanings are connoted. In regard to 'urban semiotics' (Gottdiener 1994), this function-oriented interpretation needs to be generalized. According to this viewpoint, the essential or substantial meaning, corresponding to the 'nature' of the signifier, is denoted.

— This indicates that meaning is not only a construct on the part of the individual who receives the message, but is simultaneously objectively predetermined – which thus subjectively limits interpretive freedom. In this context for instance, a luxuriously and graciously designed villa denotes the security, privacy, or intimacy of the family. It is in this respect no different from a modest apartment in a multi-family residential building. The connotation features, however, what the signifier is associated with subjectively – or what is projected onto it; the mere titular or rather ephemeral, variable, accidental meaning. The villa can connote affluence, abundance, or exclusiveness, if these are the associations or projections of the observer.

Semiotic reading of space: Chinese neighborhood as case

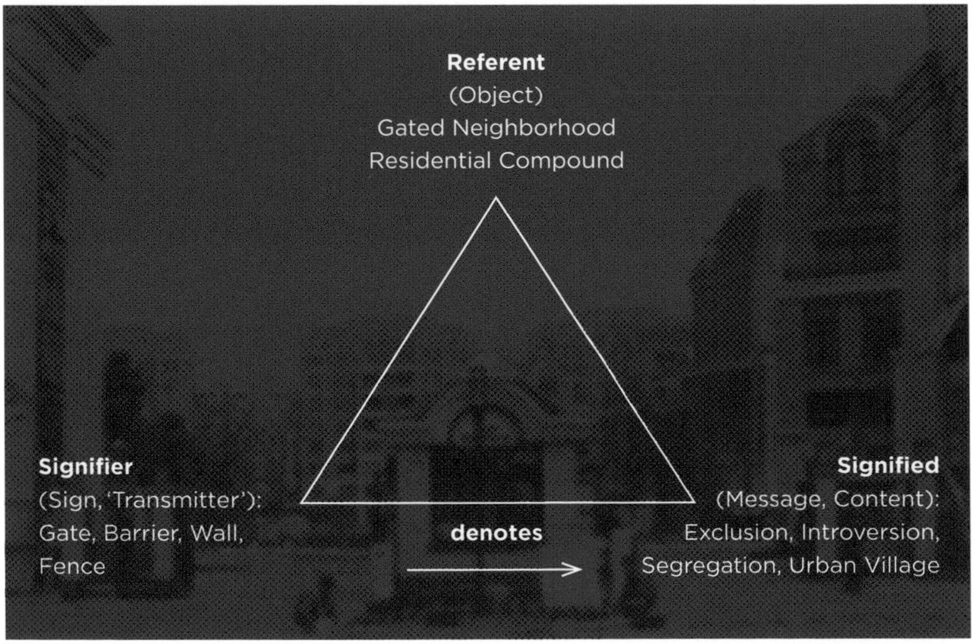

Referent
(Object)
Gated Neighborhood
Residential Compound

Signifier
(Sign, 'Transmitter'):
Gate, Barrier, Wall,
Fence

denotes

Signified
(Message, Content):
Exclusion, Introversion,
Segregation, Urban Village

— Gates, barriers, walls, and fences can be, for instance, understood as indicative signifiers that refer to a closed spatial unit, which may be a military installation, an industrial park, or a housing estate. If the referent is a residential area in China, then the corresponding signifiers (which are denoting in an indicative mode) are e.g. community, exclusion, or introversion. The following illustration exemplifies this interrelation.

— To give a further example in urbanism: regarded as an iconic transmitter, slab housing construction with prefabricated elements denotes social mass housing, serial mode of construction, modern standards of hygiene, or monofunctionalism. It connotes, however – and now the interpretations become more subjective and transitory or limited in time – collectivism, monotony, or also marginalization.

— Denoted meanings, although partly produced by the observer, claim inter-subjective validity. Connoted meanings on the other hand are subjectively assigned to the signifier that triggers the associations or projections. Denotations of 'dwelling' are objective and may be considered universally valid. All over the world, at all times and in all cultures, people built dwellings to live in, and it is correct to consider human beings as entities requiring dwelling. The term's anthropological and transcultural dimension refers to dwelling as a generic concept. In real life, on the other hand, we do not deal with a dwelling as an unchangeable Platonic real Form, but with an enormous variety of dwelling forms: with its subjective and objective differences of production, distribution, and use.

— In the context of this book, when dealing with the subject of dwelling, cultural aspects are doubtlessly in the spotlight. Dwellings are not only different due to individual taste of their builders or owners, but also due to socio-cultural preferences and practices. We can thus not only find an endless variety of individually different forms of dwelling. We also discover that they can be grouped together according to shared characteristics. The following example deals with such a socio-culturally defined group: the Chinese dwelling. Which messages does the Chinese dwelling denote?

— A dwelling in China is also simply a dwelling – and as such, similar to dwellings in Europe (and anywhere else across the globe). However, Chinese dwellings also transmit their own messages, perceived as alien by Europeans. Their meaning is not understood without difficulty, because they are expressed in a spatial language visitors from afar are not accustomed to. In this situation, visitors tend to impose their own (Western) interpretive pattern upon Chinese spatial phenomena. Subjective interpretations (connotations) are transformed into denotations of the Chinese dwelling, and Europeans believe they understand what they see or experience. A false conclusion! What is thus achieved is not more than pseudo-understanding, or even: a blurring of experienced reality, fabricated by an invalid projection of Western or foreign interpretive patterns.

— In principle, the same is true for the perception and interpretation of the Chinese city. In order to understand it, we must know its spatial code. If not, the danger exists of transforming it into a 'screen' for both subjective and merely superficial Western projection. The city displays characteristics similar to text consisting of letters, syllables, and words. To comprehend it requires knowledge of the language in which it is written. This is exactly what this book sets out to accomplish: to improve and deepen our knowledge of China's spatial language – with the goal of enabling us to separate the essential from the accidental.

— This aspiration is certainly not a simple task. It also requires substantial knowledge in cultural and intercultural terms. The reason is that China's urban signifiers are transmitting without interruption, but do not offer an instruction of how to decode them at the same time. In order to read the city, to understand its urban code, the semiotic toolkit alone is not sufficient. Or, in other words, the semiotic method assists in producing the desired meaning or sense, yet does not accomplish this by itself. As previously indicated, the receiver of urban signals always contributes to the process of origination of the sense they contain. Only through assigning sense (also described as 'semiosis'), can urban signals be transformed into meaningful messages, i.e. into understanding. But how can observers protect themselves from producing simple projections or arbitrary sense?

— It is possible that the individual urban sign reveals, when observed, part of its mystery by offering a kind of 'user manual' in order to formulate an 'explanatory hypothesis', as Ugo Volli describes the inference process of abduction as defined by Charles S. Peirce. We hence interrelate the term abduction (in contrast to induction or deduction) with the possibility of discovering the sense of transmitted code in an at least hypothetical or semi-logical way. In this respect we can assume that the different modes of transmission of urban signs will, in their own way – iconic, indicative, or symbolic – offer pathways to sense that we should dare to venture. To determine meaning that may be based on an explanatory hypothesis (at first, a completely hypothetical answer to a question that requires meaning) is therefore the "basic semiotic act" (Volli 2002, 13ff). In our opinion, apart from other hypothetical, associative, or semi-logical techniques of sense retrieval, the technique of 'superposition' as suggested by Walter Benjamin seems to be particularly helpful for determining the meaning or sense of cultural or rather urban signifiers.[14] Superposition describes the capacity to 'remember the new', i.e. to see what has been and is to come within what is present (Benjamin 1991, V 1, 493, 576; V 2, 1023f).

— To superpose thus means to regard the elements of the contemporary cityscape as elements of an encompassing cultural memory and simultaneously as station stops on the urban voyage into the future. In order to be able to assign sense in a meaningful, non-extrinsic and non-projective way, we need to take possession of this memory that has always been inscribed in animate and inanimate things. We think that it is necessary to introduce the technique of superposition within observations on urban space informed by semiotics.

— Two different generators of meaning or sense can enrich the process of urban semiosis. On the one hand, the body of knowledge provided by social and cultural sciences, and Chinese history (cultural history in particular) on the other hand. We require interdisciplinary knowledge of China's history, its traditions, its society, its way of thinking, its actions. Only if we refer to this vast body of knowledge will we be able to decipher the messages offered by China's built urban environment in an informative way. We therefore reinforce the mode of perception informed by semiotics for observing spatial phenomena with an integrative, holistic body of knowledge on the particular characteristics of Chinese history and culture.[15]

— To return to our example, if a dwelling features an interior courtyard (such as a tíng yuàn, comparable to the Roman peristyle), but lacks a decorated facade, then it transmits a completely different message than a dwelling that displays an ornamental facade, yet has no designed interior courtyard. The first, as encountered in the Chinese sìhéyuàn with its introverted conception, irrefutably denotes the pre-eminence of family and community. The latter, however, with its extroverted gesture, refers to the presence of the individual in bourgeois society.

— During the colonial era (but also in the present) an intermingling of Western and Eastern spatial languages occurred in China, creating spatial hybrids, similar to courtyard houses with ornamented facades. This species is, sphinx-like, capable of double denotation, Western and Eastern, introverted and extroverted. In the section titled 'Orient meets Occident – hybrid residential areas', we introduce, among others, Shanghai's lilong and Harbin's jingyu block as examples of this kind of spatial-cultural hybridization.

— Things become complicated when we, in our semiotical intent, direct our attention towards the city. The reason is that the terminology of primary and secondary functions as proposed by Eco cannot be applied to this signifier without difficulty. This is due to the urban multitude of combinations and overlapping functions. Urban complexity increases the differences between the essential and accidental. Against this background it may sound surprising that, in regard to denotations (understood as strictly objective attribution of meaning), the 'city' as a generic concept permits just as little room for interpretation as the term 'dwelling'. From a universal point of view, the city most of all denotes (bourgeois) society (Hegel, Marx, Weber); or according to Georg Simmel's definition (Simmel 1992) "the presence of the other and the stranger"; or as Lefèbvre states, 'centrality'.[16] If we choose the historical category 'metropolis' instead of the generic concept of the 'city', Bahrdt's (1961) theorem of 'incomplete integration' provides an essential understanding. According to this theorem, the development of the metropolis, while speeding up individualization, simultaneously furthers the disintegration of family-based social integration.[17]

— There are cities – imagined or real – that are incapable of adhering to the denotations described above.[18] The urban utopias of classical Modernism may serve as examples. Henri Lefèbvre classified these urban utopias, e.g. Le Corbusier's elitist 'Ville Contemporaine' and 'Plan Voisin' or his more socialist 'Ville Radieuse', as 'planned space' (*espace conçu*). They are more akin to collectivist space-machines than spaces in which society and culture reify. This assertion can be generalized in the context of Modernism: the modern city as such denotes facts that it is incapable of adhering to. Idea (e.g. of equality) and reality (of equality) do not correspond. The transmitted and received message corresponds neither in an iconic, nor an indicative, nor symbolic relationship to the sender. What is denoted rather matches a projection, wishful thinking, or an ideology than the (assumed) signifier's potential of providing meaning. If we don't want to transform the city as carrier of meaning into a projection surface for completely external content, then we must recognize that the number of strict allocations of meaning (denotations) is limited.[19] In this sense, the Modernist city, according to the dictum of the Charter of Athens, may connote urbanity, it however does not denote this fact, or merely so in a fragmentary way.

— The city, for instance in regard to Lefèbvre's statement, denotes centrality. But we also have to pay attention to the cultural dimension of the signifier (centrality). When comparing centrality of North American, European, and Chinese cities, we can observe the following: in the American city, the commercial centrality of 'downtown' or the CBD (central business district) dominates; in the traditional European city, the public centrality of the center with market place, city hall, and church is prevalent; and in the Chinese city, 'linear centrality' with hierarchically structured spatial successions, comparable to the Roman city of antiquity, persists (Hassenpflug 2006a).

— Which other messages does the Chinese city transmit? Compact city? Gated city? Cellular city? Media city? This book intends to offer answers to these questions. However, there is no simple answer based on one or a limited number of firm denotations. The city, being a hyper-complex object of research due to the cultural and historic materials it is made of, prohibits this a priori.

— Beyond this, in the case of China we are confronted with unique urban dynamics. In the past thirty years the degree of urbanization of Chinese society has skyrocketed from barely twenty percent to almost fifty percent. By its very nature, this hyper-urbanization influences the transmission quality of the Chinese city, of its elements, and its structures. By reinventing themselves as a culture nation (represented by the capital city Beijing) and a global economic power (represented by the commercial cities Shanghai and Shenzhen), the Chinese also open the debate on their idea of the city.

— China is in the process of reinventing the city as such for its own purposes – and is willing to explore unusual means to achieve this goal. On the other hand, we can assume that the idea of the city in China possesses a certain resilience, where a more or less unchangeable set of traditions, social patterns, and cultural rules are effective that significantly limit the flexibility of the idea of the city. Thus, China's common desire of orienting itself on the West in urbanistic terms always reaches its limits in the inertia rooted deeply within its culture. We have again and again encountered this inertia, these forces of gravity, in our analysis of cities and spaces. But this not only helps us to understand China's urban present, it also indicates that China, despite all changes, will remain faithful to itself, in dimensions both surprising and tremendous.

TRANSFORMATIONS
OF EMPTY URBAN SPACE

2

PAJAMAS AND CLOTHESLINES
— In Shanghai, summers are very hot, just as everywhere else in China. It is very likely that you will see men and women wearing light, airy pajamas on the street, in the middle of the city, during daytime. The first time I ran into a man dressed like this, accompanied by a woman wearing jeans and T-shirt in Shanghai's Yangpu district, I wondered whether he was a patient who had just, for a moment, left the campus of a nearby hospital. But there was no hospital nearby. Moreover, during this tropically hot day in June, I saw even more pajamas-wearing passers-by. My thoughts were, no, this would never happen in Europe. People would consider it embarrassing or a sign of moral dereliction!

— Only shortly after running into the carefree pajama people, I noticed something else that I had actually been used to already: along the sidewalk, clotheslines were tied between trees, fences, and lamp posts, and an entire household's laundry ranging from bed sheets via shirts and pants to underwear was nonchalantly flapping about in the dusty and exhaust-polluted city wind. This heterotopic, idyllic streetscape forced me, just like every other pedestrian, to step off the sidewalk and continue walking on the street, only to flee from the bustling traffic back to the safety of the sidewalk a few steps later.

— We don't need detailed studies to understand the connection between the pajama people and the sidewalk clothesline. Both represent a unique innocence in dealing with this urban space that we tend to describe as public; a careless transgression of the border that separates private, personal space from the open urban theatre stage. There are plenty of opportunities to watch people having a nap on the sidewalk next to their little soup kitchen, on a discarded car seat, or sitting around an upside-down fruit crate, playing mah-jongg or a card game. Audible clearing of throats and spitting belongs here as well. Without much ado, almost all functions of dwelling are extended into the urban streetscape, just as in a village. The sidewalk serves as kitchen, bedroom, living room, as a place of candid 'intimization' (cf. Busch/Ebrecht 2005). The sidewalk, that much becomes clear, is only in a beginning stage of becoming a 'public' sidewalk. It is a proto-public space.

**Sidewalk with
clothesline and laundry
in Shanghai**

— Another indicator for the ease of crossing the border between private and public is the custom of music being played through mostly visible, but occasionally hidden loudspeakers in green spaces, in public gardens and parks. In Germany, this involuntary 'public address' would be considered a nuisance and seen as an act of audible environmental pollution. In China, a country unusually tolerant of noise (in detail, Hassenpflug 2006d), music in public green spaces is seen as a contribution to the ambience, comparable to the 'beautification' of entry plazas with plastic flower beds, plastic palm trees, and plastic bamboo. It is also similar to the everyday 'enchantment' of flowers, bushes, and trees through intensely colorful spotlights or extravagant lighting fixtures by night. Typically Chinese! Or maybe not?

Sidewalk as living room

— But not only functions of private dwelling, also those of the workshop or store counter are exported into the streetscape. Sometimes sidewalks are transformed into a workbench for repairing bikes, motorcycles, TV sets, and shoes; or a workshop for assembling doors and windows; or a storefront advertising decorative pet fish, songbirds, and cats; where dumplings, jiaozi, and pancakes are prepared and sold; and a mobile barber shop is opened. Not even counting the myriad of traders and farmers who transform the sidewalks into veritable informal bazaars with an almost endless product range, late at night, when the police aren't on duty.

— But the opposite happens as well. Some of the residential compounds of the new middle class include, even though categorized as purely residential within land use plans, an astonishing number of offices, stores, and service providers of all kinds, ranging from architectural office to brokerage firm to multifunctional wedding planners, combining barber shop, make-up studio, wedding video and photography, master of ceremonies, and limo drivers into one comprehensive service. Customers stream past the guarded entrance, gate, and fences and carry a hefty dose of 'publicness' into the otherwise rather introverted residential areas.

— China's lack of concern and even negligence in dealing with urban space generally assumed to be public is reflected in the still limited number of such spaces within cities and, if present at all, their condition. There is a remarkable amount of more or less designed places, especially open urban spaces in and at shopping centers, devoid of any kind of amenities. In the meantime, piazzas under open skies or glazed arcades have become a popular and ubiquitous design element in China. But the dormant potential they offer as public space is either not recognized or not considered worthy of appreciation. In contrast, they are highly interesting to commercial enterprises, who aim to utilize every little bit of them. If you want to sit down and rest, you'll have to do so in a restaurant or café – which are, by now, omnipresent.

Meeting point beneath a highway, Changsha

— The low degree of attention that public urban spaces receive is also demonstrated by the visual and sanitary condition of many small-scale green spaces situated along streets of all sizes. They are often covered with trash and refuse, unkempt, filthy, beaten down. The street cleaners don't make a particularly good impression either. Which visitor to China has not seen them? Poor women (occasionally also men) wearing a face or breathing mask, with large straw hats, equipped with a primitive broom made of twigs of the eight-leafed broom flower, rice straw, or something similar, swirling street dust around for minimum pay. If, nowadays, you can find many well-kept green spaces in the large metropolises of the East, then it is because of an increasingly professional waste removal service dedicated to the sanitary character and beautification of the city's visual appearance, diligently picking up what others had discarded earlier without thought or care.

— Public urban spaces with a welcoming character, purposely designed for encounter, meeting, communication, scheduled and spontaneous gathering, for playing, or simply for seeing and being seen, are still scarce in China – especially in less favored, old urban areas. The scarcity of public urban space becomes apparent when a larger number of people seeks entertainment together, be it for gymnastics such as taiji (tai chi or taijiquau), for fun, for play, or also very popular, for evening dancing after work and when temperatures have decreased to tolerable levels. The Chinese love doing these things; they are a cheerful, casual, sociable, and peaceful people. However, due to lack of suitable places, we see people exercising, playing, or dancing beneath highway bridges, on abandoned parking lots, or noisy traffic islands.

Night-time dance beneath a highway, Harbin

— Public space is urgently needed, especially against the background of a continuously growing middle and upper class with related lifestyles and spatial demands. However, there is little 'publicly' usable space available in China, and its condition is often so deplorable because there are no traditions of how to deal with it. Behavior is ambivalent: people want this kind of space, because they need it; but they reject it, because it speaks a spatial language that they don't understand. Community space, neighborhood space, family space: yes! Space for civil society: what is that? The pattern of dealing with what we term public space can thus be described as torn between rejection and desire.

— The claim that the way of dealing with public space in China is either careless, inattentive, or rather disrespectful, is based on the assumption that this kind of space is actually perceived as 'public'. This assumption is, however, not correct. For the Chinese, the space beyond the places enclosed by walls and fences in which they live and work and teach and learn, the space beyond family and community, is still primarily a 'non-space' or 'non-place',[20] an urban void or 'blank' which at best has a functional meaning, for instance as traffic space. We define this space as open space. Open space is a space that needs to be traversed or passed in order to enter another meaningful space 'out there'.

— In one of his writings on the urban history of Suzhou, the former 'Venice of the East', Xu Yinong notes that open urban space in China has been, since time immemorial, associated with disorder, with a space beyond the attention and care of Chinese society (Xu 2000).[21] What does disorder as a characteristic of public space mean? Simply take a look at the hyperactive character of metropolitan street life. Despite all traffic regulations in force in China as well, the law of the strongest prevails – with a clear pecking order: from pedestrian to bike, motorcycle, car, bus, truck, to limousines of the high and mighty, painted black and with tinted windows. Pedestrian markings on the streets are mere decoration, horns are honked, push comes to shove, overtaking on the right side, driving on the left side – no matter whether legal or not!

— In the northern Chinese metropolis of Harbin, along the premises of the Harbin Institute of Technology's School of Architecture and Urban Planning and Design, we could watch how taxi drivers, among others, turned the sidewalks into additional street lanes during the obligatory traffic jam at 4 pm. Whoever might think that pedestrians would try to resist this just has to witness how they are literally driven away by honking horns and threatening gestures, like chickens on the dirt road of a country hamlet. The sidewalk is not an unconditional 'public' space.

— However, generally meaningless open space is attributed importance when it is appropriated by the living practices of family and community; when it becomes an extension of the kitchen, of the dining room, of the store counter or workshop. Especially highly mobile labor migrants, flooding into the metropolises of the eastern part of the country in vast numbers, consider urban residual spaces in their countless forms as an opportunity for informal appropriation (and survival). Through the activities of this floating population group, yet also through commercial and non-commercial uses of local residents, these spaces are socially programmed in a way highly informative for urban planning (Ruff 2007; 6ff).

**Sidewalk as bypass,
Harbin**

— Without the appreciation provided by family and community, by everyday life, or commerce this open space remains grey, empty, without content, and devoid of meaning. What thus appears as vagueness in defining the borderline between private and public is in truth only an expression of the cultural hegemony of the family or the community. The clothesline along the sidewalk is nothing other than private land appropriation that gives space with little or limited sense at least a temporary meaning.

— Western discussion on Chinese public space always includes an element of projection. It results in attributing to the Chinese city an aspect that it does not claim for itself or has only begun to claim. What we identify as public urban space in China could, in a formal sense, be described as 'civic' space, as space subject to public law. However, in truth, in the everyday perception of the Chinese, it is only thought of as open, i.e. undefined urban space. It is the space that fills the expanse between meaningful spaces with nothingness. Open space, weak in meaning, differs decisively from closed space with strong meaning.

A pedestrian sidewalk
– what is that?

— Public urban space on the other hand is a term that incorporates Western norms such as civil society, democracy, participation, 'freedom to the city', and similar concepts. In this regard, the use of the term public space in the case of China is limited to the degree that China is moving closer to adopting the corresponding norms. However, a hermeneutics of the Chinese city should, for now, be based on a strategic concept of the dualism of open and closed urban space.

— Chinese urban planners are absolutely aware of the problems regarding the lack in quality of open spaces and the absence of a culture of how to use them. Significant efforts have been undertaken to define open spaces as public spaces. As a result, the subject matter of public space receives increased attention in professional circles.

— Numerous publications and conferences deal with the subject – even though, in the absence of an enlightened public culture of debate, little is actually being discussed. A number of actions have been taken: in Shanghai, honking has been prohibited by law. With the EXPO 2010 in mind, wearing pajamas 'in public' is also no longer permitted. Indicators and benchmarks have been developed and corresponding monitoring systems have been installed. The largest cities, for instance, attempt to increase the amount of green space per capita from about 3 to 6 square meters. The southern Chinese coastal city of Zhuhai boasts a record-breaking 30 square meters per capita, and Shanghai has set itself the goal of providing 10 square meters per inhabitant before the World Exposition begins in 2010. However, the treetops along the avenues, the green strips alongside the heavily used main roads, unusable as leisure or recreational space, private golf courses and parks on university campuses, hotel complexes, and government resorts had to be included – or, as in the case of Shanghai,[22] the near-complete conversion of the agrarian counties into districts (i.e. urban areas with a resulting high degree of green space), in order to meet the envisioned quota.

— Whether parks or green spaces are open at all is, by the way, debatable. In general, visitors have to pay an admission fee. This is specifically the case in public parks that surround Imperial burial grounds (for instance, Bei Ling and Dong Ling in Shenyang), as well as for the gardens of rich trader families and the gardens of the Mandarin palaces and villas, formerly inaccessible to the general populace. Without paying the admission fee, there is no entry. Shanghai's new central Century Park in Pudong too can only be entered after buying a ticket – not exactly typical for a public space in Europe. Passing Shi Ji Park at daytime, observers may be amazed by watching numerous joggers run around the park, along sidewalks and bike paths, in order to avoid paying the admission fee of 30 RMB (approx. 3 Euro) and still benefit a little from the advantages of Pudong's 'green lung'.

— As reaction to increasing criticism of admission fees for 'public' parks, Shanghai has responded and decommissioned the gate houses of some parks. Entrance is now free. At the same time, restrictions on areas for commercial use by vendors inside the park have generally been loosened. Visitors no longer pay an entry fee, but now have to circumnavigate stands and food stalls – and are sometimes quite surprised that they leave more money in the park than when they still had to pay the entry fee. We shall return to commercialization as the most important factor in the use and design of open urban space later in detail. Interests of political representation and private land appropriations as noted above follow, yet at a distance.

— Let us summarize. What Western observers seek to interpret and classify as public space is, for the most part, open urban space. In the understanding of the Chinese, this space does not deserve respectful treatment. It is the city's pack mule, is abused, beaten up, and worn out. The only alternative to this misery are the smaller or bigger community based – political, commercial, and non-commercial – land appropriations through which empty space is transformed into a socially relevant space. There is actually no real use for public space (at least not yet); the reason being that the telos of any activity in urban space is family and community – and not the individual and society. In order to do business, attract customers, and secure delivery of goods, open urban space is necessary. But public space?

OPEN AND PUBLIC URBAN PLACES

— In Chinese cities, we mostly find two kinds of places, the 'noble' or 'illustrious' and the 'commercial' place. Both are the product of a transformation of open space by sensemaking and appropriated in terms of symbols of power or economy. These appropriations turn empty, meaningless or merely functionally determined space into a space of social activity. Besides these two main types, we can observe the emergence of a third type, resembling an embryonic form of public urban space: the neighborhood or community place.

— The 'noble' place, with Tian An Men Square as its prime example, is a powerful symbol of the new China. Most of all, it is of immense size, scale, and grandeur. It makes the human body seem smaller as it is, preferably serving for mass demonstrations, parades, or mass ornamentation (Kracauer 1977).[23] It is without a doubt a hypostasis of the idea of a 'national collective' (Volksgemeinschaft) and therefore an element of spatialization of a 'hypermoral society' (Gehlen 2004).

— A variation of the 'noble' place significantly closer to civil society or public urban space can be found along the banks of the Huang Pu in Shanghai, at the Bund. Here, we discover an open urban space with spectacular flair. It owes this impression not only to the breathtaking skyscraper-lined silhouette of Pudong's new central business district Lujiazui and the calm flow of the broad Huang Pu, but specifically and decisively to the nostalgic facade interplay of the mostly British colonial architecture of the Bund. This old-fashioned European backdrop forms a most exciting contrast to the hyper-modern skyline of the new China on the other side of the river, thus staging a unique spatial narration of modern Chinese history. On the other hand, especially these spatial characteristics promote a rapid as well as thorough commercialization of the area.

Tian An Men, Beijing

— The 'commercial' urban place uses any media that attract attention in order to draw customers into restaurants, cafés, bars, tea houses, boutiques, and galleries. Most of all – aside from music, neon signs for advertisement, video screens, and the exotic character of the foreign turned into images – an emerging medium that we could describe as urban ambience seems to serve this purpose best. This medium is composed of images that may, for example, combine the intimacy of a Mediterranean piazza and the extroversion of a European market square with the brand logos of American coffee shops and fast food franchise restaurants as well as the *qipaos* of Chinese waitresses in front of the numerous restaurants into a multicultural, theatrical stage backdrop. Xintiandi, a renovated lilong fragment in Shanghai, is a well-known example of this type of Chinese place – frequently discussed and visited by Western tourists.

— In this kind of narrative space production – to be described as 'citytainment' – commerce is the driving force of placemaking. By doing so, it preferably employs the charisma of an urban spatial milieu. Thus, we regularly encounter this place type also in the context of shopping centers, mushrooming everywhere, in which more or less awkward attempts are made to generate urban ambience by simulating Western examples. In most of the equally brand new pedestrian areas, we can also find linear versions of the open commercial place, with the shopping avenue Nanjing Lu in Shanghai as most prominent example, bathed in a delirious sea of lights after sunset.

— Both place types, the 'noble' and the 'commercial', can be classified as open urban spaces. They reflect the dualism of centralistic state authority and economic liberalism, both leaving their mark on the nation today. Designated by authority or commercial interest, open space is subject to a creation of sense and meaning that transcends mere functionality, weakness of meaning, and neglect.

— This designation as public space or civil space is, however, barely related to the attribution of meaning mentioned further above. We say barely, because saying nothing would disregard the 'public' potential of these spaces. Take, for instance, commercial space. It provides space for exchange processes. These actions take place beyond the social immediacy of family and community. Exchange processes as such are therefore not formative of community. Rather, they are, as form of interaction of economic subjects, equal with respect to the law (isonomic), constitutive of society (as a nexus of individuals). Commercialization is thus indispensable for the genealogy of civil – and therefore public – spaces. The market always has been the crucial precondition for public space, and the market square (Marktplatz, Piazza, Plaza) is its prototypical reification.[24]

— Also, in China we must acknowledge that the institutions of community (family, national collective) are the driving forces of a sensemaking that transcends 'society'. This is most of all apparent in commercially driven valorization of open space, as business transactions are controlled by families or family substitutes. This form of community-based commercialization has been described as 'Confucian' capitalism, which indicates that the success of business and trade is preferably internalized on the level of community (vergemeinschaftet) – and not on the level of society (vergesellschaftet), which, incidentally, could be regarded as one reason for growing social disparities.[25]

— Since the opening of China, significant efforts have been invested in designing high-quality public urban spaces (Hassenpflug 2004a). But achieving this goal still seems to be difficult, as numerous examples show, for instance the Municipal Square in Shenyang or the Big Wild Goose Pagoda Square in Xi'an. When it comes to open urban places, designers are quick to orient themselves on Beijing, where Tian An Men Square, located south of the Forbidden City, has been expanded into a square of tremendous dimensions, as ordered by Mao Zedong in the late 1950s. He created a model for today's Chinese urban square, object of admiration of powerful city leaders. Tian An Men Square, featuring the Chairman Mao Memorial, a replica of Lincoln Memorial, became the pinnacle of the 'noble' square, a desirable object of self-promotion of great men – and resulted in a corresponding number of copies.

— In its dimensions and appearance, Tian An Men is the opposite of a civil place. It is neither market place nor plaza nor square, but a demonstration of power reminiscent of Baroque spatial design, a communist version of the Champs de Mars (a parade and drill ground) or a Place Royal. It is a place that denotes centralized authority, the spatialization of the claim to power, which we can recognize without difficulty as rooted in the tradition of the Empire. If Tian An Men Square still occasionally hints at vestiges of 'human scale', then it is due to the incredible masses of people, city dwellers as well as tourists and guests both domestic and international, who assemble here before the gates of the Forbidden City, the National Museum, or the Memorial of Mao Zedong. It is these people who alleviate some of the square's strictness with their spontaneous and unplanned movements, their getting together, their drifting apart, their colorful attire, and their different hair and skin colors.

— Similar aspects are relevant for the Big Wild Goose Pagoda Square in Xi'an. It is also so enormous that people walking across it can actually lose their orientation. The government in Beijing, as a wise travel companion assured me, was not amused about the square design in Xi'an; according to their opinion, a city in China has no right to dare build a square that is almost as big or even bigger than Tian An Men.

Big Wild Goose Pagoda Square, Xi'an

— At the same time, the Big Wild Goose Pagoda Square – as many comparable 'noble' places in the country – benefits the city's inhabitants, as it offers all kinds of small and big advantages of urban life they can use and enjoy: for encounters and relaxation, for taiji and jogging, for dancing, playing games, wheeling and dealing, and of course, not to forget, for flying kites. The Municipal Square in Shenyang or the People's Square in Shanghai are not really different. These places achieve a character in the city that could be described as proto-public. Whereas in the China of old there had been no freely accessible public places at all (except for temple squares or bridgeheads), the 'noble' squares, similar to the commercial places, come close to the idea of public urban places. In general, they are open to a corresponding appropriation by city dwellers.

New public neighborhood
park in Shanghai

— In current development plans for the urban periphery, commercial neighborhood centers or community centers next to residential compounds are frequently completed by adding a new type of public space, the open neighborhood or community places, often also conceived as open community park.[26] While neighborhood parks in older urban areas are completely enclosed by fences, can be locked up, and are generally only accessible after paying an entry fee, the neighborhood or community places are, in contrast, usually openly accessible, not fenced in, and mostly non-commercial. In spatial terms, these places relate to the neighborhood similarly as commercial neighborhood or community centers do. Just as in these, a low or high number of corresponding neighborhoods defines whether they are 'neighborhood' or 'community' centers. The neighborhood or community place is the open antithesis to the closed neighborhood courtyard.

— The rise of neighborhood and community places in China is equally as unsuspecting as it is important. It denotes nothing less than a gradual emergence of public space. As a result, this type of space signals the introduction of elements of civil society, i.e. the strengthening of society (Gesellschaft) and the individual as opposed to community (Gemeinschaft) and family. These neighborhood and community places comprise thoroughly designed landscape architecture, include grassy knolls, tree groups, flower beds, and bushes in a balanced relation, and occasionally feature pavilions and pergolas, sufficiently equipped with furniture or other amenities and areas for recreation. The degree of coverage is high compared to European city or community parks, which hints at Chinese influences that we should explain in detail (cf. the section on 'rocks and plants' in this chapter).

— The open community places and parks are a recent development, which is why we find them only in new developments. Inquiring on their lifespan or sustainability is still merely academic. In any case, they offer a plethora of benefits especially sought by families with children in a metropolis, space for sitting and talking (the grownups), or for playing hide-and-seek (the kids), and so forth. At the same time we can see that maintaining these spaces is not as simple as it seems. This isn't even because of deficits in public sanitation (frequency of cleaning and maintenance operations) – although, in a country with a still nascent culture of civil institutions, such a diagnosis may not come as a surprise. Reasons are rather based on type of use.

— The condition of neighborhood courtyards or closed community places, both located inside residential compounds, is the responsibility of so-called neighborhood committees, representing the municipal authorities on the neighborhood level. As a result, the appearance of these enclosed spaces is clean and orderly. Also, regardless of this particular responsibility, the inhabitants of the surrounding area treat these spaces respectfully. Inhabitants of 'compounds' feel responsible for their care and take action of their own volition. In contrast, use of open or rather public neighborhood and community places is less respectful: waste paper, bottles, cigarette butts, and other kinds of trash are carelessly left behind after the evening picnic, often exacerbated by a significant lack of available trash cans.

— In China today, a mature urban culture of how to use public spaces has not yet developed – at least not in the enlightened European understanding of space for the citizenry, for democracy, or for civil society. The general and still deeply rooted disregard for open space is antithetical to this. If family space intervenes into open space in the way described at the beginning of this chapter, extends its dominion into it, and overwhelms it, then this indicates that community and society can be interpreted as in a state of incomplete separation. At best, we can speak of a stage of proto-publicness.

— In the middle kingdom, since time immemorial, it is and has been the family that decisively determines social life – and therefore life in those spaces that we generally consider to be public. Even social interactions based on and defined by institutions, contracts, and legal codes are preferably intermingled with community interaction, for instance networks (guanxi), which are much more significant here than social networks in Europe. Any businessman can confirm how important a joint dinner is for successful contractual negotiations. Only by initializing community and friendship at the dinner table, can contracts (as social-formal act) receive a community-related legitimacy (analogous to the family), without which they are not worth the paper they are written on. This kind of intervention of the community-related into the society-related is also relevant in spatial terms. We refer to the siting of the Chinese restaurant – or even, food temple – within open urban space.

— Open spaces in the city are analogous to written contracts. We find the explanation for the indifference of city dwellers towards them within the dominant reality of community and family. However, this nonchalant attitude soon turns into careful consideration when open space is valorized by the presence of the family, the community, or the political symbolism of its dramatization, and most of all by commercialization of its use. This kind of valorization transforms the Cinderella of 'open space' into the princess of Chinese urban space.

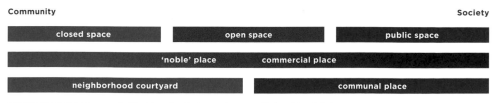

China's place typology: a field of tension between 'community' and 'society'

ROCKS AND PLANTS

— Until now, we have discussed urban or community places from the perspective of social semiotics. What is still missing is the perspective of a comprehensive cultural semiotics or, formulated in reference to architectural artifacts, a culturally informed iconology. So let us take an exemplary look at designed neighborhood and community places in an attempt to understand their iconic messages.

— The text left behind by today's designers of public spaces, gardens, parks, and open spaces of all kinds does not permit easy reading. Not necessarily because of the presence of countless individual signatures, but because of the simultaneity of different Western and Eastern spatial languages. Thus, we have to take another look. And then we discover that Chinese urban gardens seem, in general, to possess an increased artificial character, more decoration, and a higher power of imagery than comparable Western examples.

— There seem to be generally more paved areas, more luxurious furniture, and a greater number of covered areas. More often than in Western examples, bridges, pavilions, pergolas, plazas, and rock formations are present, many and broad paved walkways, more concrete, stones, and gravel, more technical equipment with lighting of all kinds, as well as loudspeakers that ceaselessly bathe the ambience in music (or even, muzak). Plans for these spaces preferably feature organically curved shapes, trees are placed casually into groups, occasionally on suggested hilltops – these green spaces appear to be in the tradition of Picturesque gardening. At the same time, the setting seems informed by Baroque style: there are axial pathways and geometrical formations, numerous trimmed hedges, shrubs, and trees – and repeatedly, rectangular bamboo beds.

— It is possible that the dissolution of design paradigms into eclectic, organic-geometric hybrid constructs is a result of the International Style's influence on landscape architecture. In this case, however, it seems as if the goal is not simply to create forms and combine them but, at the same time, allocate meanings immanent to materials and their dramatization. A hint of Zen or Ikebana can occasionally be felt, an echo of the language of the traditional Chinese garden, which, as a cultural feature, seems impervious to the individual landscape architect's (or whoever designs these urban places) design gesture. In order to read this correctly, we should refer to the culture of the Chinese garden. We reinforce this perspective by taking a look at early modern traditions of European garden design.

— In Europe, the emancipation of urban thought by the cultural revolution of the Renaissance led to the practice of rational design, i.e. of ideal spaces, cities, gardens, and landscapes. Absolutism with its hybrid character, simultaneously feudal and bourgeois, adopted the idea of subjective – and thus perspective – space, and developed it into the grammar of the space of power. This marks the beginning of the Baroque garden, defined by geometry. By demonstrating the predominance of subjective rationality, it made mankind's dominance of nature its core theme. In its iconography of power, its central axes, pathways, labyrinths, tree-lined avenues and cropped hedges, etc., it exemplifies the absolutist alliance of necessity between bourgeois rationality and feudal domination: making the court bourgeois and the market feudal (Elias 78, Vol. II, 222ff). We only need to look at Hubert Robert's paintings of the park of Versailles to immediately recognize that it was contemporaries who already rejected the pretension of the French garden's spatial gesture. Thus, a counter-movement emerged, which found its most important reasoning within the Picturesque gardens of the gentry, the semi-urban, semi-bourgeois low and middle aristocracy of England.

— While the geometric artificial character of the Baroque garden should be interpreted as a metaphor for control over nature and symbol of absolutist power, the English garden relates to a reflexive kind of control over nature, over the cultural determination of its form. Being a counter-design to the French garden, it celebrates 'natural nature', nature in harmony with a culture that doesn't reveal its rationality, dominance, artificiality. In other words: in the Picturesque garden, the built Arcadian, pastoral, bucolic landscape image, the artificial is induced into the natural until it is completely immersed within it and thus vanishes: what remains is the illusion of a seemingly 'natural nature'.

— As contrast, let us take a look at the classical Chinese garden. What the French and English garden separate, is united here: the Chinese garden demonstrates a completely artificial character, and at the same time seems perfectly natural. It doesn't hide its artificial character, its cultural origin, i.e. the human ability to control nature and transform it. Equally, it does not veil its 'naturalness'. Rather, it demonstrates an exaggerated and therefore completely 'natural nature'. The task is the materialization of an all-encompassing unity of culture and nature. Thus, the Chinese garden displays an idea of the Picturesque in which the artificial and the natural, the rational and the emotional are in a state of perfect harmony.

— In the history of the Chinese garden, the organic is immersed by the artificial, the natural by the synthetic, in a way that a priori defied differentiation – completely the opposite to the European tradition of the art of gardening, oscillating between the concepts of the geometric Baroque garden and organic picturesque garden. Whereas the Baroque garden denies nature precisely what is intrinsic to its character, i.e. its capriciousness and remoteness, the Picturesque garden rejects the idea of an artificial-synthetic 'second nature' as cultural endeavor. The practice of the Picturesque garden places itself in the service of a presumed objective aesthetics of nature.

Chinese garden
in Suzhou

— English and French gardens are thus the exact opposite – and therefore display something genuinely European: the conceptualization of dialectics as battle, conflict, as antithesis.[27] Thus, the art of gardening becomes a battlefield of conflict between culture and nature while at the same time ignoring that the one (culture) is always present in the other (nature). Only the awareness of this unity of contradiction within a design process will be able to generate a design language appropriate to its task.

— And this is precisely what the Chinese garden achieves in a unique way: spatializing the harmony of antagonisms. Not too surprising since, for instance, the French post-revolutionary architect E. Moll planned spaces for four gardens in the center of his ideal republican city: a French garden in the west, an English garden in the north, a botanical (scientific) garden in the south – and a Chinese garden (Harten/Harten 1989, 174ff). All of them were supposed to be represented equally within an enlightened republican city.

— In the Chinese garden, as in no other type of architecture, the artificial appears absolutely natural, the natural, however, equally artificial. There is no differentiation between man and world; nothing can impair the 'prestabilized' (prästabilierte) harmony of culture and nature. When materialized, this world view is articulated in a doubly coded dramatization: on the one hand, in the form of an assembly of natural elements, artificial to the highest degree; where unhewn blocks of natural stone are shaped into wildly romantic landscapes comprised of miniature pinnacles, terraces, canyons; and where, in its crevasses, adventurous plants withstand imaginary storms. On the other hand, we have an equally natural composition of completely artificial elements. We find little pavilions, pergolas, waterways, or little plazas that are encircled by trees cut similarly to bonsais into forms reminiscent of mountain ridges. The result is the merging and interweaving of the natural and the artificial in a way that makes differentiation completely impossible, and this means that it turns the process of differentiation into a purely analytical or academic exercise, into a question of knowledge.[28]

— However, the Chinese garden isn't about knowledge, nor about the commitment to a specific design concept in the light of possible alternatives. Rather, the appropriation or consumption of the space of Chinese gardens is about contemplation, i.e. the 'perfection of knowledge or rather cognition', as Goethe[29] stated, no stranger to Sinology. The contemplative immersion into the aesthetics of the Chinese garden lets us experience ourselves as beings that encompass nature in their thoughts and actions, while being encompassed by it in our natural and cultural existence (cf. Schmied-Kowarzik 1984, 35ff).[30]

— The classical Chinese garden is a courtyard garden. It is exclusive and introverted. Beyond Imperial residences, only patricians, high-ranking officials, and rich traders were capable of affording such properties. Naturally, access was only granted to invited, prominent guests. Nothing remotely comparable was available to the 'public'. Of course, by now, this has changed, and numerous previously exclusive Chinese gardens can generally be accessed by paying an entry fee.

Garden House of Goethe in Ilm Park, Weimar

Model of a castle in
destroyed Yuan Ming Yuan Park,
Beijing

— However, we do not find courtyard gardens in public space. Today, landscape architects design public space, and their design process is structurally related to the design practice of architects. They create image-heavy spaces that are more akin to eclectic style collections than the classical Chinese art of gardening. Yet it seems that elements and perhaps quotations from the classical Chinese art of gardening influence these designs. And even if not, a kind of basic mantra still persists, reflected in the already mentioned high degree of coverage and the preference for an image-laden character. It expresses a traditional inclination towards considering form and function as equal and indivisible within the design. The Western division and separation of these dimensions, which only enables their opposition or hierarchization in the first place, is something that has remained alien to the Chinese perspective, despite all alleged Westernization. This applies to architecture in general, including landscape architecture.

— German architects and urban planners tend, due to a highly advanced functionalist perspective informing their design practice, to separate function from meaning and thus from form. The formula of 'form follows function'[31] is something that is alien to the Chinese concept of harmony. Here, architectural form and functional building volume are conceptualized synchronically and assembled to a state in which the capacity to distinguish collapses. Thus, the built environment not only has to meet functional demands, it must also meet demands for content, i.e. by its character as image or sign. In this sense, every design is also a symbol or sign of promise, and architects whose design language is capable of communicating good luck, health, and wealth have a competitive advantage (Lu 2008). For this to happen, architects need to acquire a supply of iconic content, as provided by Chinese culture e.g. in the rules of Feng Shui.

— The immersion of the rational and emotional can be identified in the basic patterns of Chinese culture and corresponding cultural techniques. Let's take a look at written language as example. In Europe, written language or words refer to the rational world, images however to the emotional world. During, for instance, the iconoclasm of the Protestant Reformation, word and image became engaged in conflict, with significant repercussions as a result; the word was victorious, as it could rely on a powerful ally, the Bible, in which the first sentence of the Gospel of John states, very much in the vein of Plato: "In the beginning was the word (...)". We can still feel the results, anti-iconic and hostile towards the image, today – for instance in the 'protestant' character of Modernist or rather Bauhaus architecture.

— As the example of the Cultural Revolution has shown us, China is not immune to iconoclasm. However, we can assume that there is significant cultural resilience here to an attack on the image in the name of the word, as image and word have always existed in close proximity. There is no alphabet, no letters, and no resulting organization of letters into words. In China, there are syllables, and each syllable is an image-sign. Spoken language is similar. In a certain way, it is 'sung', as the articulation of syllables corresponds to four different tonal successions (if one counts the almost atonal 'fade out'– for instance in xiexie = thank you – then we have five 'notes'; Chinese language can actually be considered 'pentatonic'). If we exaggerate slightly, we could actually say: the Chinese speak, when they sing, and they sing, when they speak. They are emotional in their rationality and pictorial when dealing with function.[32] In contrast, the West either speaks or sings,[33] is either emotional or rational, either pictorial or functional.

SWINGING LINES AND DANCING DOTS

3

— We could almost have the impression that the urban design principles of the Charter of Athens weren't actually invented in Europe, but instead, in China. No other country in the world has built so many Siedlung-type residential slab housing settlements, with their north–south orientation, their residual setback green spaces – in China, often also 'grey areas', especially when setbacks between slabs are covered with asphalt or concrete pavers – and their small-scale functional differentiation. Not in Europe, and not even the countries within the Soviet sphere of influence after World War II until 1989.

— Evidently, the country's geoclimatic conditions, expanding north and south of 35 degrees latitude, are of decisive importance for this pronounced practice of orientation, and always have been.[34] Orientation of residential housing to the west or the east is not recommended due to sun angle and declination. In the case of east or west orientation, the sun's low position after sunrise and before sunset would cause excessive heat gains in apartments. However, in the case of south orientation, vertical surfaces provide ample protection to sunlight due to the sun's high position at noon. On the other hand, in winter, the sun's position is less steep and shallow enough in the south for sunlight and thus warmth to enter apartments. Orientation to the north is not relevant to residential construction in the northern hemisphere above 30 degrees latitude – as opposed to industrial buildings, where shed roof skylights permit intake of desired natural, diffused daylight from the north.

— A comparative analysis of large-scale Siedlungen in Germany – from the Märkisches Viertel in the west of Berlin to Marzahn in the city's east, via Bremen-Osterholz to Hoyerswerda, and from Halle-Neustadt to Munich-Neuperlach – reveals that, in Germany, the 'orientation paradigm' of the Charter of Athens was never enforced as strictly as in China. Naturally, again, the geoclimatic position is significant. In central Europe, being located in a northern part of the globe, western and eastern sunlight is less intense. This is why change in orientation from north–south to west–east has always been considered an opportunity for gaining flexibility in urban planning, for instance as a chance for loosening up spatial configurations and enabling individualization in residential development. Also, residential buildings have often been used to create borders for streets, for instance as setback building cordons along main streets and avenues, or simply as enclosing elements for ancillary streets.

— In Europe, southern orientation of residential slab housing construction generally remained piecemeal, as the concept of the 'new city in the park' was interpreted rather loosely – which doesn't imply that elements of classic European perimeter block construction with its traditional facade playfulness had been integrated instead. In terms of spatial politics, modern housing of Fordist origin rejects the bourgeois gesture and individuality of the cult of facades, including the corresponding public culture of urban space production, and is in this respect reluctant to make compromises. Thus, when approximating perimeter block construction, limits appear in the use of the elements otherwise subordinate to slab housing construction as well as in functional deliberations.

— It is therefore clear that creating a border for the street, if this was in fact intended at all, was left to the retail store, the service business, the workshop, or also the office building. For obvious reasons: orientation is less important for these functions. In modern urban planning, this aspect is considered and utilized worldwide as an opportunity for urban design, increasing density, protecting residential settlements against street emissions of all kinds, creating centrality, and mixing functions. This detachment of different urban functions from orientation is also the reason why Modernism in urban planning and design and city centers of old European origin could join forces in the medium of the pedestrian zone, as it integrates both: the structure of block border architecture based on individual lots with the requirements of Modernist spatial-functional specialization. The pedestrian area is the only monofunctional structure that permits, without difficulty, a combination of zoning with the heritage of the old European city.

— We shall return to the preconditions for an attractive Chinese pedestrian area in the chapter on urban media facades (Chapter 5). At this point, we only need to consider that contemporary Chinese urban planning – in this regard, similar to European practice – also makes use of free orientation of the above mentioned basic functions for a design-related and functional valorization of urban space: by creating borders for neighborhood compounds, by providing local supply infrastructure, or as welcome emission buffer between street and residential area.

— However, in China we do not see flexibility in using detached linear structures for a perimeter block typology in residential construction comparable to European practice. Instead, the ideals of the Charter of Athens are enforced much more rigorously. Aerial views of Chinese cities clearly demonstrate this. When zooming onto a Chinese metropolis in Google Earth or viewing it from the top of a TV tower or a skyscraper, we recognize that the expansive urban texture still looks a little bit like a parade ground. Reminiscent of rank and file soldiers, the buildings of the city seem pretty much completely oriented to the south. Similar to magnetically charged iron filings, linear housing structures generally follow an east–west axis. The number of exceptions only rises in the extreme north (Harbin) and even more clearly in the country's south (e.g. in Guangzhou).

**Fordist slab
housing construction,
Shenyang**

'Swinging line', Shanghai

— This pattern even persists in the expansive topical housing estates of the new middle class. These are located in an exterior urban ring, circumscribing the previous genera- tion of Fordist housing estates. Here we find oddly curvilinear housing structures that, from a bird's eye view, appear like meandering chains made of grey and brown strips and blocks. However, orientation is by no means abandoned, as by and large the now swing- ing and dancing housing chains still follow an east–west direction. The magnetic powers of north–south-orientation remain in effect. As a result, the organic basic patterns of the new settlements are limited to structures that are oriented to the south.

— In Europe and America – for instance within the urban planning schemes of New Urbanism – architects and urban designers started to abandon the orientation paradigm in housing estate construction (which was never really that strong in the first place), in order to dedicate themselves to perimeter block construction, to reinforcement of urban centrality, and to preservation of built cultural heritage, by making use of the potential of advanced technology and construction materials. In China, there is no comparable development. And this is the case regardless of New Urbanism, also popular as a fashion in China, and regardless of numerous European themed urban fictions – as all these imported urban constructs serve exclusively to decorate commercial spaces, where they are not bound to the orientation paradigm.

— In residential architecture, China remains true to orientation, yet in a creative way. For instance, we can witness the combination of technicist-functionalist 'Fordism'[35] and its apex, the well-known image of the 'machine-city', with the appealing shapes of organic spatial design, and appreciate this as a remarkable post-Fordist advancement of rectilinear slab and nodal high-rise architecture. We only have to enter one of the new residential settlements without prejudice to convince ourselves of the advantages of Post-Fordist linear and nodal architecture in a residential environment – despite all peculiarities in regard to employed architectural 'style', maintenance of parks, guard security, and introverted character. Setback green space has, in fact, become an element of a new on-site design strategy for park-like recreational space; there are trees, bushes, grassy knolls, and flower beds; comfortable benches, fountains, sometimes even usable playgrounds, many bodies of water, and numerous similar amenities.

— But how can we explain this strong compliance with a building code that obviously drives creative progress and that we usually classify as an element of Modernist-Fordist residential architecture? Is this indeed only the power of Modernism, fallen on fertile soil in a China that considers itself backward? Or is it pure necessity of holding onto Fordist mass housing construction? There is a grain of truth in both points of view – and we should not underestimate the energy of this former victim of colonization to reinvent itself. China wants to reach the very top, and to accomplish this is not only willing to get rid of old-fashioned urban planning practices, but also to both make maximum use of the accomplishments of Modernism and benefit from them as well.

— We count mass residential housing among these accomplishments, and it is absolutely obvious that it offers indispensable potential for urban planning and design in China with its population of far more than a billion.[36] Just recently, in June 2006 the Chinese Central People's Government (Ministry of Land and Resources) published an ordinance according to which the construction of suburban villas, single family residential construction, and other low-rise residential buildings as well as low-density residential developments would no longer receive permits.[37] The future of Chinese residential housing obviously lies in residential high-rise construction – and Fordism offers the relevant propositions in architectural-conceptual terms.

— But this isn't the only reason. Most of all (and again), history offers an explanation for the radical character of this compliance with orientation in residential architecture: in the placement of historic Chinese dwellings, orientation to the south has always played an eminent role. The hutong system, present in northern China and having received sad recognition due to its large-scale demolition, may serve as an example. On a checkerboard-like floor plan, the hutong provides an organizing system for families and neighborhoods. Ever since the Zhou dynasty (Eastern Zhou 770–256 BC), a rule has been in force according to which a particular number of families forms a neighborhood (ling or bi). A further defined number of neighborhoods, ling, form a quarter (li) and yet another defined number of quarters constitute a district (zhu). If a neighborhood consists of five families, the quarter is comprised of five neighborhoods, and the district features four quarters, a zhu can assemble 100 soldiers if each family provides a son. In the li, everyone could be held responsible for everyone else's actions – under the threat of execution (Wu, Weijia 1993, 90ff).

— The family or clan lives in a courtyard house structure, a sìhéyuàn. The interior courtyards of the hierarchically structured sìhéyuàn are closed off on all four sides by buildings: 'si' means 'four'; 'he' refers to a multi-generational household, and 'yuan' is the Chinese word for courtyard. The entry gate can be found on the structure's southern perimeter. The – parental – main house is the largest building in the structure and always accommodates the eldest generation. It is placed in the north and oriented to the south, to the courtyard. This permits a linking spatial arrangement to the high-ranking status of parents within the family hierarchy.

— While comparable structures also correspond to traditional spatial concepts of other regions, southern orientation and the size of dwelling in China are connected to a fundamental expression of social status in a way that is still valid and hasn't diminished to this day. In the new residential compounds of the middle and upper class, we can observe this interaction of orientation and size without difficulty. Almost without exception, a Chinese middle class apartment is not only oriented towards the south, it is on average also much larger than a comparable apartment in Europe.[38]

Sìhéyuàn, model

— Viewed from a bird's eye perspective, the Chinese city is no longer the city of lis and zhus. It is now the Fordist city, introduced to China through Soviet agency. While the Charter of Athens, with its ideals of prefabricated, affordable social housing, fell onto fertile soil in the communist Soviet Union, the soil of communist China proved no less fertile. Here, orientation to the south as a result of sanitary considerations, including demands for light, air, and sun, permitted a seamless integration with the ancient Chinese tradition of southern orientation and the prestige it is linked with. Within Fordist urban planning and design, a piece of the old China was always perpetuated – beyond inexpensive construction methods and high densities achieved by compact building volumes, the best precondition for the phenomenal success of modern residential housing development.

— Against this background, it is hardly surprising that the practice of oriented linear housing construction is even mandated by local building codes. In the case of Shanghai, for instance, a deviation from the 'orientation paradigm' is not allowed without a special permit. We may actually doubt that such a provision is necessary at all; the Chinese housing market demands strict orientation, and any foreign architect and urban planner is well advised to respect the Chinese desire for orientation. We will return to this aspect later in the discussion on Chinese urban fictions (Chapter 6).

— In order to make better use of light intake and views to the exterior while at the same time optimizing density (for instance, floor space ratio), we can often find a tiered, cascade-like or grandstand-like placement of buildings, in which the number of building floors increases northwards by two to four steps (mostly three, depending on the average size of blocks). Hence two to three story villas stand in front, the building type with five to eight stories is in the middle, and the 'masses', i.e. the high-rise buildings with nine, ten or more stories, are placed to the back. However, high-rise housing towers (Wohntürme) can stand in each other's way, especially regarding desired orientation to sunlight. Thus, software-based shadow mapping is nowadays in widespread use to continuously improve the tiered setback model. The tiered gradation permits small-scale differentiation of site quality within the development. The resulting arrangement therefore also reflects the financial means of the inhabitants. The upper middle class lives in the 'front row', the middle class is 'in-between', and the lower middle class is on the 'cheap seats' at the back.

**Tiered arrangement
of residential line housing,
neighborhood, Qingdao**

— But elevation isn't the only factor for differentiation. Placement in relation to parking lots, playgrounds, and setbacks to streets or green spaces influences real estate value as well. Even magic street numbers can be of great importance.[39] Despite the gradually tiered arrangement, planners never forget to place buildings around a central green space, thus expressing the Chinese tradition of introversion. In China, it is necessary to generate high densities and, as a result, buildings require a corresponding number of floors. Residential high-rise construction with twenty to thirty stories and more isn't rare. In many places, residential high-rise construction is mandatory by law, in order to prevent using too much agrarian land for urban development.

— Already today, Chinese residential architecture has begun to combine modern linear structures – and thus the sanitary concerns of the Charter of Athens – with an appealing design of living environments, at least in an initial stage: serial socialist slab housing construction with individually and variably designed residential high-rise buildings; orthogonal-rigid floor plans of modern residential development with organic floor plans of the 'city in the park', linear housing with commercial block border construction; monostructures with functionally versatile border structures. The desolate Fordist settlements with their purely functionalist structure and seemingly frozen slabs have thus started to move; the lines ('linear' buildings or Zeilenbauten) begin to swing, the dots (high-rise buildings with small, 'nodal' footprint or Punktbauten) start to dance.[40]

— The rise of Japan, Korea, and Taiwan already served as an indicator for the West that copying and emulating neither comprise a national character among eastern Asians nor a dead end, but a stage in the current process of catch-up development. Urban planning and design might be one of the first disciplines in which China surpasses this stage. And there is evidence to the claim that this has already occurred – of course, with the support of prominent examples vastly important for Chinese urban planning, Hong Kong and Singapore.[41]

— In summary, we can say that China has adopted the heritage of Fordism – which is, however, transcended and even advanced in a post-Fordist way by the swinging lines and dancing dots of the new Chinese housing estates.[42] In the light of the dramatically increasing degree of urbanization worldwide, it may not be long before China takes on a leading role in urban design with its type of settlement planning. Already today, in the mega-urban landscapes of the Pearl River Delta, the Yangzi Jiang Delta, the metropolitan region Beijing-Tianjin, the northern axis of Dalian via Shenyang, Changchun, to Harbin and along the Yangzi Jiang, spatial models of settlement are designed and implemented that offer solutions for the future, in the form of high-density, vertical, yet highly livable mega-cities.

— Because poverty is traditionally stigmatized in Chinese culture, creativity in urban design is mainly focused on the growing middle and upper class. In this regard, Confucian China differs distinctly e.g. from Catholic Latin America, where society sees poverty as far less offensive. Here, the social acceptance of poverty offers a reason for the increased attention that particular population groups receive from architects and urban planners. In China, the focus is on upward social mobility. Run-down, poor urban settlements are regarded as transitional environments, mainly inhabited by the so-called 'floating population' and labor migrants. Therefore, not much thought is invested in how to deal with these spaces. It doesn't have to stay this way, though. But it is striking that the formalization and valorization of informal dwellings (favelas) and the advancement of social housing construction and housing for the poor constitutes a permanent focus of urbanist theory and practice in Latin America.

'Dancing dots', downtown Shanghai

CLOSED URBAN SPACE

4

CLOSED NEIGHBORHOODS

Exclusion is a key word in the text of the contemporary Chinese city. It is, in fact, a closed city, consisting of omnipresent walls, fences, and gates; a cellular landscape of partial spaces cut off from one another: spaces of production and service industries, public facilities such as court buildings, city administration, and agencies of all kinds, educational facilities (e.g. schools, universities), social facilities (e.g. kindergartens, hospitals) – and most of all housing estates, the so-called residential 'compounds'.[43]

—   In the metropolises of contemporary China, the majority of residential compounds is enclosed. This is hardly surprising, considering that the Chinese word for housing estate (zhù zhái xi'o q) is translated as 'closed neighborhood'. Enclosure is elemental to the understanding of the word neighborhood or residential district and is materialized in the creation of residential compounds.[44] In a certain sense, these closed neighborhoods represent villages within the city; they are rural elements that constitute the Chinese city.

—   "In spatial terms, the MRDS (MRD = Micro Residential District, a synonym for residential 'compound' – D.H.) are precisely defined areas", writes Barbara Münch, "which are not only limited by walls, fences, or buildings, but are deliberately provided an insular character through streets and green spaces. As the courtyard houses and the old danwei before them, the modern residential districts not only define exact borders, but also a clear separation of interior and exterior. As a result, their interior access pattern is not part of the urban street infrastructure. Also, they always feature a core, whether it be a school, a cultural center, or simply a large green space, which symbolically establishes the differentiation between interior and exterior" (Münch 2004, 45).

Hutong access road,
Beijing

**City wall,
Xi'an (Ming dynasty)**

— Against this background the following numbers will not come as a surprise: "Chinese suburbs are becoming 'gated suburbia', ranging from luxury gated compounds to more 'ordinary' commodity housing estates. From 1991 to 2000, about 83% of Shanghai's residential areas have been gated. In the same period, in Guangdong, 54,000 communities became gated, covering 70% of residential area and 80% of population [...]" (Wu, Fulong 2006, 1). Since the survey used for this publication was conducted, the degree of enclosure is likely to have increased significantly.[45]

— Housing estates are not only enclosed spatially by walls, fences, commercial strip buildings, etc., but are also organized towards exclusivity in social terms. Every residential compound is required by law to form a neighborhood committee (Lü Junhua, Shao Lei 2001, 270f). These committees, situated at the lowest level of the hierarchically structured urban administrative system, consist of representatives of so-called living or house groups, generally four to five persons. Their tasks include providing support to management on the neighborhood level in guaranteeing security, sanitary conditions, and integrity of the premises.[46] House groups are separated from each other by the internal access system and green spaces and can thus be distinctly identified within space. Since they are grouped around the interior courtyard of the compound we also speak of a structure of 'four dishes and one bowl of soup' (cf. Lü Junhua, Shao Lei 2001, 271).

— But the Chinese city today is also an open city.[47] It features open areas and generally accessible open spaces. Almost everything related to trade and mobility is located within this open space. We can generally consider streets and places in the urban centers and subcenters as open spaces that relate to the closed spaces of the city just like trunk and branches of a tree to its dense foliage. In the open spaces serving for trade, the predominant part of interaction between economic subjects takes place, and they thus become the spatial point of origin for the formation of a Chinese bourgeois society of the future. From an urbanist perspective, the open city should be evaluated as a great accomplishment of contemporary Chinese history. In a process that has lasted about one hundred years and began in the late years of the Empire, the Chinese city, formerly more akin to Kafka's 'Castle', has become more and more permeable, more open – and therefore more urban.

— Dwelling is exclusive, trade is inclusive. Closed and open spaces are the two defining spatial elements of the contemporary Chinese city – their binary code, so to speak. In the following, we will focus our attention on these two aspects; first, the closed Chinese city, the foliage; and then the open city, the trunk and the branches, reaching out in all directions.[48]

—   Within the practice of enclosing space, a number of influences both historic and recent overlap. But first, we examine the historic influences.

—   Even more distinctly than the contemporary city, the Imperial city was a complex of omnipresent walls, a hierarchically structured cellular pattern segregated along social strata and comprised of family and neighborhood units with defined 'cellular membranes'. In this system, we can identify the spatial representation of a 'hypermoral' (Gehlen 2004) society based on community morals informed by Confucianism. Each level in the hierarchic system of family – neighborhood – quarter – district is divided by walls from each successive level. The quarters (ling) were closed off at night, just like the city itself. Depending on the city's status, additional interior walls could complement the external city walls. Each wall represented the Imperial order. The greater the length and quantity of city walls, the more important a city was and the higher its status in the state hierarchy.

—   This definition indicates that the historic Chinese city is significantly different from the European city in history, where walls generally delineated an independent, self-governed legal domain, often almost complete independence from feudal authority. This more or less articulated autonomy of the old city comprises the historic roots for its contemporary legal status as local authority or regional administrative body and its corresponding planning competence.

—   In Imperial China, nothing comparable existed. "Chinese cities were never corporate entities with their own legislative bodies [...]" (Friedmann 2005, 95). According to Friedmann, as local administrations found themselves confronted with mounting difficulties due to the country's size and population number, a government of "benign neglect" developed that delegated policies of local well-being to local elites – except for tasks such as the implementation of big governmental projects or the onerous collection of taxes (Friedmann 2005, 7f).

—   In regard to the degree of enclosure, the Imperial capital city of Beijing was surpassed by no other Chinese city, except perhaps the historic Chang'an (Xi'an). Beijing consisted of four hierarchically structured partial cities enclosed by walls: the palace city (the 'Forbidden City' with its internal hierarchical structure), the Emperor's city, the capital city, and the southern city (as the developed part of an originally planned outer city). As Imperial residence, the Forbidden City was inaccessible to mere mortals. The same is true also for the massively walled and heavily guarded Emperor's city with its concentric layout. It comprised something akin to a government district and was not open to regular city dwellers without permission. The nine gates of the third city, also concentrically built around the Emperor's city and the capital city and secured by walls 12 meters in height, were closed at night – as all other gates as well. The fourth city finally, a fragment of the never to be completed fourth concentric city, had the function of an interface to the exterior, to the countryside. It was walled and guarded as well.

— As symbols of Imperial rule, incriminated as feudalist, city walls in Beijing and elsewhere were widely demolished and removed from the streetscape during the Mao era. What has remained are the closed areas – initially in the form of closed producers' cooperatives or production units, the so-called danwei, and later the 'gated communities' of the new middle and upper classes, the residential 'compounds', and all the other closed spaces of production, service, and education mentioned above. The danwei, or rather dayuan, are urban versions of agrarian production cooperatives. As walled and introverted cells, they turned their backs on open urban space. Thus, they express the fact that urban open space simply isn't public space. The danwei embody the attempt to create a comprehensive spatial unity of dwelling and working.[49] These producers' cooperatives include dwelling, work space, plan economy distribution outlets, kindergartens, schools, health care centers, and recreational facilities: "The Chinese concept intended for all inhabitants to be completely self-sustaining within their dayuan, the urban planning area unit of the danwei, so that they actually would never have to leave them. […] This means that the cities continued to grow additively in the form of walled units, which were, for their members, not only replacement collectives, but also offered them new territorial communities" (Münch 2004, 44ff).

— Since the early 1990s, i.e. in the course of the general economic opening of China, the danwei were, however, gradually depreciated and disbanded. Their functional structure disintegrated and was differentiated by means of zoning into a variety of functionally specialized urban spaces for housing, working, shopping, learning, recreation etc. As institutions of collective social life, they had already to a large extent vanished towards the end of the old millennium. In this respect they have been replaced by the new 'gated communities', the residential 'compounds'.

— After looking at the danwei, our conclusion is that the ancient tradition of enclosed quarters persists without significant historic interruption within the current practice of residential development. In Chinese cities today, housing is exclusively planned, built, and marketed in the form of gated neighborhoods. The residential area secured by walls and gates is still the standard in China today – and not, as in e.g. Western Europe, an insignificant exception. There are probably no other metropolises in the world with a comparable amount of barriers than in the land of the Forbidden City.

— Residential compounds are completely closed off by walls, iron fences, hedges, and similar means, and often additionally equipped with video cameras, infrared sensors, and comparable security technology. Access to residential compounds is similar to entrances of military installations with their gates, speed bumps, rolling gates, and booms, their guard personnel with quasi-military uniforms, their guardhouses and sentry boxes. Thus, the interior access system of neighborhoods is completely cut off from the traffic infrastructure of open urban space. However, this appears more martial than is actually the case: "[…] the level of security control varies. According to a nationwide survey of community management in 2005, only one third of residential areas are strictly controlled. About 4.3% allows only homeowners to get in; about 26.3% have strict control and require no-owners to register; and 37.6% only have nominal control, and others had very loose gate control […]" (Wu, Fulong 2006).

Neighborhood gate,
Qingdao

— The data featured here may indicate a relaxed attitude in the guarding of residential compounds. And in fact, these compounds are often much more open than they seem at first glance. Quite often, as already mentioned before, these dwellings are even used as places for all kinds of commercial activity. It's quite possible to find laundry services, mom-and-pop stores, and brokerages within compounds, in ground floor ateliers specifically dedicated to such uses. In order to bridge the gap before they move in or until they have sold their previous property, apartment buyers often let labor migrants rent their unfinished apartments – without discernibly aggravating their neighbors or the compound management. Visitors receive a friendly greeting from the guards, and cars can enter without specific controls. However, license plate numbers and date of arrival are registered, because only short term free parking is permitted in many neighborhoods.

— When we inquire on reasons for this permeability, danwei, with their functionally integrated structures, appear to be potential ancestors of these residential compounds. However, when following Münch, then it seems as if their outdated influence was gradually disappearing. In due time, closed neighborhoods would transform into pure residential zones, and would therefore become more akin to Western or rather American 'gated communities'. Yet, there would be important differences. The Chinese neighborhood, which could be described as a product of a gradual historic development, was not only accepted by people from all walks of life and social strata, but shared as a way of life. In other words the Chinese closed neighborhood as such would denote no tendencies towards social segregation. What a startling and poignant contrast to the situation in the United States would this be! We could then interpret American 'gated communities' as a spatial reaction to increasing social polarization and resulting tensions in a historically spatially open society. While residential quarters in China were subject to functional specialization and thus transposed a number of uses into open urban space, the trend in the USA was headed in the opposite direction: an increasing number of functions was introduced into these exclusive spaces (Münch 2004, 47; cf. Kögel 2004b).

— But the permeability of compound borders, a fact that we can observe frequently, may also refer to the symbolic nature of this enclosure. In a number of cases, it seems to have evolved into an independent form that has gained autonomy from its content, i.e. security and control. In the meantime, many residential compounds seem merely a parody of their American counterpart. Fulong Wu comments on this laconically: "Despite a gate, security is not a concern" (Wu, Fulong 2006).

— The closed neighborhood is 'natural' to China, for the historic reasons described above. It is neither questioned, nor are there any alternatives. At the same time, influences from North American 'gated communities' on Chinese closed neighborhoods can't be completely dismissed. The medium for this influence seems to be the American 'way of life', widely admired in China – and, in the eyes of the Chinese middle and luxury classes, with the 'gated community' as seemingly important component. The United States, we are told again and again, are a successful nation. To be successful as well, it appears to be a wise choice to follow its example. If successful Americans live in gated communities, living in such a closed neighborhood as well seems like a good idea.

— According to a Chinese planner's statement on this subject, there are further reasons for the resilience of the 'gated neighborhood' in China. This form corresponds to the needs of governmental or private developers in a number of ways. For one, the format matches the plot sizes, i.e. the area blocks that are the result of site development. In addition, each block, for purposes of successful marketing, is supposed to display the developer's signature and feature unique sales propositions. Thus, each quarter attains the status of a product with a brand identity, at the same time offering the promise of association for the compound's residents. Therefore, the equation one block = one compound = one brand = one identity is formulated. In order to adequately dramatize the uniqueness of the particular quarter, the task is to provide it with an unmistakable character. And separating it from the environment contributes to this task just as much as 'branding' through repetitive decoration, color choice, architectural 'signatures', or uniform roof decoration.

— However, within the term 'closing off from the environment' we detect the influence of something different, perhaps much more decisive. The word 'environment' is the key, in this case referring to the open urban space beyond the gated space. This open space has remained irrelevant, even alien to Chinese mentality, until today. Within a world view deeply informed by family or rather community, open space is at best a functional space, a space in the shadows of the Chinese way of life characterized by the precedence of community and widespread absence of (individualistic) society. It is crossed, passed, and transgressed by car, bus, bicycle or on foot, in order to reach the other side of it, the inviting, tempting side where all important things happen: family, relatives, friends, topped with a fine dinner, because dinner is heavenly!

'Dinner is heavenly', Fushun

Serial villa development, Qingdao   **Serial villas in Luodian, Shanghai**

— Let us not forget the upper class villa neighborhoods. For Western observers, their serial luxury is breathtaking: Europeans are used to recognizing the villas of their upper and luxury classes as solitary, unique designs. They interpret these as the homes of wealthy members of the bourgeoisie, as villas that express personality, individuality, and independence through the uniqueness of their respective architectural gesture. But even though villa areas may be concentrated in sites with ideal topography and climate, the individual buildings hardly constitute any kind of neighborhood context. In spatial terms, the demonstration of the ego ('I') dominates the denotations of a neighborly 'we' based on shared lifestyles.

— How astonishingly different the Chinese villa compounds are in comparison! Here, we find numerous, in some cases up to a hundred and more, almost identical villas in simulated or fictitious 'styles' (Tuscan, English, Nordic, Spanish, fairytale, etc.) with expensive impression in repetitive configurations like soldiers on a parade ground. The only aspects that occasionally keep them apart are roof colors or color and style of drapes. Also, they are not surrounded by individual hedges or fences belonging to the house, but are placed freely and openly similar to lines and dots within a surrounding green space or buildings within closed vertical neighborhood blocks. This is due to security being organized within the neighborhood collective.

— European observers are, however, used to seeing the luxury of an expensive European villa pointedly protected by an individually designed enclosure. Münch offers a hint on the background of this peculiar Chinese modesty or disregard. She notes that the "typological form" within the new residential compounds may have "changed radically, however, a certain continuity exists in the architectural significance of the single or solitary building: Today, as during the Imperial era and the Mao era, these buildings are not results of individual architectural design, but building volumes that are arrayed as exact copies within a MRD" (Münch 2004, 45). Therefore, the serial character of contemporary residential construction not only indicates that the practice of Fordist residential development has been perpetuated, but also that the ancient tradition of the semi-urban, half-village, half-urban fabric of courtyard structures (i.e. the hutongs of Beijing) is still alive.

— The interplay of exclusion and inclusion becomes apparent once more. The Chinese middle and upper class family demonstrates its wealth within a community, within the membership of a collective that lives in an exclusive neighborhood. As signs, the villa replicas cater exactly to this desire. In China, wealth rhymes with collective and community. The West is the complete opposite! Here, a villa signals individualism – and therefore distinction – by separating itself from other villas through uniqueness, fence, and hedges. The urban open villa suburb of Europe is diametrically opposed to the village-like, closed villa neighborhood of China. We now realize that the Chinese luxury neighborhood is the habitat of a Confucian proto-bourgeoisie.

INTROVERTED NEIGHBORHOOD COURTYARDS

— In order to understand contemporary production of Chinese urban space, the term 'introversion' is indispensable. It is a socio-spatial key word par excellence. The adjective 'introverted' means 'to turn inward' or 'oriented towards the interior'. In architecture and urban planning, introverted spaces or introversion as spatial practice have always played a significant role.

— Introverted spaces, for instance courtyard houses, denote community or a lifestyle defined by a community ethos. This is the case when the courtyard house constitutes a dominant form of dwelling that defines the habitat. This was also the case in the historic China of the Imperial era, it remained this way in the form of the danwei during communist modernization, and it has remained so until today: in the form of the residential compound or MRD with neighborhood courtyard. It comes as no surprise that, according to Lü Junhua and Shao Lei, only a few years ago the Chinese Minister for Construction, on the occasion of a pilot project in Kunming, called for reinforcing the concept of the interior courtyard.[50]

— The strict enforcement of the Charter of Athens in China belongs to the past, despite all compliance to strict orientation. Since the opening of the country, a remarkable advancement of Fordism has taken place. The social, socialist or collectivist slab council estates defined by rationalism turned into both picturesque and vertical Postmodern neighborhoods of swinging lines and dancing dots. This transformation occurred simultaneously with a partly abrupt, partly gradual (endogenous) dissolution of those former Chinese producers' cooperatives (danwei) that were characterized by integrating Fordist housing estates into a functionally comprehensive socio-spatial communal system.

Neighborhood courtyard, Yangpu district, Shanghai

**Neighborhood courtyard,
Pudong district, Shanghai**

— This transformation is also induced by exogenous factors, most of all by influences from eastern Asia, for instance Hong Kong, Taiwan, and Singapore, which offer guiding principles, fashions, and stylistic inspirations (not only) for residential development that the country has, since its opening, taken advantage of. Based on loose, organic, or also figurative, yet always auspicious patterns (most popular forms seem to be fish, turtle, or snake), the 'line-and-dot'-arrangements of the new residential buildings feature post-Fordist variations of the dominatingly southern oriented slab housing estates of the past. We can see eclectic designs ranging from moderate to extreme. The resulting 'softening' of floor plans is complemented by developments such as the tiered arrangement of linear housing structures and the culture of roof decoration.

— The most spectacular advancement of modern residential development in China is, however, the neighborhood courtyard. It has become a marketing success, and no current residential development project can do without it. The neighborhood courtyard is a green space situated at the center of a residential compound, rich in furniture and decoratively designed, featuring circular flower beds, fountains, and veritable parks. The architecture in the compound is arranged in groups and built around this interior space in multiple layers along a west–east axis. The central green often protrudes like fingers into the setback areas, occasionally expanding into ellipsoid shapes circumscribing cultural centers, occasionally also a school, and always pergolas, playgrounds, fitness and workout equipment, or simply benches.

— In ambitious middle and upper class compounds, we often discover large interior courtyards that feature, comparable to landscape gardens, ample bodies of water, green spaces, canvas-lined pavilions, pergolas covered in vines, ritzy waterworks and benches, trick fountains, bridges and pontoons, occasionally even restaurants. The design is usually based on an eclectic mix of English, French, and Chinese garden concepts (Chapter 2), complemented by a selection of decoratively employed elements from the stylistic repertoire of Modernism and Postmodernism.

— At first glance, the neighborhood gardens, comparable to public parks, bear little relation to traditional Chinese gardening culture. An appealing design style dominates, with an iconographic concept that may best be described as a mix of tamed Baroque and decoratively softened landscape architecture. The Baroque influences have been relieved of their symbolic expressions of power, and the artificial character of these arabesquely designed gardens is palpable. No trace of a Chinese garden, if we disregard a few endemic plants and a few insignificant references, for instance the way trees and shrubs are groomed and cut or the occasional use of craggy rocks.

— But here as well, looks can be deceiving. Something has remained. Western observers may note the unusually high degree of coverage, already witnessed in the neighborhood and community parks. The extensive use of rocks and the rich equipment with decorative small-scale structures of all kinds (small temples, galleries, pergolas, summer pavilions, etc.) is an a priori of classical Chinese garden design. These elements are indispensable materials of a dramatization aiming at a harmonic and balanced relationship between the artificial (culture) and the vivid (nature).

— Contrary to this, the aesthetics of contemporary neighborhood gardens seems rather nondescript. In today's residential compounds, we are no longer dealing with miniature mountain ridges or rocky garden landscapes, with summer pavilions or protected spaces for meditation and contemplation beneath majestic trees. Here, we instead see surfaces covered in asphalt, concrete pavers, tiles and stones of all kinds, pathways, little plazas, wooden ramps and pontoons with various covered areas encircled by quickly growing low-maintenance foliage green. The degree of coverage occasionally increases so much that the centrally located neighborhood park or courtyard seems more like an urban square. Here, not only a harmonization of differences takes place, an almost typical blurring of the line between place and park in Chinese space production, but also that blur or haziness or uncertainty in defining function and form of urban public or open space already mentioned above.

Left:
Access passage,
Xing Cheng

Right:
Family courtyards,
Xing Cheng

— In terms of formal classification, neighborhood courtyards are semi-public spaces. They exclusively serve the compound residents and their guests. The residents, when buying their apartment,[51] also purchase a percentage of the green spaces, and thus are required to continuously pay fees for its maintenance and care – generally as part of security costs.

— In typological terms, neighborhood courtyards represent the tradition of Chinese introversion. What used to be the courtyard house (sìhéyuàn) is now the residential compound. As a result, the interior courtyard of the former family residence evolved into the now semi-private neighborhood courtyard. In China today, hardly any new compound is built without this central spatial element – especially for marketing reasons. Customers from the blooming Chinese middle and upper classes have internalized this picturesque form of introversion as much as the architects who design the residential compounds and the teachers who provide the corresponding design education. The interior neighborhood courtyard receives everything; public space and the street, on the other hand, are given nothing – but there is a growing number of exceptions.

— The (merely seemingly vanishing) practice of introverted spatial design is perpetuated in the form of centrally located parks, spaces for recreation, playgrounds, bodies of water, and fountains. Although there is no model analogous to the northern Chinese courtyard house (sìhéyuàn) or its central and southern Chinese variations in modern neighborhood design, the residential compound (MRD) as such has inherited the interior courtyard – and its corresponding interior orientation. The former family courtyard has thus evolved into the semi-public neighborhood courtyard as a unique and independent urban spatial form.

— We presume that an empirical survey may verify Bahrdt's theory of "incomplete integration" (Bahrdt 1961) in the new middle and upper class compounds. Anonymity and loneliness are not unknown in the urban villages of today's China, just as translocal forms of social integration through modern communication technology and automotive mobility are not unknown practices. On the other hand, Chinese closed neighborhoods seem to have a much more distinct capacity for social integration than European open residential areas in the urban periphery. In many residential compounds, actually something akin to a palpable neighborhood identity seems to be emerging – despite high rates of fluctuation.[52] The already mentioned neighborhood committees seem to play an important role in this regard.

— The built amenities of the neighborhood courtyards are, if present, welcomed and strongly frequented. People meet each other; speak to each other, play games, and exercise. There are numerous taiji groups and occasionally people meet to play music together or to dance on suitable surfaces in the neighborhood courtyard. Reasons for this visible form of social coherence may be the quality of the spatial amenities, the social homogeneity of the residents, the group identity of neighborhoods, supported by numerous measures, and, not to be underestimated, traditional solidarity within a neighborhood or residential district. We should also consider further community identities beyond the family as the center of social identity; 'we'-identities that, similar to the layers in an onion, circumscribe the family identity: a neighborhood-based 'we', a friendship-based 'we' (guanxi), local 'we', and a national 'we' integrated in a shared culture.

ROOF AND LIGHT SCULPTURES

— Eye-catching and sometimes intrusive, we can often see spectacular roof constructions and roof decorations that play a surprisingly important role in the residential compounds of the new middle and upper classes. The symbolic meaning of roof decorations is also quite literally highlighted by colorfully illuminating them at night. Especially Western visitors are surprised by these roof sculptures, overloaded with electronic decoration. The shapes range from simple pavilions and terraces to occasionally almost fragile pergola cornices, arcades, figurines with naturalistic impression, to expressionistic sculptures, signs, and miniature copies of Greek temples complete with columns, architraves, and tympani. Mostly in older buildings with gabled or hipped roof construction, existing roof ridges, hips, valleys, and eaves are simply and literally redrawn with bands of lighting, following the example of the Forbidden City's palaces at the Tian An Men in Beijing. In the case of flat roof and pitched roof constructions (typical of Fordist housing) colorful light chains are applied to roof edges, or lighting fixtures of all kinds are attached to facades. When people feel that a building lacks a proper hat, this way it may at least have an illuminated one at night.

— How can we explain this pronounced love for highly visible, expressive roof decorations? The word 'hat' offers a fundamental indication. In China's history, social status was expressed especially through headdress. Among the types of headdress that served as sign of rank we find not only hats, but also roof construction and decoration – no big surprise! Roof decoration in China has always been considered a kind of headdress, a sign of rank for those who reside or live beneath it. The higher the position in the social hierarchy or the greater the spiritual meaning of the institution that is 'wearing' the 'hat', the more significant the roof decoration is, according to color, material, and form. Roof decorations that quite literally project meaning were available to the mighty, important, and successful.

— We know from architectural history that roof construction had an enormous importance in Europe as well – until it became redundant, in the eyes of functionalism, as an object of aesthetic attribution. We remember, for example, gabled roofs or domes of temple buildings of classical antiquity, the builders of which were called architéktôn (architects), which is a combination of the words archós (leader, chief) and téktôn (carpenter, artist, craftsman, builder). However, in Europe's history, roof decoration never received the same degree of importance and creative dedication as in China.

Temple roof,
Hunan University campus,
Changsha

Roof decorations, Shanghai

Branding by illumination of roof sculptures

— In general, Fordism in China ended the tradition of roof decoration as well, mostly in residential construction. But now, in times when the country attempts to reinvent itself, the ascending middle and upper classes remember the capital for distinction that is signalized by expressively designed roof decoration. They want to see a reflection of their own success within roof decorations suffused with meaning.

— The practice of lavish roof decoration can only be understood when taking the cultural relevance of the traditional Chinese roof into account. Historic roofs were – despite their dynamic and elegant appearance – difficult and costly to build. They served not only for weather protection, but also (by use of roof charms or roof figures and the color of roof materials) as protection from evil spirits and as a social sign of status.

— Weijia Wu provides us with insight that deepens our understanding of the 'hat' in Chinese architectural culture. The walled city is seen as symbol for the legitimacy of Imperial rule, and Imperial rule is interpreted as a large roof that covers everything beneath it (Wu, 202f). A settlement without a wall is not an Imperial residence, thus has no (metaphoric) roof function, and is therefore not a city, but instead a village (according to a decree of the Song dynasty, 960–1279 C.E.), even if its population number makes it a metropolis and even if it covers a geographic area of corresponding size.[53] This interpretation of the city wall as representation of the roof, i.e. the Emperor, is emphasized by wall pavilions generally situated on wall corners and above gateways and equipped with expressive roof decoration.

— The 'disenchantment of the world',[54] on the advance in today's China as well, has not been able to expel this playful inclination towards symbolism. The strong anchoring of Chinese everyday culture in family and community seems to strengthen the collective memory. The Chinese love their opulent roof decorations – and casually use them also as signs of identification and orientation within the sheer endless cityscapes of their megacities. The 'good life' is not only expressed in good meals, a big apartment, and a big car, but also through a residential compound with unique roof decorations. In residential compounds (MRDs), the subject of roof decoration and lighting is fused with the strongly expanding practice of branding neighborhoods, i.e. the combination and blending of local identity with brand identity. Roof decoration and lighting sculptures are thus to be considered strategic elements for developing corporate neighborhood images.

— At this point, let us briefly discuss the close interrelation between roof and facade in history, rooted in design, proportion, and building volume. The increasingly important role of roof decoration for developing strategies that offer distinction to neighborhood residents is a factor that evidently also informs facade design. It is literally drawn into the practice of branding. In the newest residential compounds, we can see how an integrated architectural language assumes the role previously played by the roof exclusively. Residential compounds occasionally display a highly elaborate architectural language; roof decorations directly adopt this language and, as a result, their visual impact is minimized in relation to the facade. In this regard, roof decoration becomes an integral part of a distinct architectural language, and at the same time a distinct means of communication.

BRANDING COMPOUND LIFESTYLES

— Roof and facade as signs confirming rank, prestige, status, and success constitute an aspect of transformation of neighborhood identity into brand identity. 'Transformation' indicates that the neighborhood culture historically informed by socialism is gradually declining within the emerging social upwardly mobile middle class and is replaced with a more iconically oriented identity based on distinction through dramatization. In the course of this change, the abstract-collective superego is replaced by an equally abstract-individual one. Brand cult is essential for this.

— However, due to its positive connotations, the idea of neighborhood in itself is an important resource for the concept of a neighborhood-related brand identity – and is thus immediately placed in its service. "The notion of 'community' is a selling point for gated suburbia in China" (Wu, Fulong 2006).

— Life in a closed compound today is less a question of vital neighborhoods, perceived belonging, and controllable security, but rather of the right packaging, the projected image, and connected to this, the internal identity. Neighborhood is an ingredient of proper, status-oriented packaging and is simply indispensable according to the Chinese ethos of family and community. So far, according to Fulong Wu, literature has not dealt with this aspect of 'branding' in modern Chinese urban planning. "What is lacking in the literature is to see how the cultural politics (the politics of 'niceness', politics of the aesthetic, politics of 'good life', or in a word politics of 'urbanism') is unfolded in the construction of gated community [...], how the Chinese suburbia is becoming a new way of life. We see gating more as 'branding': labelling and decorating the quality of life 'behind the gate'" (Wu, Fulong 2006).

— Branding begins with roof 'hats'. Developers who market the residential compounds of the new middle class focus on roof decorations as brand images with a recall value of lasting effect. Branding is continued within the architectural language of facades and in neighborhood names, since street names and numbers are not suitable for a media-based strategy for distinction, particularly considering that suburban arterial roads and tangential streets are often many kilometers long.

— For purposes of marketing in an equally large and competitive real estate market, the practice of giving neighborhood blocks 'fancy' names has been established. This book was, to give an example, written in a building within a neighborhood given the rather pretentious name 'Shanghai International Maritime Garden'. "Core to the concept is the brand – all these prestigious spaces have a name, not an ordinary street name such as 'Beijing Road' and 'Nanjing Road' but a label of life quality – Yosemite, Orange County, Riviera, Fontainebleau, and McAllen" (Wu, Fulong 2006).

Renowed names as brand identity: neighborhood gate, 'Weimar Villa', Anting, Shanghai

Tuscan style as compound
brand identity, Ningbo

— Germans may rejoice, as Germany is present as well. China already has a 'Weimar Villa'. It is located on the outskirts of Weimar's partner city, Anting New Town, which is part of the city of Anting, the Detroit, or perhaps better, the Wolfsburg of China. It wouldn't be a big surprise if we also encountered a neighborhood under the name 'Heidelberg Village' in China. However, it is more likely that the name would stem from one of the 'Heidelbergs' in the United States or Canada. "The new rich [...] began to seek difference and diversity; gated suburbia, tactically promoted by the real estate developer as an 'exotic' and 'stylish' new living space, meets such an imagination for a good life. The gated communities are branded through a mélange of metaphors such as 'classic', 'continental', 'authentic'. 'European' and 'North American' lives, have indeed become the de-contextualized and diverse built forms" (Wu, Fulong 2006).

— Due to the market-oriented nature of residential development, architecture and urban planning inadvertently become instruments of targeted and successful marketing. This orientation also draws both into the transformation process from neighborhood identity to brand identity. Urban planning and architecture become instruments of the reification of signs and codes provided by TV and the Internet within the global village of virtual spaces, and thus enter the minds of viewers – in order to be unveiled there within dreams that supply the imagery for the 'good life'.

— Let us summarize: contemporary urban planning in China is, to a high degree, charged with symbolism. Naming of neighborhoods, roof decoration, architectural copies, even the identity-providing and guaranteeing potential of the term 'neighborhood' become components of a brand awareness that is deliberately created and targeted by developer agents. People live in a gated neighborhood, its name is 'New Venice', roof decoration is impressive and unique, people drive BMWs, and the apartment covers 180 or more square meters. In the neighborhoods of China's new middle and upper classes, architecture has always been media architecture, and the new cities therefore media cities. In the following, we will continue to deal with the subject of media architecture and media cities, first in the context of the open city, where we encounter the phenomenon of the media facade, the urban TV screen, and finally in the context of the practice of citytainment, which has evolved considerably in China.

ORIENT MEETS OCCIDENT – HYBRID URBAN QUARTERS

— The intermingling of Chinese and European spatial practices and styles is nothing new at all. As early as in the pre-colonial Imperial era, for example, Baroque buildings and gardens of French origin were added to Yuan Ming Yuan Park in Beijing, the Qing dynasty's summer palace that took 150 years to complete.[55] To this day, observers can clearly recognize decorations composed of Western and Eastern elements (see image) in the many marble ruins on the estate, destroyed by European colonial forces during the Opium War.

— While the encounter of cultures in Yuan Ming Yuan Park happened in a rather accidental manner, this process of encounter is of a substantial nature in the case of the residential structures in Shanghai called lilong. The lilong combines – clearly visible within the second generation[56] described as 'intermediary form' – the Western-extroverted public street with the Eastern-introverted quarter and its interior courtyards.

— The lilong developed under the influence of colonial powers, most of all England (since about 1840) and France (starting some years later), but also, to a comparatively limited degree, the United States (the same as France). They comprise closed residential quarters with two to three story residential buildings, as such comparable to the northern hutong. The quarters are separated from the surrounding environment by walls, can be accessed on the exterior through gates at public or commercially used streets and in the interior through a hierarchically organized network of primary and secondary passages. The apartments are accessed through ancillary passages running in west–east direction via stone gateways oriented to the south called shikumen[57] (in the earlier forms!). These lead to interior courtyards, separated from the passage by a tall wall. In the newer lilong, shikumen and wall are replaced by a front garden featuring gate and fence. The older lilong feature a further interior courtyard which was reduced to a simple light shaft in the course of time, yet included a well in its earlier versions.[58]

— Here, we focus our interest on a particular detail that has received insufficient recognition in architectural and urban planning literature. We mean the clearly articulated facades and facade decorations, based on Western influences. These are oriented towards the shikumen passages or back alleys, thus transformed from pure access corridors into a kind of public space: into public or semi-public space, in the middle of the closed, introverted, non-public neighborhoods. It is this simultaneity and mutuality of Chinese courtyard townhouse architecture and Western decorated facade[59] that comprises the unique and frequently discussed magic of the lilong. Within the newer lilong, due to the front gardens and a significantly improved infrastructure, a quality developed that still meets highest demands of urban residential lifestyles.

View towards a 'lilong' quarter, Shanghai

Ruins in Yuan Ming Yuan Park.

Only a closer look reveals the mixture
of Baroque and Chinese Motifs, decorations
or images.

Inside lilong settlement, Shanghai

Jingyu block, exterior, Harbin

— In the jingyu block in the central Daowai district of the northern Chinese provincial capital Harbin, we can find a comparable example of hybridization of building culture, significantly further developed in terms of its language of forms. Here, Chinese dwelling and construction types mix with Russian influences into a much more balanced form in terms of cultural contributions. While at the lilong elements of extroverted European urban culture face interior fountains ('Divine Fountains') and passages, in Harbin we stand on public streets in front of facades indicating lot-based perimeter block construction, partly decorated in lavish eclecticism ('Chinese Baroque'). But when we walk through the strikingly large gates, we find ourselves, after a few steps, in a characteristic Chinese interior courtyard, a kind of enlarged sìhéyuàn with a main building oriented to the south, two side buildings and expressive wooden steps leading to the upper floor. This courtyard house structure offers room for seven families when including the upper floor of the building segment facing the street. The ground floor of the building segment oriented towards the block border generally serves commercial purposes, i.e. as workshop or store.

— In the Russian-Chinese multifunctional hybrids of the jingyu blocks, the union of extroverted urban space of Western type and introverted, family-oriented Chinese courtyard houses is expressed in uncanny clarity. Here, the sizes of courtyard houses are oriented on the representational demands of the public facade. Also, means of enclosure such as walls, fences and guarded gates, as in the classical Chinese residential quarters (li), the hutong, the lilong, or the new residential compounds, do not exist. This function is performed by the block border.

— The illustrations show these gems of architectural or rather cultural hybridization in a deplorable condition. There are many reasons for this: the value of these urban planning hybrids is not recognized beyond academic circles. Here, the long-term economic potential of local architectural cultural heritage succumbs to short-term commercial thinking. Beyond that, these inner city quarters, especially in their current condition, do not reflect the dwelling and lifestyle preferences of the new middle classes, rapidly growing in Harbin as well. At present, no provisional buyers are in sight, which is why developers (including the city authorities) aren't interested in the restoration, maintenance, and valorization of the quarters.

— Finally, and this is where we come full circle, these inner city quarters have become the 'bridgeheads' for labor migrants who are streaming into the city. And actually, the run-down condition of these quarters and the corresponding low rents are exactly what make them interesting to this clientele. Here, people seeking fortune come together – and when they have found it, they buy their own apartment, register, and thus make room for new labor migrants. During the winters, in Harbin as cold as in Siberia, the jingyu block residents use the refuse that heaps up in the interior courtyards as heating material.

Interior courtyard, house, jingyu block, Harbin

OPEN URBAN SPACE

5

LINEAR CENTRALITY OR THE MAGIC OF THE GOLDEN CORRIDOR

— If we interpret cities as signs, then they primarily denote centrality – in various forms: nodal centrality, linear centrality, dispersed centrality, etc. In general, urban centrality refers to a place of highest symbolic meaning, optimum accessibility, and at the same time, greatest scarcity. Thus, urban centers are generally also the most expensive and, in fact, the prime locations in the city or cityscape.

— In Europe throughout history, a kind of centrality has developed that has a nodal form and is public in terms of content. First in the agora of the Greek polis, an 'embryonic' urban space, then in the Roman forum with its representational character, and finally, in the process of reurbanization after approximately 1,000 C.E., in the ensemble of market place, church, and city hall, which spatially defines the European city to this day. In this ensemble, an urban society founded in Christian faith and bourgeois self-determination saw itself spatially represented in an adequate way.

— In the United States of America, which never shared the feudal and old bourgeois traditions of Europe, but rather considered itself its republican counter-design, commerce became the prime motor of urban development from the very beginning. The market's powers of urban formation produced the 'central business district' (CBD), a place where the company headquarters of 'big business', banks, shopping centers, hotels, lately also cultural institutions and wealthy urbanites in fancy residential high-rise buildings assemble in order to add the symbolic capital of centrality to their image – and of course, vice versa. In the Chinese city, however, linear or axial centrality is the characteristic form, suitable for the design of hierarchical spatial sequences. There are two prominent reasons for its significance in Chinese urbanism.

— The first reason is a historic one. How could it be otherwise! Following cosmological laws, similar to those applied in the founding of Roman cities, classical Chinese cities, including necropolises, were also arranged and oriented according to spiritual aspects. Cities were based on a rectangular plan with north–south orientation and two (or more) central axes intersecting in the city center. These clearly remind us of Cardo and Decumanus, the central axes of Roman cities in antiquity. Usually, the 'bell tower' or 'drum tower' is located where the two main axes meet, i.e. in the very center of town. These, together with city walls, are the preeminent symbols of the omnipresence of Imperial power. The Emperor's palace or governor's residences were often placed on the northernside of the axis running in west–east direction, mostly integrating the north–south axis. The historical main axis with east–west orientation is highlighted in its significance by providing access to temples, such as ancestral temple (usually in the east) and harvest temple.

— Exact regulations on the hierarchy of function and meaning served to determine size, arrangement, and equipment of each building and each street. Hierarchy was always translated into a linear spatial sequence. This linearity indicates the importance of a singularly legitimate perspective: the Emperor's. Thus, in its arrangement, the city represents the unchangeable order of things, determined by the Emperor (Wu, Weijia 1993). Linear or axial centrality has persisted in the spatial memory of Chinese capital cities (Beijing, Xi'an, Nanjing, Hangzhou) and in many other cases of Imperial city founding to this day. In fact, it has imprinted itself in the collective memory of the Chinese people.

— With this we already approach the second reason for the popularity of linear centrality in Chinese urban planning. Axial centrality with its related hierarchical sequence of space allows the centralistically legitimized, 'hypermoral' or 'papaistic' (Gehlen 2004) and thus strictly hierarchically organized Chinese society of the Imperial era (in fact, it would be more correct to speak of a national community – Volksgemeinschaft) to spatially reflect and recognize itself in an adequate way. Since the basic social structures of this society haven't changed significantly in the past one hundred years, despite Republic and Maoism, the still 'hypermorally' shaped Chinese society of today continues to mirror itself preferably in the hierarchical spatial sequence of central axes. Moreover, linear centrality seems to be strongly interrelated with the often obviously Baroque appearance of city halls, all kinds of government buildings and, not to forget, of illustrious places and noble squares while keeping in mind that the latter spatial figures are historically much younger than the ancient axes.

— The old and new capital city of Beijing as example demonstrates how significant the power of linear centrality is to this day. The sports, service, and housing facilities in the city for the 2008 Olympics were placed, almost naturally, along and on the northern part of the historic north–south axis, the former Dragon Axis. However, this was only the beginning of a complete renewal, elongation, and revitalization of the northern part of this axis. Looking southward, we see the gigantic Tian An Men Square, one of the largest city squares of the world, located in front of the gates of the Forbidden City, and rather naturally, on the north–south axis. When Mao Zedong ordered the construction of this huge, open square flanked by buildings with political meaning (Great Hall of the People in the west, National Museum in the east), he not only envisioned an antithesis strong enough to offer resistance to the symbolic presence of the enclosed complex of the Imperial palace, but also to reorder the central-spatial hierarchy by interrupting its spatial sequence. The precondition for this goal was utilizing the historic axis.

— But we should not forget the equally important east–west axis. It intersects the north–south axis exactly at Tian An Men, prior to Mao's expansion only a small square in front of the Forbidden City's main gate. This axis is the second focal point (actually, a 'focal line') of the city's efforts to control Beijing's centrality dynamics. In the 1990s the idea was born to provide the capital city of the new China with a fitting gateway to the world in the form of an American-style 'central business district'. It became clear rather quickly that only Chaoyang district offered an appropriate site for the city's new commercial center, exactly where the third ring road intersects the east–west axis, i.e. Chang'an Street. In simple terms, the business center has to place itself along, and thus be subordinate to, the historic axis. The decisive aspect was integrating it into the axis of Chang'an, 'The Nation's First Street'. Orientation to the airport and to the embassy quarter in the eastern part of the axis was of secondary importance. This placement, however, made

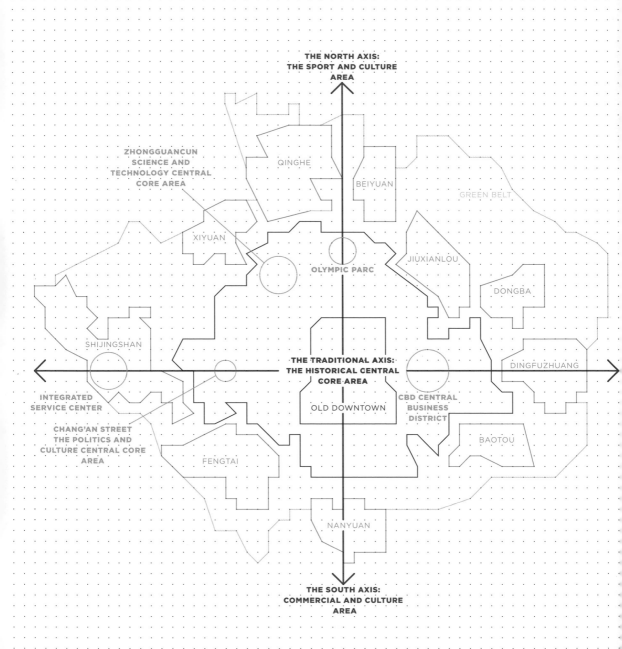

THE NORTH AXIS:
THE SPORT AND CULTURE
AREA

ZHONGGUANCUN
SCIENCE AND
TECHNOLOGY CENTRAL
CORE AREA

QINGHE

BEIYUAN

GREEN BELT

XIYUAN

OLYMPIC PARC

JIUXIANLOU

DONGBA

SHIJINGSHAN

THE TRADITIONAL AXIS:
THE HISTORICAL CENTRAL
CORE AREA

DINGFUZHUANG

INTEGRATED
SERVICE CENTER

OLD DOWNTOWN

CBD CENTRAL
BUSINESS
DISTRICT

CHANG'AN STREET
THE POLITICS AND
CULTURE CENTRAL CORE
AREA

FENGTAI

BAOTOU

NANYUAN

THE SOUTH AXIS:
COMMERCIAL AND CULTURE
AREA

Central axes, strategic plan, Beijing

clear from the very beginning that Beijing's CBD, although intended, could never become an American-type urban super-center: Beijing's supercenter is already allocated or rather occupied, today and in the future, by the 'Great Cross', the intersection of 'Dragon Axis', running from north to south, and Chang'an Street, spanning from east to west.

— If we take into account that there are already three other so-called CBDs in Beijing, we also have to acknowledge that this CBD is the highest-ranking among these centers. Why? Because it incorporates Beijing's so-called 'Golden Cross' in the intersection of Chang'an Street and Second Ring Road. Along this central axis, however, the new CBD has to fight for its position in the hierarchy of symbolic places. Chaoyang district's Party Secretary explains how this can happen: "Our CBD is not an 8 hours CBD. If the people working here in day time are gone with the wind after they ring out, the CBD would be a nightmare city zone. Our target is to make our CBD a livable international business community. We will call it 24 hours business community, which is full of life and busy beside working time" (www.bjcdb.gov.cn). The important word here is community. The positive connotations of family, collective, introversion, and exclusion are aspects of its shining radiance. A good CBD is a 'gated community', a family unit, a compound, or an urban village: helping each other in work and leisure time and, beyond that, joining work and leisure together in harmony. Work is playtime, and playtime is work. The CBD as symbolic place of 'Confucian capitalism'![60]

— Following the logic of centrality and hierarchical spatial sequence, the east–west axis needs an adequate counterweight in the west. The matching balance seems to be provided by the 'Science Park' (considered similar to Silicon Valley in the San Francisco Bay Area) and the bank district along western Chang'an Street. But things aren't that simple; what are the implications of having a bank district in the west of the Forbidden City and, to its east, a CBD project burdened by extreme expectations? According to rumors, IBM and Google have moved into the new CBD – however, they had only visited the area briefly and then returned to their old location. That one of the banks of western Chang'an had decided to move into the new CBD is not official yet. Thus, the CBD, with its share of spectacular buildings, not only suffers bad luck, but is also a problem within the centrality construction of the city of Beijing as such. Because, what is a CBD without banks? The strong wing could turn out to be the weak one.

— Beijing's previous mayor, Liu Qi, described how people imagine the cross-shaped center's meaning in somewhat awkward, yet fitting words as 'one line, two wings' (he couldn't speak of a dragon with two wings; Chinese dragons can fly but actually don't have wings). A bird with a strong wing, let's say the Science Park and the bank cluster, and one weak wing, for instance the projected CBD, will have difficulty flying. The future will show what the syncretic composition of a CBD on the 'Golden Cross' means for balancing the city's 'body'. Will something similar happen as in Paris, where La Défense gave Americanism a stage on unfamiliar grounds – with certain unwelcome results, such as vacancies, expensive resuscitation measures, and the creation of office ghettos? Or can the east–west axis yet exact its integrative power?

— There may be only one 'Great Cross' in China – due to the capital city's singular position. However, the magic of oriented linear centrality and its hierarchic spatial sequence is effective everywhere. Thus, there may be more than only one 'golden axis'. Shenyang's 'Golden Corridor', devised and designed by planners from the College of Architecture and Urban Planning (CAUP) of Tongji University, Shanghai, is one of China's most renowned examples. It is on average 2 km wide and about 12 km long, is centered by Qingian Street, and runs based on its original plan from north to south, from Beiling Park to the Shenyang International Exhibition Hall in Hunnan New District on the southern banks of the Hun He (Hun River). The city has implemented this plan with great enthusiasm and, in the meantime, has extended the Golden Corridor all the way to Shenyang Taoxian International Airport.[61]

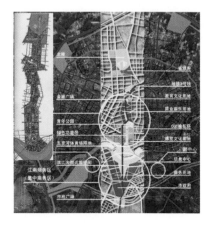

The 'Golden Corridor', Shenyang

— The Golden Corridor not only poses an answer to the question of urban centrality, which is still underestimated in China even now. It also answers this question in a typically Chinese way: the center of the Chinese city, as we already know, is preferably a linear space, historically comprised of two (or more) axes intersecting each other in the city center. Of Imperial origin, it is charged with the promise of good luck, organizing space into hierarchical sequences of meaning, following the concept of linearity. The choice of Beiling Park as one termination point and the exhibition center, or the airport, as the other may indicate that planners had, from the beginning of planning the Golden Corridor, a legible succession of urban 'sensemakers' in mind.

— However, the corridor has one irritating characteristic – and this confusion refers to, among others, the understanding of urban centrality in contemporary China. The irritating thing is that the historic Imperial palace of the early Manchurian Qing dynasty (Gu Gong) is not acknowledged within its centrality. The Golden Corridor does not integrate Gu Gong (China's 'Forbidden City' no. 2), instead it is placed at a distance of two to three kilometers to the west of the historic main axis. We can conclude from this irritation that the east–west axis that could integrate the Imperial palace is actually missing. But can an Imperial palace be placed along a west–east axis? Of course not! Obviously, the city of Shenyang and its consultants underestimated Gu Gong's significance, or they simply didn't consider the former Imperial estate to be of sufficiently great relevance. However, the global public thinks otherwise, ever since declaring the Forbidden City of Shenyang, just as the successor palace in Beijing, a UNESCO world heritage site. The Golden Corridor integrates the Municipal Square and Shenyang North Railway Station – but, as we have already noticed, not the Imperial palace, even though it is still important to the local identity of Shenyang's inhabitants. The new axial center orients itself on the city's spatial conditions that developed in the course of industrialization, but it is incapable of combining the new with the old China in a convincing way.

— The concept of the Golden Corridor does not relate to the concept of a radial concentric centrality; and due to the dominance of axial hierarchy, the latter has never existed in historic China. An analysis of Shenyang's current urban structure (of 2007) indicates that a nodal center as the core of a radial concentric urban structure would actually be quite a good solution. Shenyang's main center is divided into three partial centers with the capacity to become a single mega-urban supercenter: comprising the above mentioned Imperial palace Gu Gong, the area surrounding the Municipal Square, and the area surrounding Shenyang North Railway Station. Designing such a supercenter has, however, never been attempted – for obvious reasons. Such a cluster of three partial centers can't be translated into a linear-hierarchic spatial sequence. It demands more spatial equality, obviously more than Chinese planners are willing to concede at present. To generalize: the notion of nodal centrality seemingly cannot rely on strong advocacy in the mental landscape of contemporary Chinese urbanism.

— On the other hand, the Golden Corridor is a success, as it addresses some important issues for metropolitan development in contemporary China and integrates them into a coherent form. This includes the 'great street' (Qingnian Street), which is, in fact, a derivate of the formerly Imperial axis. It also includes a great 'river jump', an urban development concept that, in China today, is more or less a 'fashion' – we will deal with it in detail later.

— In closing, we would like to add an example of how naturally the goal of strengthening axial centrality is pursued in contemporary urban development planning. When architect Zhang Lingling of the School of Architecture and Urban Planning at Harbin Institute of Technology (currently Dean of the School of Architecture and Urban Planning at Shenyang Jianzhu University) received the commission to design a structured center with a defining landmark for the ascending industrial city of Jilin (next to the capital and automotive city Changchun the second largest city in the northern province of the same name, Jilin Province), he rather naturally adopted the almost forgotten historic north–south axis in the attempt to revitalize it. In doing so, he was not only capable of integrating an important bridge across the Songhua Jiang (Songhua River), but also including a gothic cathedral built by the French into the north–south axis. With the creation of the 'Century Square', he provided the signal for a spatial restructuring for which the north–south axis, now in the center of attention, serves as a 'backbone' (Zhang, Lingling 2004).

OPEN NEIGHBORHOOD SPACES

— The closer we get to inner city spaces of Chinese cities, the more walls and fences of compounds disappear to make room for generally accessible, open spaces. The number and size of stores and shopping centers also increases, as well as the number and size of restaurants, office buildings, hotels, and in general, of skyscrapers, turning Chinese megacities into veritable urban mountain panoramas. More and more often, we also see green spaces that offer views of public facilities; squares unfold in front of and inside shopping centers; and finally, we even discover pedestrian zones – not only in Shanghai or Beijing.

— Two questions arise: which functions can be assigned to open space? And how do closed and open spaces relate to each other? We can answer the first question quickly. We find open spaces chiefly where there are commercial uses: retail, shopping centers, supermarkets, street vendors, services of all kinds, from barber via luxury hotel to restaurant, brokerage, etc. We can also find open spaces in the vicinity of public buildings such as museums, galleries, concert buildings, libraries, registration offices, and city administration buildings – however, not in the proximity of kindergartens, schools, universities, or government buildings. In the past markets were closed and, when opened, strongly politically supervised facilities or, during the Mao era, almost completely shut down. The open spaces of Chinese cities today are different – they embody China's opening towards market economy.

Commercialization of a former
lilong Quarter, Shanghai

— Returning to the relation between closed and open space, Shanghai's new developments offer a significant typology of open, commercially defined infrastructure that shares a relationship to closed neighborhoods. But they differ in the degree of centrality, in which size and functional diversity or also, instead of functional diversity, the degree of specialization increases with the degree of centrality. A neighborhood center for four to twelve neighborhoods is, of course, smaller and less differentiated than a multifunctional district center with a catchment area comprised of forty to eighty superblocks.
— In the following, we will distinguish between perimeter block strip, neighborhood pedestrian street, neighborhood center, community center, and multifunctional center at district level. Currently, we can still include the old village road within suburban areas. However, its days are coming to an end.
— We can tell that the overall structure originates in a neighborhood planning system based on American models. We can also consider this a result of China's opening, as popular neighborhood planning introduced from the New World during the era of the Republic was discontinued after the communist rise to power in 1949 (Kögel 2007).

Integrated perimeter block strips
— The culturally rooted orientation paradigm in residential construction results in a palpable limitation of alternatives in urban planning and design. These, however, are regained in part through commercial buildings that are not subject to orientation rules. Thus, a remarkable symbiosis takes place in Chinese urban planning, between housing estates with strict orientation and commercial strip buildings independent from orientation. In China, slab or linear housing structures and perimeter block construction do not contradict each other, especially not in ideological terms. Instead, both types complement each other harmoniously.

— All residential housing structures within neighborhoods, whether row or high-rise, are more or less oriented to the south. Thus, housing rows are lined up in east–west oriented strings – also when they are 'swinging' and 'dancing'. In older settlements, this spatial grammar generally resulted in block border slabs directly bordering streets along the northern and southern neighborhood perimeter,[62] while western and eastern perimeters mostly featured a dual sequence of setback green space and housing slab ends.

— The freedom in urban planning derived from the flexibility of commercial functions already served to combine housing and all kinds of shops in older Fordist residential developments. The open 'flanks' of slab developments were occasionally closed by strip buildings, offering space for small stores and workshops. This achieved three important goals for Chinese city dwellers: firstly, local supply could be organized in a spatially sensible way, secondly, the enclosing effect of tangential perimeter 'brackets' matched the inhabitants' expectations on exclusion and security, and thirdly, the perimeter 'brackets' served for a most welcome protection against all kinds of street pollutants and noises. Whoever has experienced the crashing noise of one of the (still existing!) old-fashioned one-cylinder rural 'danwei trucks' passing by can imagine how much this kind of protection was appreciated.

Commercial perimeter
'bracket', Shanghai

— While adapting to the basic structure characterized by enclosure, orientation, and introversion by defining the block borders, a radical conceptual contrast to the orientation paradigm results along the eastern, western, and also northern neighborhood perimeter. By providing a flexible element of urban design and construction, the commercial uses offer highly welcome freedom of design to the Chinese city. This allowed functional diversity with clear spatial allocation of roles to emerge: the interaction of closed residential quarter and open, commercial borders.

— In the course of neo-Fordist change, this basic structure has been significantly advanced and refined. The 'brackets' along row house ends bordering the street are nearly ubiquitous in China today. Many older quarters have been retrofitted with them. In newer residential planning, they are integrated from the very beginning. Today, Chinese cityscapes are no longer imaginable without these 'brackets', clearly visible design elements that herald the dualism of closed and open urban space.[63] Also, the integration of commercial spaces in the slabs along the northern and southern quarter perimeter is, by now, commonplace.

— But not only that: northern and southern perimeter buildings are now even planned as purely commercially used architecture. They serve, similar to the western and eastern 'brackets', the same function as walls or fences surrounding a neighborhood.[64] Today we can find many easily accessible, centrally located, and large neighborhoods that are completely enclosed by such retail and commercial strips and no longer need walls and fences. The only remaining 'traditional' elements are the gates. Of course, we also find quarters with two or three 'brackets', and neighborhoods with only one or even no 'bracket' are also common. For two-story villa neighborhoods for instance, strip shopping buildings along the block borders are not really needed due to the small number of customers. Beyond that, they may even decrease the high site quality of the villa compound. That is the reason why such villa compounds expose their barriers, i.e. fences, hedges, walls, and combinations thereof quite visibly. Moreover, these settlements are protected by broad green belts covered with bushes and trees in order to separate them visually from the open traffic space.

— Why is this commercial infrastructure so valuable for contemporary urban design? The answer is obvious: commercial infrastructure connected to neighborhoods counteracts the visual barrier effect created by walls and gates. A residential quarter that hides behind strip shopping malls does not have such a strong 'gated' impression. Due to the functional diversity that commercial uses add to quarters, they also seem significantly more urban than quarters comprised of neighborhood monostructures closed off from open space. Also, inhabitants of a quarter enclosed by one or more strip malls benefit just as much from the available local supply services as residents from adjacent quarters.

— The precondition for making use of this spatial advantage is, however, the size of the housing estates; their sheer number of dwellers. Both closed residential area and open commercial 'bracket' together comprise a superblock, which we can regard as a legacy of the disappearing danwei. Shopping strips attached to quarters, as direct urban planning

Commercial
perimeter 'bracket',
Shenyang

OPEN URBAN SPACE / 5

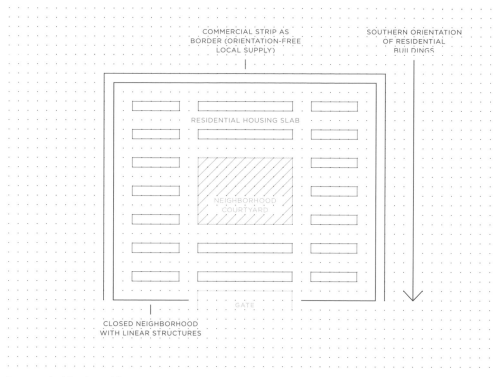

COMMERCIAL STRIP AS
BORDER (ORIENTATION-FREE
LOCAL SUPPLY)

SOUTHERN ORIENTATION
OF RESIDENTIAL
BUILDINGS

RESIDENTIAL HOUSING SLAB

NEIGHBORHOOD
COURTYARD

GATE

CLOSED NEIGHBORHOOD
WITH LINEAR STRUCTURES

Compound with oriented linear structures and non-oriented commercial 'brackets'

strategy, can counteract the barrier effect only to a limited degree, because they strongly depend on objective, contextual, and locational conditions, e.g. population number of compounds. In general, and according to the overall situation, future compounds will exclusively comprise residential high-rise buildings with high population number and corresponding density.[65] As a result, small-scale proximity to residential areas will offer profitable retail opportunities. Accessibility is yet another hard factor, but residents still vastly prefer neighborhood streets, with their opportunities for parking and pedestrian crossing, to higher-order city streets.

— Elements of landscape architecture are also employed for directly effective urban planning concepts aimed against the barrier effect, such as placement of green and tree or bamboo strips, integrating existing watercourses (found often in Shanghai, located close to the mouth of the Yangzi Jiang), or simply by accentuating the avenue-like character of higher-order streets.

— Commercial infrastructure has an enormous effect on a cityscape's impression. As fences and walls are, more and more, replaced by perimeter block strips or lines, spatially small-scale neighborhood infrastructure provides a certain balance, a harmonious urban design rhythm of closed and open spatial elements. As a result, we can observe how the quality of life in contemporary Chinese cities is decisively shaped by their commercial elements. This confirms a fundamental insight of urbanism: retail or trade facilities have always been and still are significant components of urban form. Thus they are of secular, perhaps even universal historical significance.

The neighborhood pedestrian street

— A neighborhood pedestrian street is an 'inverted' version of the organized perimeter block strip described previously, switched from the outside to the inside. Münch also considers it an example of the integration of urban space into the closed neighborhood (Münch 2004, 45). In this case, perimeter block construction is effectively turned inward. We can also see it as commercial variation of the interior pedestrian passages of residential quarters. In any case, this peculiar pedestrian area combines elements typical for perimeter block strips and residential construction. The perimeter block strip includes, for instance, stores, bars, and workshops packaged in a homogeneous architectural language with orientation freedom and serving as barrier between closed housing area and open urban space. The residential compound on the other hand provides the meandering geometry and introversion in the form of a cul-de-sac. By referring to the spatial elements of the neighborhood, the pedestrian area becomes an element of introverted spatial design.

— The neighborhood pedestrian street opens, in all cases, to the superordinate city street. It is publicly accessible and usable, and attracts customers by the same means as other shopping avenues and pedestrian areas. Its public character is, however, counteracted by a certain intimate nature, not only because it adapts to a quarter's particular design. It is also underscored by the especially neighborhood-oriented product range (drug store, children's clothing, toys, sports goods, restaurant, mobile phones and accessories, bakery, candy store, etc.), elaborate street furniture, and also local leisure infrastructure (ping pong rooms, music studios, etc). The neighborhood pedestrian area becomes Janus-faced – it looks in both directions at once: to the exterior open realm and the closed private sphere.

— Whether this form of neighborhood-oriented shopping infrastructure works well is something this study can't verify yet, due to a lack in corresponding research. My occasional visits to these locations indicate a rather desolate picture. However, selective visits only permit selective impressions. Proximity to residential buildings, lack of space, and distance to more heavily frequented higher-order streets and shopping centers narrowly limit the placement of attractors or magnets (such as department stores) on introverted pedestrian streets. This certainly explains the difficulty in luring translocal customers into these shopping streets. On the other hand, the high customer volume that compounds themselves offer could sustain a certain number of small stores.

**Neighborhood pedestrian street
in Pudong, Shanghai**

Neighborhood pedestrian street
in Pudong, Shanghai

— Recently we discovered a higher-order variation of this form of neighborhood pedestrian street, the spatial integration of very large vertical residential compounds and big shopping centers, i.e. so-called community centers. This connection of local supply with supply on the community or rather district level is obviously supposed to boost the corresponding neighborhood real estate into the premium segment. This type is actually no different from other community or district centers. We find an open or closed piazza, surrounded by a number of department stores serving as attractors for customers to numerous smaller stores, boutiques, barber shops and hairdressers, bank branch offices, restaurants, and cafés.

Neighborhood and district center
— Urban planning regulations state that every group of neighborhoods in the new suburban developments of Chinese metropolises has to receive a shopping and service center ranking above the decentral shopping strips or 'brackets'. We can identify two types, distinguished according to size, number of stores, product range, and mix of functions: the small neighborhood center and the large community center. The community center itself is superseded by the district center, which, due to size and variety of forms, is generally located at the core of an existing or planned city center or sub-center contributing heavily to its centrality.
— Neighborhood centers are usually found at the intersections of major traffic arteries. Their core is comprised of a shopping center, often called 'mall' in reference to American models, and includes a large supermarket (in Shanghai often joint ventures with British supermarket chain Tesco or French retailer Carrefour), seasoned with numerous smaller specialty stores, service facilities, and most of all, Chinese fast food restaurants. Parking is scarce or simply missing. Instead, supermarkets offer their own bus shuttle service and also a comparatively well developed delivery service; neighborhood centers reflect the still relatively low, though rapidly increasing rate of car ownership in China.
— Neighborhood centers are often also central nodes for the commercial perimeter block strips of adjacent residential areas. Their product range seems to be dominated by brokerage firms. The agglomeration of stores of all kinds creates a certain mix and vital character. This is amplified significantly by public facilities, especially kindergartens and schools, as well as informal farmers' markets offering fruit and vegetables, or the small, often tiny food stalls, cook shops, BBQ vendors, and pancake bakeries run by labor migrants. The agglomeration effects of neighborhood centers are irrefutable.

Neighborhood center

— Their becoming a center is based on urban planning decisions that usually match investors' and developers' interests. Corresponding agreements are made early in the process. Spatial points of origin are often representative buildings that, due to their elaborate garden complexes, are typologically rather reminiscent of public buildings. Actually, however, they are the sales pavilions of local real estate developers who, to improve marketing, surround themselves with a grand ambience. On the upper floors of these buildings, we occasionally find higher-quality restaurants. After apartments have been marketed, these buildings are, in general, completely and irreversibly converted into restaurants. Characteristic for community centers is the available range of supply functions of paramount significance. We usually find open retail centers with stores that are mostly grouped around a square from which one or more pedestrian streets extend like fingers. At least one anchor store is present in the form of a large super-market, a department store, or an agglomeration of restaurants of all kinds (from fast food via ethnic food to Chinese gourmet restaurants). Next to the typical retail stores we also find movie theaters, fitness centers, beauty salons, etc. The models for these commu-nity centers are American malls. As already mentioned, it is no coincidence that many of these Chinese reproductions carry the word 'mall' in their name.

— Accessibility is a decisive aspect for siting community centers. In a country with a still relatively low rate of car ownership, at least a subway station should be close by, an intersection of major streets, or a large taxi stand. It is no surprise that we find the largest shopping centers at subway hubs, often with a direct connection to the subway tracks. Also, community centers often seek the proximity of exhibition areas or trade fair complexes, civic institutions (museums, art galleries), large hotels, and specialized or wholesale retailers. Existing functions often attract other functions, and this effect is increased by the high number of barriers in surrounding urban space. Subway stations trigger the transformation of these places into gateways to the urban quarter that serve to attract residents. Such places are both equally profitable for taxis and motor rickshaws on the one hand and for small-scale, informal trade and services on the other hand.

— A prime example of a new community center is Big Thumb Plaza along Fangdian Lu in Shanghai, in the residential area north of Century Park in Pudong. Here the attempt was made to create an urban square, an open space for civil society, following the example of the open American community center. The shopping center occupies an entire block. The centrally located Plaza and the adjacent small streets and squares are car-free. Big Thumb opens towards a vividly frequented taxi area along Fangdian Lu and offers pas-sages to a cobblestone street for delivery and parking in the north, and to another access street in the east. However, there is no subway station nearby. This deficit is balanced by the high population density of the adjacent neighborhoods and unusually large below-ground parking facilities.

— It is interesting to see how most of all Western companies assemble around the main square, spearheaded by Carrefour, in its own words a 'hypermarket', as well as Starbucks, Pizza Hut, and two small bakeries that offer French bread and pastry. Numerous restaurants concentrate in the shopping center's wings: Japanese, Korean, and Chinese. Also, there are boutiques, beauty salons, and a bookshop named 'Heidegger Books'.

— Big Thumb illustrates the attempt by Chinese planners to create an urban place modeled after the open American community center. However, lacking a deeper understanding of its funcional structure, only a superficial image of this kind of center is transposed. The inadequacies are evident: Big Thumb Plaza only has one anchor store, the Carrefour. As a result, customer frequency in the mall's periphery declines, in part drastically, or even ceases completely.

— The square itself is graciously equipped with long benches for sitting and relaxing. Sitting there for a while you can watch how, in the local Starbucks, people read the newspaper, are engaged in conversations, usually drink a cup of coffee, and all somehow look like Westerners, yet not like tourists. In contrast, Chinese coffee store customers demonstrate startling differences in their public behavior: they constantly fumble on their cell phones, gaze into their laptop monitors, talk in a concentrated and business-like manner, write notes, and every now and then sip on their juices, teas, or chocolate drinks, however rarely on cappuccino, espresso or latte macchiato. They pay little to no attention to what is happening around them. Hanging out, strolling about, public communication, and such kinds of urban practices are to this day still rather Western behavioral characteristics. This does not come as a surprise! As we know by now, there is no tradition of public space in China, no urban routines in making use of this kind of space, and thus no tradition of flâneurship or public discussion based on civil society. Reading Chinese newspapers in a coffee shop means receiving filtered information and mandated opinions – political debates in public are generally not considered necessary. The freedom that the Chinese people have been granted until now has been for the most part limited to economic activity – and this opportunity is grasped excessively.

Community shopping center, Big Thumb Plaza, Pudong, Shanghai

— In the evening, the front square is as busy as Munich's Christmas market: parts of the square are closed off to give children inline skating lessons. This is, of course, a commercial operation, and the task is to sell inline skates. Next to it, a few polished and shiny cars with wedding decoration and flower bouquets approach, and some men and women dressed like models step out. It's time for car advertisement! However, if we move back a little from this happening, we suddenly stand alone in the dark. Asian restaurants close around 9 pm. When they turn off their lights, we suddenly realize that there is hardly any street lighting present.

— A different kind of Shanghai community center is located in the south of Century Park along Longyang Street, situated at the Maglev station side facing the city. The magnetic levitation train developed by Thyssen-Siemens, still called 'demonstrational' in Shanghai, provides a connection to Pudong International Airport. In this no man's land at the new compound's terminal, particularly German companies attempt to set the tone, for instance the wholesaler Metro or the hardware store OBI (Tengelmann Group), which was forced after a while (possibly due to problems in coping with barriers of Chinese business culture and customer preferences) to discontinue business and sold its assets to the British B&Q company.

— Not only numerous local supply retailers have established themselves in this location, but major corporations and services oriented towards the entire city as trade area settle here as well, including Shanghai New International Expo Center, one of the biggest worldwide in terms of exhibition space. The community center along Longyang Street has the potential to become a higher-order center. However, it fails to reach the level of communal supercenter or rather district center. A necessary, highly integrated shopping center comprising department stores serving as anchors and equipped with small-scale interior organization is absent. The location has not yet reached its apex. Right now, it seems like a functionally determined community center. It doesn't really want to be 'urban' yet.

The sutlers of urban growth

— A very special form of shopping avenue or shopping strip for middle and upper class suburban neighborhoods is provided by what seem to be 'villages'. According to scale, size, materials, buildings, and spatial impression, they don't appear to belong to their otherwise brand new surroundings. These 'villages' generally look impoverished and comprise structures for trade and commercial use, specializing in the new residential area's short and long-term needs. This secures their 'rural' inhabitants' income, at least for a limited amount of time. We can identify two types of 'village' settlement.

— Firstly, these are, in fact, villages that border or have become encircled by rapidly expanding metropolises. As we will show in detail in the example of Shenzhen's villages (Chapter 7), they can develop an astounding socio-cultural capacity for adaptation to their new environment. However, the particular stabilizing preconditions in Shenzhen (for instance, ongoing collective land use rights for the entire village property) are not uniformly available throughout China. The villages that we look at here are mostly residences for a limited time only. After their land, gardens, and fields are slated for development (a process which often starts with converting a rural county into an urban district in the course of local municipal restructuring), their inhabitants are ordered to leave their homes and are reimbursed for the loss of their land use rights. The villages are vacated piece by piece, demolished house by house – until only one or two building strips along the main access streets remain. These can then become, for a more or less limited amount of time, local shopping streets and local supply centers that retain certain village qualities: small scale, extreme diversity, colorful mix, in a highly popular format. Not surprisingly, these vital streetscapes attract fruit and vegetable stores, butcher and seafood shops, small 'supermarkets', mom-and-pop stores of all kinds, in addition to textile vendors, restaurants, florists, mobile phone stores, bank branch offices, and repair and craftsman workshops of all sorts.

— Secondly, we are dealing with informal settlements created by labor migrants in tow of new residential developments expanding into the countryside. In the past, sutlers followed troops on their path to war. Today, these settlements follow the construction cranes and mortar trucks, construction managers and workers. Their huts and sheds are built preferably along major access streets. They display their goods to both construction workers as well as new residents driving by. And, despite their poor appearance, they often develop into highly specialized shopping strips capable of reacting flexibly to the various needs of the new development's tremendous construction activity.

— The existence of this 'village type' is not based on agriculture, but on trade and craftsmanship. To be even more precise: the residents of these informal settlements offer niche products and services to the new development expanding around them. They sell paint, nails, screws, door signs, gravel, tiles, cement, flowerpots, brooms, and many other items usually in demand in such places. Demand is generated especially by the elaborate decoration works that take place before residents move into a new compound. Apartments in compounds are usually sold as shell, before their interiors are finished. It is the first owner's task to actually complete the interiors, and they eschew no costs or efforts. In return, the residents of sutler settlements are optimally prepared for the resulting need for cleaning materials, decorations, tools, cables, lighting fixtures, air conditioners, etc. Aside from stores that offer all necessary items, craftsman workshops provide welding services, glass cutting, tailor-made window grilles, repairs of small machinery and tools, and much more. They benefit from being close to their customers. Often one or more food stores join these commercial villages specialized in niche demands for the construction of middle and upper class residential compounds.

— But the remarkable thing about these informal settlements is not only their symbiotic relationship with the new residential developments. What is particularly astounding is the spatial openness of their residential buildings. They are presumably among the few residential quarters in the booming metropolises that are still actually open. Of course, this 'openness' reflects their commercial reason for existing, but we must acknowledge the important fact that open living in China today rhymes with informality and rustic or rural poverty. From the point of view of the Gründerzeit (the period of incipient industrialization during the nineteenth century in Europe), the small villages that follow developer's land appropriations, much akin to the little cart of Brecht's Mutter Courage, are merely an element of open space. Their legitimacy stems from their commercial function. They exist because they are a welcome lubricant of urban growth, no more. The people who live here come from the poor hinterland. They can't afford to live in a closed neighborhood. And because they can't afford it, they don't receive the city residency permit, but remain 'country folk' in the language of the official household registration (hukou) system. They have to accept life in the city's residual spaces, thus programming it

View of a sutler strip
through a neighborhood
gate, Shanghai

socially in a meaningful, most informative way. That they are permitted to do so indicates that people actually need them.

— On the other hand, we should not overlook that many a family active in sutlers' settlements produces an income that, after a few years, enables them to buy an apartment and thus, according to the rules of the hukou system, also purchase residency permits for the Chinese city. The temporary mobile villages indeed keep the Confucian dream of family wealth awake and even make it come true. For the duration of this current Chinese Gründerzeit, they will be an epiphenomenon of the nation's urbanization.

— We need to distinguish the villages in new developments described here from the 'ethnic' enclaves or 'migrant villages' identified by John Friedmann (Friedmann 2005, 57ff). Those 'villages' are permanent and can be found in all Chinese mega-cities. They comprise mostly informal settlements of people from the same region, in some cases even family members from the same village who decided to leave and pursue their luck in one of the metropolises in China's east. In this regard, these 'villages' are, to a certain degree, comparable to overseas 'Chinatowns' that offer a home away from home, not only to Chinese in general, but often also families or clans of specific villages, regions, or provinces. "Ethnic enclaves are called 'villages' (cun) and some are preceded by the name of the province from which the migrants come. Thus Beijing has its Henancun, Anhuicun, Xinjiacun, Zhejiangcun, and so forth, whose inhabitants think of themselves as tongxiang or compatriots ('homies') and stand ready to help and support each other [...]" (Friedmann 2005, 70).

MEDIAPOLIS

— If open streetscapes are not to completely deteriorate in the light of the tremendous primacy of uses focused on the interior, but rather to display an incredibly vital, colorful city life that many people find attractive, this is due to the characteristics of commerce and its incessant wooing for customer attention. In order to better understand how trade impacts city space, let us take a step back and look at the bigger picture.

— In Chinese cities, building facades oriented to the street principally have no meaning. They usually 'face' the street space without any 'facial' articulation. A cult of the facade, i.e. an interplay between decorative facades and the street space they dramatize, has never existed here. What a contrast to Europe, where this interplay, based on the evolution of an individualized society, is constitutive of urban aesthetics! Both the almost completely missing care for the aesthetic potential of facades and the general lack of interest in the streetscape mirror the historically persistent disregard for public street space. A cultural reference for the aesthetic valorization of open urban space through facade ornamentation is absent. There are some cases of buildings that border streets, and since the early twentieth century even clearly articulated perimeter blocks. However, these are most of all related to functional spatial practices and the imperatives of real estate economy. They are unrelated to the dramatization of public urban space. If block border based strip shopping malls, for instance, protect a residential area behind it from noise, dirt, and the invisible emissions of the street, then we can, in terms of functionality of city streets as complex of traffic space and bordering buildings, consider this an appropriate structure. For a number of reasons: for purposes of local supply, emission protection, and enclosing residential quarters.

— In China, however, this complex is not related to a culturally articulated form of relationship between street and block border where this space becomes a theater stage. As a result, the spaces of streets and squares seem disparate, torn, fragmentary, and transitory to European visitors. And vice versa: the facade play of old European cities is viewed as exotic by the Chinese, and therefore as a possible means for producing social distinction. The related images are consumed with tremendous enthusiasm and in all imaginable forms: from the free interpretation in theme parks via the ambitious transposition to the relentless copy[66] (see Chapter 6).

European extroversion:
facades in Mühlhausen,
Thuringia

— If countless shopping streets (in China, almost every open inner city street is a usually crowded shopping street) are emphatically considered vital, vibrant, dynamic, and occasionally also picturesque in an Oriental way, then we won't find the reasons for this in an embracing interplay of facades theatrically dramatizing public street space in a culturally specific manner. The case is different here! The cause is, not difficult to recognize, the unhindered and unrestrained use of images, signs, and symbols. Countless little, medium-size, and large stores, workshops, and service facilities use them to attract the attention of rapidly passing swarms of pedestrians. And if, in the case of main shopping streets (Nanjing Road, Huia Hai Road, Lujiazui in Shanghai), the front facades of buildings don't provide enough room for advertisement, they are simply covered with

Storefront, Shanghai

oversize TV screens. Or, as in the example of Huai Hai Road, immovable video screens are mounted every 50 meters along both sidewalks. As a result, excessively colorful stage sets are produced, regardless of any theatric intent, and occasionally bordering the tumultuous, the chaotic, and the delirious.

— In the light of dancing images and signs, the equally manifold theater of urban life unfolds in the less affluent areas as well – to Westerners, the spectacular mix of repair workshops, food stalls, fruit stores, barber shops, newspaper stands. And in front of them, the people: we often see older, occasionally also younger women and men sitting on rickety fruit crates and wobbly stools. Talking, playing games, working. It is these scenes from everyday life of a nation still trying to find its way between abject poverty and glittering richness that transform the Chinese city street into a vital urban theater stage, even when its bordering background merely displays pure function. Against this backdrop it's no surprise that quite a number of Chinese visitors to Europe experience our (partly even shrinking) cities as too empty, dull, and lifeless, even similar to a kind of 'concrete cemeteries'.

— The world of trade is like a circus, and this becomes especially apparent by night. Even those grey, dirty sidewalks and building walls, looking chaotic or dull during daytime, sometimes even decrepit, unfold a magical-colorful charm; obviously something that only eastern Asians can achieve, by turning on the light chains, the illuminated signs, the spotlights, the storefront lightings. In their halo, borders of streets and squares emerge; to us, they are facades of light.

— Without much ado, the facade enters the stage after all, via the media of advertisement and light, and thanks to the Chinese disposition towards colorful, glittering diversity. Modern Chinese perimeter block construction – either as 'bracket' or as integrated form (as component of residential quarters) closing off the Zeilenbau-type open-ended rows towards the street – does not use decorated stone facades in order to dramatize the urban space. No, instead, it creates stage backdrops comprised of advertisement messages, images, pictograms, brand logos, lettering, figures, lighting objects, and manifold bric-à-brac. Walls become animated collages, multicolored websites, TV screens. The skyscraper sceneries of several waterfronts already serve as gigantic video screens, offering advertisement, infotainment and even short films, thus propelling our understanding of what 'media city' actually means into a new dimension.

— Our conclusion is that a new type of open or rather public space is emerging. It is emerging in this laboratory comprised of the dynamic city of today's China, a space dramatized by media architecture of some kind instead of facades. These media facades display the rapid advance of extroverted practices. It is then logical to a certain degree that the capacity for public dramatization offered by Chinese skyscrapers – in Shanghai: Lujiazui waterfront – is made use of today. We see office towers that become video screens by night, each window representing a pixel. We see skyscrapers that turn into light sculptures after sunset, at a scale that defies comprehension. Chinese media facades are already at the point of literally outshining any and all comparable light spectacles in New York or Tokyo. We should point out the role of Hong Kong: as these words were written, about thirty skyscrapers, sides facing the ocean, are turned into video screens after sunset – a tourist attraction that certainly does not miss its mark.

— In China today, the media city of the world of tomorrow is arising. This finding is emphasized by yet another observation. We are talking about the configuration and equipment of metropolitan avenues and arterial roads. With their eight to twelve lanes, their green borders lined with shrubs and trees, their additional lanes for mopeds and bikes, their bus lanes and parking bays, their bordering multistory buildings, their glass skyscrapers, their spectacular public buildings behind huge sculptures made of polished steel or marble, and cast iron lancet post fences fronting vertical residential areas, they become urban cityscapes from the future.

— Of course, these boulevards primarily reflect the mobility needs of the globalized mega-city of today. But that is not the whole story. Similar to media facades, the functional space of the street is transformed into a media space of tremendous expression by its impressive arrangement of spatialized image messages, pictorial visions, and envisioned worlds of the future. The non-place of the street is thus fueled with meaning. The formal character of the public street space is, however, not transcended. Yet, the described dramatization transforms it into the stage for an act of self-confidence in anticipation of a spectacular future. As a public space for civil society, it is without value. But at the same time, it announces the grand ambitions of a global power of the future.

Screens, Huai Hai Lu, Shanghai

Nanjing Lu by night, Shanghai

— The 'great street', as we choose to call it here, is no boulevard, also no copy of it. It is a relative of Tian An Men, of the noble square, the stage set for mass ornamentation. It is the ambassador of the mediapolis. For the ruling city elite, it is as important as the great square; so important in fact that for it to become reality the destruction of entire quarters, even of the inner city itself, is taken into account. Against this setting of arguments it is no surprise at all that, for example, the city government of Shanghai considered it particularly important that the size of Century Avenue in Pudong had to surpass the size of the Champs Elysées in Paris (Arkaraprasertkul 2009).

— The city of Changsha in Hunan Province provides another example for this practice of staging 'great streets'. Changsha is the location of one of the oldest Confucian universities, largely preserved and outstandingly restored by the architect Liu Su. According to the guiding principle of the great street, representing the grandeur of China, the local small-scale, multifunctional inner city texture comprising open residential quarters was almost completely eliminated. It is true that the inner city had burned down almost totally as a result of Japanese bombardment in World War II. Also, in the days before China's opening, funds were not available for high quality restoration and reconstruction. Yet these facts can't serve as excuse for a current urban planning practice in which the inner city is claimed as reserve area for the construction of big streets beyond any reasonable scale. The current interventions are slightly reminiscent of West German reconstructions of bombed cities following paradigms of functionalist modernization. They ruined the historic centers of many a city in a sustained way. Beyond that, Changsha happens to be located in the south of China, in subtropical climate. The huge asphalt surfaces of the many-laned streets heat up enormously, impacting the microclimate in the remaining small-scale inner city structures. These 'great streets' have little to do with sustainable urban development.

— One cannot reject the impression that the 'great street' and 'noble place' not only reflect the spatial requirements of mega-cities with millions of inhabitants. Rather, we can consider them the petrified emanations of a vision that congeals into ideology: media city as ideology.

POSTMODERN ECLECTICISM IN URBAN PLANNING AND DESIGN
— In closing this chapter on open urban space, an example from the works of Harbin's City Planning Authority serves to demonstrate the interplay between basic and infill structure in the plan for Harbin's New City in the west of the Songhua Jiang. The street structure is based on a grid reminiscent of the typical American urban grid, connoting democracy and equality of opportunity in its rejection of all spatial hierarchy. This plan, however, has a different message. It transmits the iconography of power. The central area of the plan shows a Baroque axis as strong center of gravity with a hierarchically structured sequence of representative administrative buildings. A government building (the new town hall of Harbin city) residing at its termination point strikes a palatial pose. The axis begins at a riverbank avenue, traverses a green zone composed of square gardens arranged in a rosette pattern, then meets a round plaza that occupies the middle level of hierarchy – to finally connect to an equally circular 'noble place' divided by a 'great street'. A geometrically curved bridge spans across the street and leads to a baroquely designed garden serving as entry plaza to the main building, its pose commanding respect.

Model, new government quarter, Harbin   **Model, new city center, Shenzhen**

— This hierarchic sequence is supported by a sinusoidal curved street with the main building at its apex, connected to the orthogonal main pattern by two further curves towards the model's borders. In this spatial context, we can actually consider these two curved streets as quotations of old, curvy European city streets. On closer inspection, however, we can recognize bordering green spaces with designs that clearly feature Picturesque characteristics along the waterfront and the river banks. We see irregular-organic curved bodies of water and grass areas with loosely placed shrubs and trees in clear contrast to the geometric layout of flower beds and hedges in the axial area.

— Along the model's borders, we also discover numerous neighborhoods that clearly display all previously discussed characteristics. They are integrated in a spatial syntax comprised of 'great street and vertical block'. Even though not explicitly shown here, at this point we can assume that the quarters will be closed. We may not see dancing dots, but still more or less clearly swinging lines oriented to the south, and most of all, plenty of old-fashioned Fordist slab housing. And at an even closer look, distributed within the neighborhood blocks, we can actually discover the so-called neighborhood courtyards. In addition, we can assume that the compounds have noble names, distinctive roof decoration, and other elements representing their respective collective brand identity.

— A comparable eclectic compilation of axiality, linearity, hierarchy, nobility, verticality, pervaded by a mix of Baroque and organic patterns is also displayed by the plan for the center of Shenzhen. The construction of the city hall with its spectacular swinging roof, quoting the ancient Chinese art of roof construction, was completed a couple of years ago (see model photos).

URBAN FICTIONS

6

— In the following, we will differentiate between four basic types of urban fictions: firstly, the rather ambitious mimetic transposition of the European city to China. Here, we will introduce one of the satellite cities of Shanghai's 'One City, Nine Villages' plan, the project 'Anting New Town'; secondly, a travesty of Chinese new towns by use of European facade 'wallpaper', the projects Taiwushi New Town (a quarter of the 'one city' Songjiang) and Luodian New Town, both also part of Shanghai's polycentric growth plan; thirdly, a parody of a Chinese neighborhood by use of copies of urban ensembles and prominent buildings in the example of Holland Village in Shenyang; and finally, the city in the theme park, the 'Disney' variety of citytainment. As example, we will briefly introduce the well-known theme park 'Window of the World' in southern Shenzhen.

SHANGHAI'S NEW SATELLITE CITIES
— Towards the end of the millennium Shanghai's city government, to alleviate permanent population increase in the core districts of this mega-metropolis with its eighteen million inhabitants, employed a method of relieving urban growth that could be called 'classic': the creation of satellite cities. As a result, the new strategic development concept for the city, titled 'One City, Nine Villages', was agreed upon within the context of the tenth Five-Year-Plan.[67] It was expanded as '1966-Plan' within the eleventh Five-Year-Plan. The construction of the city of Songjiang (the 'one city') and nine smaller cities ('towns' or 'villages') with a projected number of 5.4 million inhabitants is intended to decrease the inner city population (approximately eight million inhabitants) by approximately 1.1 million people (according to the numbers of 2000) by 2020.

— Beyond that, these plans are supposed to enable controlled urban development. The keyword here is 'polycentric growth': the ten new cities (1+9) are intended to be 'self-sufficient' or functionally integrated, meaning that each one of them must provide an adequate number of local jobs, public infrastructure (kindergartens, schools, health care institutions, etc.), retail, etc. This is aimed at preventing overwhelming commuter traffic between urban core and periphery. Polycentricity is further supposed to safeguard remaining agricultural land, reduce sprawl, promote the creation of green spaces, and especially concentrate traffic as well as control it more efficiently. A large-scale traffic development plan is an integral part of the 'One City, Nine Villages' plan, focused on sustainable urban development. Beyond that, within the context of EXPO 2010, Shanghai has not only adopted the plan, but also highlights the relevance of satellite cities[68] both within and beyond the urban fringe for the dynamic change of spatial and lifestyle demands of the growing middle and upper classes in China.[69]

— This plan can thus be described as 'classic' since it returns to models and practices of satellite city plans from the era of large-scale urban development in Europe and North America. In this context we should mention not only the creation of philanthropic factory towns in Great Britain, France, and Germany,[70] but also the Garden City movement of the late nineteenth and early twentieth century,[71] and the so-called New Town movement starting in the 1940s and relaunched in the 1960s (New Towns Act 1964), resulting in many examples such as Bracknell or Milton Keynes in the United Kingdom and Marne-la-Vallée or Évry Ville Nouvelle in France.

— One must also include 'New Urbanism', originating in North America, as a reference model of Chinese urban planning and design (Ziegler 2006). Not only because it is explicitly mentioned within the context of Shanghai's 'One City, Nine Villages' plan, but also because it is highly important for the subject of citytainment in China. New Urbanism with its historicist character refers to a paradigm change within the understanding of urban development that can be summed up from a European point of view as follows: away from the faceless functionalism of classic Modernism onwards to a 'reflexive Modernism' (Hassenpflug 2006c) in which tradition and modernity can be reconciled. But this also means: away from fostering centrifugal forces of urban development, and onwards to supporting and creating centripetal dynamics! However, the idea behind New Urbanism isn't actually satellite city planning for growing cities, but instead an antagonism to 'urban sprawl', a return to the city, to density, to public space, to centrality. It is essentially opposed to what has been created in the name of early industrial and Fordist satellite city planning.

— The emergence of 'New Urbanism'[72] within the context of Shanghai's satellite city plan cannot be explained in simple terms. In China, we can find neither urban sprawl comparable to the North American situation, nor the narrative of the 'common man' and the 'frontier' (Hardinghaus 2004) that we could interpret as the context for this kind of migration to suburbs. But just why does New Urbanism still play a role? For the time being, two brief explanations will have to suffice, not without referring to the detailed observations in Chapter 8, which provide further reflection.

— A first explanation is offered by the unusually ambitious, almost experimental expectations placed on the 'One City, Nine Villages' plan. The 'one city' and its satellite cities are not only supposed to demonstrate technically advanced construction methods in the areas of ecological viability, sustainability, energy efficiency, use of materials, etc. but also demonstrate concepts of urban aesthetics connected to predominantly Western lifestyles. This demand is, e.g., interpreted in the pictorial representation of the culturally 'typical' ('typical' American, German, Italian, Nordic, etc.) within the medium of urban planning and design.

— The second explanation leads us to the phenomenon of the rapid emergence of a strong and, of course heterogenic, Chinese middle and upper class and the accompanying change in functional and aesthetic demands placed on residential space. Reflecting upon their own Chinese history is still biased to a certain degree due to the traumas of more recent history. Thus, the gaze is all the more liberated and outward bound in the open China of today and absorbs schematics and fashions of urban aesthetics, especially of the Western middle and upper classes, and preferably of the United States of America. "The selling point of Chinese new (sub-) urbanism is a 'new way of (good) life', distinguishing itself from the outdated socialist utopianism." The developers, according to Wu in his informative essay on 'branding' of the new Chinese neighbor-hood unit, "are becoming 'community builders' like their North American counter-parts and attempting to capture the imagination of the upwardly-mobile middle class. Through the imagination of simulated landscapes, often copied from foreign places, the developers are shaping a new myth of Chinese suburbia. The gate, especially built into spectacular and iconic styles, serves as visual anchor in the imagination of (sub-)urbanism" (Wu, Fulong 2006).

— The essence is that China, according to the 'One City, Nine Villages' plan with its theme cities, is still searching for itself – and Shanghai envisions itself as the head of the Chinese dragon, surveying the world from above, obliged to stride forward and discover new perspectives.

— Ten theme cities in ten districts have been projected, intended for development as artificial 'in vitro'-cities according to the guidelines of master plans as a result of both contracts and competitions. They are informed by 'total' planning in the vein of plan economy (and, thus, the exact opposite of incrementalist urban planning). According to our research, these currently include the following projects:

No.	Name	Theme	District
	Songjiang City/Taiwushi	English town	Songjiang
1	Anting	German town	Jiading
2	Bao	Australian town	Chongming County
3	Fengcheng	Spanish town	Fengxian
4	Fengjing	American town	Jinshan
5	Gaoqiao	Dutch town	Pudong
6	Luodian	Scandinavian town	Baoshan
7	Pujiang	Italian town	Minhang
8	Zhoupu	Euro-American town	Nanhui
9	Zhujiajiao	Chinese town	Qingpu

— The 'One City, Nine Villages' plan has been carried out for a number of years now – mostly with government funding, since private investors are only remotely enthusiastic about these kinds of model projects. As changes are continuously made during imple-mentation, the results are no longer consistent with the original planning.[73] Also, the number of planned satellite cities has obviously gone far beyond the number of ten. Further, remaining historic villages, towns, and small cities within the periphery of Shanghai receive increasing attention. Their potential as tourist sites has been discovered – and the attempt is made to secure these locations through large-scale restoration and revitalization plans. One of these 'villages' already appears within the 'One City, Nine Villages' plan (Zhujiajiao). For the above-mentioned reasons, it actually isn't that easy to find out which of the nine satellite cities is in fact currently included in the plan.[74]

— However, we can be completely sure that the three case studies are included. These are Anting (Jiading district), Taiwushi ('Thames Town' as part of the Songjiang New City in the Songjiang district) and Luodian (Baoshan district). All three of these projects have, from the beginning, been part of the 'One City, Nine Villages' plan of the city of Shanghai and have also been largely completed.

STRAIGHT OUT OF GERMANY: ANTING NEW TOWN

— Anting New Town is a product of 'mimesis' (a type of imitation to be explained in this paragraph) in urban planning and design – and as such, one of its kind.[75] The project represents the ambitious attempt to materialize the idea of the German city in China. Anting New Town is not a copy of an actual German city such as, for instance, Rothenburg ob der Tauber, Ulm, Celle, Görlitz, or even its 'sister city' Weimar. It is also not an assemblage or a collage of copies of German building ensembles or individual buildings. Instead, Anting is supposed to represent the German city 'as such'. Talking philosophically one would say: within the medium of urban planning, urban design, and architecture, the German city is to be exemplified; an 'ideal type' is to be erected in concrete, glass, asphalt, and stone. That's mimesis: the ambition to copy an 'ideal type'. A truly titanic effort!

— In a certain way, the Frankfurt-on-Main-based architectural and planning firm AS&P created this task for and by itself. It seems to be based on the firm's interpretation of a contract for the development of a 'German city' in the Province of Jiading. The clients themselves probably envisioned a simple copy of a city, a piece of the historic city center of Weimar including Frauenplan and Goethehaus, Schillerstrasse and Schillerhaus, Marktplatz and city hall, Anna Amalia Library and Stadtschloss, etc. In other words, an assemblage or collage of urban building blocks placed on an open urban theater stage, rimmed with closed neighborhoods. Obviously, Albert Speer and his design team decided differently. Within their master plan, they sought the combination of two concepts both highly ambitious and with high quality demands.

— For one, they chose an 'organic city plan' as basis, a typified spatial structure of the medieval European city. This seemed possible since the German city shares this spatial grammar in its traditional layout. Also, the medieval urban morphology is still characteristic for the urban core (important for both image and identity) of most German cities. In addition, Germany is, to this day, still a landscape of small- and medium-sized cities – a circumstance that becomes more apparent than usual when comparing the German cityscape to its Chinese counterpart with its many mega-cities and their millions of inhabitants. Also, AS & P subjected their master plan to the high quality urban planning and design standards applied in Germany. This particularly regards sustainable urban development, i.e. energy efficiency, quality of materials, reduction of all kinds of emissions, waste separation, a balanced supply of green and recreational spaces, short walking distances, and not to forget, a rational design clearly based on the functionalist tradition of classic Modernism.

Model,
Anting New Town

— Whereas the first principle informs mostly the basic structure of the projected city, the second principle influences the infill structure. Both basic structure and infill structure together create the image of the city. In the following, we focus our attention on the first concept. To proceed, let us recall the most important elements of the basic structure of the European city. These are as follows:

the center is defined socio-culturally, i.e. market place with church
(as representative of 'sacred' urban space) and city hall (as representative
of 'civil' urban space) define the spatially 'inclusive' public city center ('Stadtkrone')

the nodal center comprises functional diversity and mixed use

small-scale perimeter block construction based on lots and property ownership
is dominant (orientation to the south is of minor importance)

streets and places create the 'stage' for public space by use of gable-end
facades with decoration and ornamentation (extroversion)

while density decreases towards the center, size, height, and prominence
of buildings increase

the building volumes of public buildings are oriented vertically (elevation of gable or eave)

streets are non-linear or curved in the sense of 'organic' city layouts [76]

city walls, moats, and fortifications are an iconic representation of a strict,
not only spatial but also cultural distinction between interior
and exterior (formerly between bourgeois city and feudal countryside)

— A first glance at both the original models as well as the part of the city that has been completed up to now in the first (German) construction phase more or less clearly features these characteristics. There is a central place, designed by German architects GMP, with a church and larger buildings for public and commercial use. There is perimeter block construction with vertically oriented buildings featuring pitched and hipped roofs, curved streets, gable end facades and a border in the shape of a moat or trench. Also, the noticeably colorful character – the buildings are painted in red, yellow, blue, and ochre hues – cites the colorful character of the European city of times past. Anting feels surprisingly open. Walls and fences enclosing residential areas do not exist. The designers seem to have seriously attempted to imprint the idea of the German or European city into the earth of Jiading – and in regard to the structures mentioned above this attempt has been successful; to a certain degree, in a certain sense, 'in abstracto'.

**Excessively broad, curved street
in Anting New Town**

Mixed use buildings,
Anting New Town

— On second glance, however, the completed part of the project displays significant departures from the envisioned European principles and, in fact, massive signs of dissolution. The intention to import the essence of the German city by use of perimeter block construction has suffered in a way that we can see and feel – an impression that is not softened by the perimeter block structures on site, but actually aggravated. By taking a look at the area one can recognize that a struggle for the actually indispensable block border has taken place and that compromises have been made. Large parts of the city have been changed into linear structures and in addition, to solitary, serially arranged villas. Blocks are stretched, to a certain degree torn apart along their western or eastern periphery, or can only be identified as fragments.

— The streets are too broad and the buildings too Modernist to provide the impression of visiting an old-fashioned, historic town center. Many buildings with pitched, hipped, and shed roofs are oriented with their eaves facing the street. Also, the few unadorned gable ends, reduced to pure abstraction, are hardly capable of effectively dramatizing public urban space. The street curves feel aesthetically weak considering their width. In the end, the first completed construction phase of Anting New Town feels like a late Fordist residential development forced into the corset of a medieval basic structure. The result is slightly reminiscent of Kirchsteigfeld in Potsdam by architects Krier Kohl, however much less historicist, more like a hybrid of old-fashioned German ('Altdeutsch') and Bauhaus.

— The strangest thing about the urban space in Anting New Town in its entirety is the way it oscillates between seclusion and openness. Following the European ideal, Anting New Town presents itself as open urban space. Walls, hedges, and fences were omitted in accord with the German traditions of urban planning and design. At best, the moat surrounding the New Town can be interpreted as a barrier in the sense of a closed city.

— But is this degree of openness possible in China? Don't forget, residential buildings comprise the majority of built structures in the city. Of course it isn't possible! So, the residential quarters needed to be closed, somehow. Consequently, small red guard houses – of course with security personnel – have been set up at driveways and junctions to side streets. But where does open urban space remain, which belongs to closed space as the key belongs to the lock?

Zeilenbau-type
open-ended rows
instead of closed
block borders,
Anting New Town

— What happened? Why does the transposed structure lack graphic clarity so much? Why isn't there even a faint impression of the character of German town centers in Anting? Is this because Albert Speer actually intended to build a modern German town, a city that he would design that way in Germany (if someone actually could still build cities like that in Germany)? Or is this just because the plan, even though paying reverence to an archaic basic structure, has been covered with a modern infill structure? Has Anting New Town, as a German small town, fallen victim to Shanghai's building code? Or is Anting simply still too new, not vital enough, has it simply not been appropriated enough by its inhabitants?

— The displeasing result of the 'transposition' (Cai/Bo 2004, 45 ff) of the idea of the German city raises many questions – and prompts many answers. But the key to these is not based as much on the intentions of the German planners and architects and, one should add, their Chinese partners. It is primarily based on the Chinese culture of appropriation, production, and consumption of space. Three key words are of importance here: orientation (1), exclusion (2), and introversion (3).

1   Orientation

— The paradigm of southern orientation was not unknown and was actually integrated into the transposition of the idea of the German city to China. However, its meaning was underestimated. But the planning process was already under way before the planners became aware of the significance of this aspect. This in part led to drastic adjustments. Shanghai's planning and building code may have played a role here. In compliance with obviously deeply rooted everyday cultural practices, variances are not allowed without special permission. The city finally conceded to permitting a variance covering thirty percent of the residential construction (Cai/Bo 2004, 74).

— The block border can only be used effectively for framing or dramatizing street space with residential structures if southern orientation is guaranteed. An analysis of traditional and modern Chinese urban planning and design could have taught planners about how little flexibility is actually available here – and that other means are necessary to secure the enterprise of 'transposition'. For instance the separation of dwelling and commercial functions and making use of the thus gained orientation freedom, and the placement of commercial uses in the block borders on a north–south axis. Instead, not only did planners hold onto the mixed use concept. Also, a large proportion of stores was placed in linear housing structures on an east–west axis. This indicates that the potential of commercial uses for creating block borders in north–south direction has neither been recognized, nor has it been utilized.

— Against this background, it is not surprising that someone was forced to hit the brakes while the project was already under way. Blocks were pressed together and stretched in order to generate more facades facing the south. In other cases, the eastern or western block periphery was simply omitted. These interventions transformed the closed block periphery into two (Fordist) rows and the block courtyard into (Fordist) green setback space. Thus, in the course of creating a belated and reactive compromise, there was loss on one hand, the indispensable introversion, and gain on the other hand, southern orientation. But viewing this as the birth of a new building typology, the 'Anting Block' (Dong/ Ruff 2006), may be slightly too euphemistic. The illustration displays how the original plan changed during the implementation process (Oldiges 2007).

— Our anxiety is likely to rise when we look at the models for the second construction phase of Anting New Town, comprising more than 50 percent of the total area of the city, considering the large number of residential buildings oriented to the west. The current stage of planning here may be the reason that a construction permit has not yet been issued for this construction phase. Is there still flexibility for planners to improve orientation to the south in this part of the city? Hardly, since the 'invisible city' (infrastructure), involving a great deal of cost and work, and part of the street network have already been completed. The thus predetermined compact urban blocks offer too little space for rows along the block border oriented to the south. The only solution could be a distribution of high-rise 'dot' buildings across the site. This would, however, completely destroy the impression of a German or European city the planners have been striving for.

Anting New Town before (2000) and after (2004) construction – stretching and opening of blocks

2 Exclusion

— It seems as if, from the beginning, the cultural significance of the dualism of closed or open space or the urban dialectics of exclusion and inclusion hadn't really been part of the design at all. Anting was planned as an open German city with integrated functions. The mix of residential and commercial uses within an open urban space was obviously intended to express the ideal of a German urban way of life. Closed neighborhoods were not included in the plan. The broad moat that encloses the entire city can, however, be interpreted as the intention of enclosing Anting New Town as such – and therefore turn it into the equivalent of a neighborhood. In regard to residential functions, urban community and neighborhood would then become one and the same.

— In China, residential areas are neighborhoods – and they have to be enclosed. This is a socio-cultural imperative. In Anting New Town, however, this ideal cannot be attained. The attempt to create lively urban spaces with mixed use leads to the immediate integration of commercial use within residential areas. Anting New Town needs to be open due to the integrated commercial uses. This, however, is not permissible due to its residential functions.

— Thus, choosing the European ideal of the functionally integrated, open city caused an irresolvable conflict. The means for exclusion seem similarly ambivalent: gates are necessary for residential use – so they are present. They need to go, because they inhibit commercial use. How to elude this dilemma? The way out is (as in many cases) miniaturization! The residential community Anting New Town was – according to the spatial conditions as determined by the master plan – segmented into numerous smaller neighborhoods. Each of the subsequently created neighborhoods received a gate: a barrier with speed bumps and a delicate toll bar, at least. But a gate without the usual symbolically charged visual appearance including arch, columns, gate house, etc. – a gate without walls and fence. An oddity! Thus, we find small, red, mobile gate houses everywhere that fail to hide their provisional character. Slightly 'gated'! Not adequately gated for residential use, but too gated for commercial use.

— From a semiotic perspective, the corresponding messages are equally ambiguous. The miniature gates were without a doubt established as indicative signs that communicate exclusion. Since they are not permitted to function for exclusion due to the mixed use in the surrounding buildings, they are disqualified as indicative signs of exclusion. The only thing they perhaps indicate at all is the call to ignore them. As this indication neither is nor can be voluntary, what remains is the symbolic function. The little gates symbolize an enclosure that doesn't exist in reality. Regarding the iconic meaning of the little gates, we should point out the uniform red paint finish and the lettering with the equally uniform Anting typeset. In these unifying forms we can identify the attempt to use the many gatelets as iconic carriers of a kind of brand identity in Anting. We then realize that all three of Peirce's formats of transmission – iconic, indicative and symbolic – overlap within these gates.

**Open or closed?
Pseudo-gates
in Anting New Town**

— Because interior exclusion is too weak, it should receive prominent placement at the city borders, for instance at the bridges crossing the moat. However, this could deter potential customers of the planned shopping center in the city interior – not particularly inviting, to say the least! Yet, if the commercial use is weakened, this could have consequences for the willingness to move to Anting New Town. As a result, retail would receive fewer customers. In effect, a vicious cycle could be triggered and the city as a whole may perhaps emerge as the loser in this game.

— But the city has not yet reached that point. At present the developers still try to make corrections and adjustments. We can recognize that Anting New Town is slowly becoming Sinicized – in the sense that eventually there will be an open city center that can be entered via two to four open streets. The entire rest of the city, however, at this point still in the ambivalent state of being symbolically open or closed (depending on whether you view it from the perspective of housing or of retail), will then be fragmented into neighborhoods and closed off. One can only barely imagine the consequences this kind of spatial segmentation would have for an open urban plan!

— In Anting New Town, the principle of the inclusive city was implanted naively into a cultural context of exclusionary practices. Thus, the extroversion crashes into the introversion. There has been too little recognition of the fact that residential space in China belongs to the closed city, and in contrast commerce and market to the open city. Accepting this dual structure would be the precondition for a successful transposition of spatial structures and qualities from Germany to China. Understanding the urban code of China and taking it seriously means to be willing to engage in the production of spatial hybrids, actively, creatively – instead of first demonstrating naïve insistence and then patching up mistakes in the light of the normative power of the factual. But it seems as if an elaborate understanding of China's urban code that could have helped avoid this situation is absent.

— If Anting New Town were, similar to the following examples of New Towns in Taiwushi and Luodian, clearly partitioned into closed neighborhoods and open commercial areas, then there would be no conflict as described above. In that case, Anting New Town would be an open city with closed neighborhoods and thus a functioning travesty of the German city as such: a Chinese city with a modern German urban stage backdrop. Instead, problems become apparent wherever we look.

3   Introversion

— In Anting New Town, according to the German ideal of the open city, no residential compounds were intended to be built in the area surrounded by the symbolic moat. As a result, there was no opportunity to consider the necessity for introverted spaces. But there is no alternative in China! And so, adjustments were necessary. A kind of emergency program provided the opportunity to re-code the interior courtyards created by the urban block periphery into neighborhood courtyards.

— The European type of block border is actually Janus-faced. Its view is oriented both ways: towards public space, which it seeks to frame and to stage, and towards the interior, to the courtyard, which traditionally receives little attention other than for functional uses such parking space, light well, storage room, place for drying laundry, small garden, green space, and occasionally playground. It is also often in a state of disrepair. The main reason for this neglect is its subdivision into lots and the processes of privatization thereby expressed. This actually prevents 'socio-spatial integration' into a neighborhood courtyard. But in China, with its integrated neighborhood planning that omits the creation of lots, these areas are of principal interest for use as family or neighborhood courtyards.

— The possibility of designing setbacks and block interiors in a picturesque way in order to meet the scarcity of introverted space was realized at last, and the attempt was made to employ it. However, interventions in the originally intended block border that led to a decrease in width of courtyard spaces resulted in limiting available options. As Oldiges' drawing shows, substitutes for neighborhood courtyards could be created only by removal of entire blocks. Also, solutions that were appealing to Chinese tastes were hampered by the fact that the neo-Fordist score of 'swinging lines and dancing dots' was a game the designers were unable or rather unwilling to play.

— Still, the attempt was made in Anting to cater to the need for introverted space by creating a number of smaller, sometimes representative, sometimes picturesque places. Many of these places with their thorough geometric design, for instance Weimar Square, featuring a copy of the famous Goethe and Schiller statue, the only 'real' copy in Anting, do not permit an interpretation as introverted space. They denote European extroversion all too persistently.

Goethe and Schiller statue, Anting New Town

Church in the center
of Anting New Town
(design: GMP)

— Let's take a closer look at Weimar Square. The presence of the Goethe and Schiller statue refers to the city partnership between Weimar and Anting. It possesses a character relevant for establishing the identity of the entire city (i.e. at the very least, the space surrounded by the moat). The statue represents an element of the 'branding' of Anting and of its image. Now consider that Anting, as foreseen, will be segmented into neighborhoods and closed off in the course of its Sinicization. In that case, Weimar Square will be transformed into a neighborhood courtyard without meaning for the rest of the city. Goethe and Schiller will then be completely incorporated into a particular residential compound – symbolically 'communitized' if you will. In that case, they will solely serve the brand identity of a singular 'compound'. A grotesque, but not completely fabricated scenario.

— Beyond this, the example of Weimar Square also indicates that the opportunity for re-coding European plazas, market places, Baroque urban squares into neighborhood courtyards from the get-go was obviously not recognized – and could not be recognized, since introverted neighborhoods were not planned. However, the fact that this appropriation comprises a way of life is visible in numerous compounds in Beijing, Shanghai, Shenzhen, and other advanced cities along the east coast. Copied places there are part of 'compound branding'.

— This aspect brings us to a further principal finding: the attribution of brand identity in China is preferably and primarily linked to residential compounds, which as result gain collective advantages of distinction. But Anting is neither a gated neighborhood nor a residential compound nor an open urban stage, but a German city based on the dualism of public and private space – and not the dualism of open and closed space! Were Anting an open urban stage, its German classicist and Bauhaus-based image capital could be allocated to the adjunct 'compounds'. But neither this open urban stage, nor these residential compounds exist – with the exception of the 'Weimar Villa' neighborhood (which is actually located beyond the moat). If Anting were dissected into 'compounds', the urban stage that is supposed to provide its image would be fragmented as well.

— In order to prevent this fragmentation, the attempt could be made to integrate Anting as a whole into one neighborhood. In that case, however, the market place would play the role of a neighborhood courtyard. It would then no longer be a market place, but no more than a non-commercial fiction of a market place; simply because a neighborhood courtyard has no commercial function. But the central market place is explicitly intended to be part of a shopping center for serving a trade area that reaches beyond the borders of Anting New Town. By doing so, it is supposed to represent European centrality and 'publicness'. Yet in this function it can't be part of a neighborhood. Thus, it is integrated into an open urban stage. But that is also impossible, because the open residential areas are the inseparable part of the German city. Any which way one tries to interpret this complex, the open part impairs the closed part, and vice versa.

— Anting is a project threatened by failure – this conclusion is valid at least for the current stage of completion (June 2008). The process of this failure can be imagined as a chain of compromises that are akin to pouring salt into a wound rather than healing it. The neighborhoods can't be closed off anymore, so the use of symbolic actions such as miniaturization is supposed to accomplish this. The central urban place needs to be open in order to attract retail. But this isn't permissible, since the integrated neighborhoods need to be closed off. By stretching blocks and their openings, more southern orientation may be gained, but at the same time available flexibility for design of neighborhood courtyards is limited. If the block border is maintained, the orientation rule is violated. If the open places still existing are re-coded into neighborhood courtyards by subsequent means of closing them off, a 'communitization' of their 'public' (social) character takes place – a risky kind of intimization of spaces with implications for establishing Anting New Town's identity as a whole.

— Despite all criticism, we shall not overlook the positive intentions and most of all the accomplishments of those responsible. For us, the list of accomplishments begins with providing the dialogue between West and East (or the German-Chinese exchange of thought and experience) with an invaluable object of experience (which, last but not least, benefits this book) by creating the real-time experiment of Anting New Town. Reflecting on this experiment contributed to increased intercultural awareness and advanced knowledge of China's urban code. The fact that the project has and still proceeds to generate a huge wave of secondary literature, books, essays, newspaper articles, blogs, etc. shows that we are not the only ones who benefit from it. But this is only one aspect.

— It is due to the unwavering commitment of those responsible, especially the leadership of Albert Speer, Jr., that Anting New Town claims high quality construction and technology standards, also including 'high-end' products. At this scale, this should be regarded a pioneering feat in China, where to this day questionable quality of materials and technical infrastructure dominates urban planning and design. If this is true, the 'German city' has the potential to become a prime example of building and construction in China. In any case, Anting New Town is a courageous project characterized by high demands on quality; in technical terms we could call it the Mercedes Benz[77] among the so far completed theme cities of the 'One City, Nine Villages' plan.

EUROPEAN TRAVESTIES OF THE CHINESE CITY
Taiwushi New Town (Thames Town)

— Thames Town can't be compared with Anting New Town. Anting is a project brimming with idealism – in this respect, typically German. It wants to be authentic, make the world a better place, propose solutions – and coincidentally, intends to demonstrate German engineering, admired everywhere.

— Thames Town is a different cup of tea, heralding Anglo-Saxon pragmatism from within every molecule of its built structure. Atkins' master plan delivered what the client had ordered. The client wishes the image of the English city? Nothing easier than that! 'Ye Olde Englishe' architecture and building ensembles are photographed, filmed, scanned, compiled, and synthesized into an entire city. Perhaps even a Modernist cherry on top? Why not! The client loves the charm of the Baroque? Got it! Thus, the central place is designed as an ideal circus with an opening along a central axis oriented towards the neighboring lake. The urban fake is then dedicated to commercial urban space.

— The neighborhoods, however, are cleanly severed, gated, and equipped with the typical security infrastructure. Presto – you have Thames Town – the travesty of a Chinese city.

— Taiwushi is an English dream, a built fairy tale. The city is a theme park that can be inhabited in a way that is similar to visiting a theater and sitting in the parquet. Life in the neighborhood at the outskirts of town offers a view towards an urban theater stage where an English play is performed. It bears no relation to the concept of Anting New Town. Even though Taiwushi New Town is not a copy of a particular English town, neither was it intended to represent the idea or subject of the English or British town as such. By no means! We suspect that a thought like that would never cross the mind of a true Brit.

Street scene with wedding couple, Taiwushi

'Cathedral', Taiwushi

— Instead, the open part of Taiwushi New Town is an assemblage of three-dimensional images, i.e. copied elements of English cities that were exactly reproduced in built form, true to scale. The kind of spatial compiling employed here is similar to the medial-spatial organizational schematics of the Disney Worlds, first analyzed by Sorkin (1992). Walking through Taiwushi New Town, visitors move within a three-dimensional, built feature film, and crossing nearly every street corner resembles a film cut. You walk through the narrow alley of a southern English town, and after your first turn into a backstreet you emerge into a typical London square adorned by Victorian townhouses. Since British cities to a large degree share the spatial ideals of their sisters on the other side of the Channel, a central place with a church and – seemingly – public buildings are also featured in Taiwushi New Town's plan. We find perimeter block construction and excessive, uncompromising facade playfulness, strongly curved and narrow alleys, all kinds of roof constructions – simply real copies of English – and thus, European – urban components.

— In other words: we find in its pure form, both on the level of basic as well as infill structure, all which has been diluted in Anting New Town, under the auspices of a modern Germany and the search for compromise with Chinese spatial requirements. Still, Taiwushi New Town appears to be an urban copy of high quality, no holds barred. Not a real city, yet a built dream, powerfully gripping the Chinese imagination.

— It comes as absolutely no surprise that Thames Town has become an El Dorado of Shanghai's gargantuan wedding industry. The pseudo-public spaces surrounding the square at the cathedral (an imitation of Bristol Cathedral) have been almost totally occupied by their cosmetics-, photo-, video-, and fashion shops and studios. On a nice day in Thames Town, one can see dozens of wedding couples at once, the bride in her flowing white, beige, or pink dress, the groom occasionally with a British top hat on his head or in his hand, sometimes couples in horse drawn carriages clattering along the cobblestones of the alleys. Just like in a fairy tale!

— In contrast, with very few exceptions, the residential areas are 'typically Chinese'. Except for the occasional use of Victorian style design elements, they effectively have nothing to do with the copies of England in Taiwushi New Town's center. They are residential areas with villas or single family houses, i.e. 'compounds' of the upper middle and luxury classes, today to be found everywhere in the periphery of big Chinese cities. Thus, the closed part of the city is clearly separated from the open part. This also applies to the residential buildings integrated into the city center and directing their facades towards staged public space. Here, the planners applied a technique that was completely neglected in Anting New Town: the small-scale connection of open and closed spaces. As a result, one can find blocks in Thames Town that feature residential use in their parts oriented to the south, yet are defined as commercial areas towards the west and east. However, this separation as such is not sufficient for residential use. Therefore, clearly articulated, prominent gate systems have been placed at entries – including liveried guardsmen in Buckingham-Palace-look. Also, the interior courtyards have received meticulously designed landscape architecture.

— The surrounding residential quarters are characterized by the following: they are closed, i.e. they are equipped with an appropriate fence, guard house, toll bar, video cameras, infra red sensors, and everything necessary for proper exclusion. All residential buildings are oriented towards the south. With very few exceptions, there are no problems with the perimeter block structure. After all, the quarters are introverted, i.e. equipped with neighborhood courtyards or introverted parks. In these areas, the only element reminiscent of Great Britain except for the guards' red uniforms is the placement of the well known red Gilbert R. Scott phone booths, as well as equally red mail boxes, fire alarms, etc., situated along entrances to the open urban space.

— Since Atkins for the most part extracted the residential quarters from the body of the English town and reassembled them as Chinese neighborhoods surrounding his 'Disneyland', a mixing of introversion and extroversion could not occur. The residential quarters are introverted (we are tempted to say, appropriate for the Chinese context) and the entire rest, the open area, is extroverted. In Taiwushi New Town, the attempt was not even made to designate historic English residential buildings as actual dwellings. Everything that seems old and English is staged as commercial space and commercial

Victorian 'row houses' bordering
an urban square, Taiwushi

Gate of inner city
compound, Taiwushi

area. If necessary, buildings bordering the urban stage are left unoccupied. It doesn't matter. They function as the backdrop of an English dream regardless, just as the buildings along Main Street in Disneyland function as the stage setting of an American dream. And maybe in the future, who knows, people from the West will move into the buildings with their bars and cafés along the urban stage.

— The differences between Taiwushi and Anting New Town are obvious. While the planners of Anting were either unaware of the binary urban code of the Chinese city or even ignored it in order to not sully the ideal of the German city, open to all sides, the British were not only aware of it, they accepted it and turned it into a central design paradigm. While the Germans achieved a wholesome image of the city from a European point of view, the disintegration into two partial cities – a city of introverted middle and upper class ghettos and a city on Disney's theater stage – was willingly tolerated in the case of Taiwushi. This provided easy legibility for Chinese customers. In order to function as a city, Anting on the other hand demands a German perspective and a corresponding lifestyle from its Chinese inhabitants.

— Taiwushi here, Anting there – the notions of transposition from Europe to China could not be any different. We can assume that Thames Town's disposition is suited much better to Chinese appropriation than that of Anting New Town, swinging between fiction and authenticity, traditional and modern, open and closed, in- and exclusive, west/east and north/south. As these words were written, not only German Anting, also British Taiwushi was more or less a ghost town, visited only by wedding couples, tourists, and curious Chinese. Statements indicate that all villas and apartments within the neighborhoods of Taiwushi have been sold – mostly to real estate brokers – and that prices are rising. In Anting New Town, shady reports state that at the most eighty percent of apartments had been sold by summer 2008 – with real estate prices slowly decreasing. In 'Weimar Villa', however, the upper class residential compound outside Anting New Town, all properties have supposedly been sold, with prices increasing in the further marketing process.

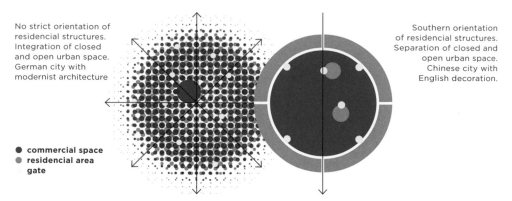

Anting New Town (left) and Taiwushi New Town (right) in schematic comparison

No strict orientation of residencial structures. Integration of closed and open urban space. German city with modernist architecture

Southern orientation of residencial structures. Separation of closed and open urban space. Chinese city with English decoration.

● commercial space
● residencial area
  gate

Luodian New Town (the Nordic city)

— If Anting is the idealistic and Taiwushi the pragmatic answer to the question of how to transpose the European city to China, then Luodian is an answer that could be described as routine, tipping towards the trivial. Just like Taiwushi, Luodian is also a travesty of the Chinese city. The satellite city is Chinese; its center is covered in Scandinavian wallpaper. That's about it.

— Luodian New Town, completed within six years' planning and construction time by the Swedish firm Sweco for about 30,000 inhabitants in Baoshan district in the north of Shanghai, is based on the same principal assumptions as Taiwushi New Town. Open and closed urban space are clearly separated from one another. The compound areas feature Scandinavian architectural language only to a limited degree at the entry gates. The densely packed neighborhoods are secured by tall fences and feature those abominable, serial-eclectic villas so prominent in China and are, of course, equipped with neighborhood courtyards along meandering waters. The city is cut apart by a broad six-lane street – with the closed neighborhoods to one side and the openly arranged urban theater stage to the other.

— In copying the Swedish or Scandinavian city, planners neither adhered to the German, nor the British way with its highly ambitious copying techniques. Instead, freely designed Scandinavian houses, yet intended as ideal type, are arranged in European-style lot based perimeter block construction. The production of this kind of block constituted no problem at all since nobody will live in the buildings that are part of open urban space anyway. Each block features an opening in one or another suitable or unsuitable location. Here you can walk through a symbolic wooden gate – to find yourself standing in an inner place, on a paved area with inlaid, mostly circular or oval green spaces.

— Nordic style is supposed to be conveyed most of all by the emblematic use of curb roofs. Occasionally, these have been amended with pitched, hipped, and other roof structures; mostly forms derived from curb and hipped roofs. The placement of bronze sculptures of nude men, women, and children is obviously considered a further symbol of Nordic culture. Naked people become a brand symbol of Luodian simply by their abundance. Obviously, Scandinavia or Sweden is supposed to be associated with nudist culture. In any case, a large sauna has already opened business in the city center.

View towards the
open urban
theater stage,
Luodian

Pedestrian street, Luodian

Wooden gates at
courtyard entrance,
Luodian

Luodian's
brand identity

Pseudo-courtyard
in Luodian

At the time of our site visit, however, it looked orphaned, was closed, and the colors of advertising signs had started to fade.

— Finally, a further symbol of Nordic culture is suggested in the form of wooden gates located at inner places. Wait a second! Wooden gates located at inner places? Is this really a symbol for recognizing the Scandinavian city? This seems kind of far-fetched, or perhaps even erroneous, because these inner places are only pseudo-Swedish: in their uniform design, they disregard the fact that European urban courtyards are fragmented due to their lot structure based on small scale private land property. The likely explanation is that Sweco attempted to provide the effect of exclusion, insinuating that it finds approval in China. Since there is a large number of European-style perimeter blocks present, there are also many inner places as well. These courtyards feature more than one entrance/exit, and many access points are equipped with two gates – one oriented towards the street and the other towards the plaza – and the result in some areas is an almost grotesque density of exclusion.

— Of course – just like Anting and Taiwushi, Luodian has a church. Something like that is a 'must' in a European-Christian city. While Anting claims that it provides a real house of God in a modern shell, and most likely Chinese weddings according to Christian rituals are by now offered in the cathedral of Taiwushi, the church of Luodian still seems to await its destiny. On the day of my visit in late 2007, it only housed a public rest room as place of profane bodily 'salvation'.

— Luodian New Town can, of course, be easily read by the Chinese. Here, the neighborhood, there, visibly detached from the residential area by a broad street and a canal, the urban fiction as open space. But different from Anting, where the ambivalence of open and closed space causes anxiety among the security agencies and services, in Luodian you can take pictures without hindrance, just like in Taiwushi, of lifeless facades 'animated' by plastic flowers and plastic vines.

— Luodian, more than Taiwushi, feels like a ghost town – and, surprisingly, even more than Anting. The reasons are difficult to identify. Is it the separation by the very broad, dividing street and the equally broad canal? Or is it perhaps the slightly too grayish choice of colors, the extensive use of wood, weathered in the subtropical sun and the monsoon rain and typhoons, too many wooden gates, or perhaps an urban fiction that altogether has a rather cheap appearance? Or is it the orbital location combined with the absence of efficient translocal traffic connections and routes to the inner city of Shanghai (which is also a big problem for Anting New Town and Taiwushi New Town)? In any case, Luodian, different than Taiwushi, seems like citytainment without entertainment. A rather weak stage backdrop!

— Should perhaps the concept of Anting with its high quality demands succeed rather than Luodian, easily legible from a Chinese point of view? Can Anting New Town perhaps, in a synergetic manner, benefit from the unconventional integration of open and closed spaces? If such a synergy could prove successful, Anting would basically outclass the other two New Towns introduced above.

HOLLAND VILLAGE IN SHENYANG: AN URBAN PARODY

— Let us now take a look at another type of urban fiction in China, the radical copies or urban parodies. One example that actually speaks for itself is the facsimile of urban scenes and important public and semi-public buildings of Dutch origin in the form of a closed neighborhood covering 200 hectares in the northern Chinese metropolis and capital city of Liaoning Province, Shenyang. Not only have entire streets, places, canals, and bridges of the Dutch city Amsterdam been recreated here, but original street lighting, trashcans, and street signs as well. We find an exact replica of its city hall, true to scale, and also a facsimile of a corvette with iron cannons on board, their barrels directed towards the recreation of the central train station located across from it. And, of course, there has to be a windmill. Along the ceiling of an access gallery, we find ambitious reproductions of famous paintings by Dutch masters, slowly losing their hue and decaying. The 'new Amsterdam' of Shenyang is a ghost town.

— Arriving at Holland Village, visitors walk through large, unguarded gates. The windows of most buildings seem blind, the colors have lost their hue, and we can occasionally see rust spots. Entire street facades feel like Hollywood film backdrops. In some areas, half-finished buildings are surrounded by extensive voids and unused areas. Few people inhabit the streets and places during daytime, gleaming in the sunlight. The only vital area is the place in front of the central train station. Yet no train departs from here, and no train arrives. Why? There are no rails. But where do all the people come from?

— The question can, in part, be answered right away. Wedding couples including entourage emerge from passing limousines for 'photo-shootings' on a regular basis, and the Chinese wedding industry has obviously taken possession of this ambience – similarly as in Taiwushi New Town. But this by itself does not explain the busy character of the place in front of the train station. One has to enter the train station in order to fully answer the question: instead of ticket booths, departure and arrival signs, newspaper stands and fast food vendors, we find orphaned sales areas and dust-covered models for marketing apartments in Holland Village's neighborhood.

— Still, we encounter hectic, bustling activity. In the halls and floors, waiters and waitresses hurry and scurry on roller skates, from everywhere to anywhere. The reason is that tables and chairs are spread out endlessly where one would usually expect platforms and tracks, beneath the glazed ceiling of what can be described as a big greenhouse. They belong to a mega-restaurant, the scale of which we can perhaps only find in populous China, with its by now enormously increased middle and upper class.

— Holland Village is a compound as city collage. Its images were taken exclusively from the architectural richness of famous Dutch cities, especially of Amsterdam, the city of canals. Similar to Taiwushi or Luodian, a distinction was made between residential and commercial areas. However, the borders have been drawn much less clearly here. The urban syntax of open and closed space is not obviously comprehensible – and this is where, albeit distant, parallels to Anting lie.

— Thus, there are typical Dutch residential houses bordering the block perimeter. These serve not only as stage backdrop, but are also designated as residential houses. However, as we know by now, they need to be oriented to the south. Yet, since a total fiction was employed, a problem arises. A street running in east–west direction results in placement of entrances facing the south on one side and towards the north on the other side.

Peace Palace
(copy),
Holland Village,
Shenyang

— At the rear of the relatively low buildings, only two stories tall and oriented to the south, there is an opportunity for locating the terrace (or balcony), important for Chinese families, to the south. This side could thus be marketed if inhabitants did not have to sacrifice the equally important northern balcony on the street side. We have to acknowledge that north balconies are still very popular as place for food storage, even in the age of refrigerators, having also dawned long since in China. It is also a welcome place to put a washing machine or similar things. People don't want to do without it.

— On the northern side of the street, the opposite occurs. Due to fictional authenticity, there are no southern balconies oriented towards the street. Only a northern balcony is, perhaps, available. That is not a minor offering, but it is not enough for the demanding Chinese customer. A bad hand in the card game of marketing.

— A further problem results from the fact that in extroverted European cities, community-oriented interior courtyards are almost absent – they have actually only survived in monasteries, Renaissance villas, and castles or similar estates, in the form of cloisters, some courtyard gardens, and horti inclusi. Due to the copy process involved, these places also don't exist in Holland Village. The indispensable demarcations, walls, and fences are absent, as well as neighborhood and family courtyards; inside and outside, open and closed, residential area and trade area are not clearly separated from one another. In many block border areas, southern orientation, indispensable for residential use, had to be abandoned. Finally, the large replicas of Dutch buildings are not arranged in a visibly articulated hierarchical spatial sequence. From an urban design point of view, they are placed arbitrarily within the surrounding urban space.

— In Holland Village, everything is ambivalent. The main entrance gives the impression of a gateway to a closed neighborhood. However, this residential compound presents itself as a theme city in the style of the Shanghai New Towns. Holland Village is a closed neighborhood and at the same time speaks the spatial language of an open city. In its interior arrangement, the estate is divided into a number of open pseudo-neighborhoods, among them villa quarters, mixed quarters (of the gradual setback-type), high-rise quarters, and not to forget, residential architecture in the style of typical Dutch row houses alongside canals, integrated into the fictional body of the open European city. Towards the city of Shenyang, however, the latter are closed as part of a single 'mega-compound'. Thus, there are contradictions wherever we look. The inconsistencies point out a deficient master plan and a lack of foresight for the consequences of importing European images into Chinese urban and residential space. Obviously there was a significant absence of intercultural competence. The overall impression of the urban copy is correspondingly fragmented. It is no surprise that this neighborhood has remained uninhabited.

— If one can still observe a certain degree of animation at the central train station or by the watercourse in front of the city hall, then this is also because none of the gates is guarded. So people enter freely, for fishing or for family outings, for visiting the restaurant, or for recording wedding videos. If the flowerbeds in the included photos still appear well maintained, then it is due to the Horticulture World Exhibition 2006 that had opened its gates not far from the Dutch urban fiction at the time of our inspection.

Fake Amsterdam central station, Holland Village, Shenyang

Canal houses,
Holland Village,
Shenyang

— Holland Village is a mostly informally appropriated ghost town, a dead backdrop metropolis, a citytainment desert filled with built urban imagery, in brief: a built dream of a town that turned into a nightmare. The marketing of apartments in Holland Village was stopped before it could begin. The project developer supposedly went bankrupt before the construction of Holland Village compound was completed. Reading the *South China Morning Post* of 19 September, 2009 we find out that developer Yang, "once acknowledged as China's second-richest man", has been "jailed for 18 years in 2003 for fraud and bribery" (Li 2009, B2).

— That the use of imported or endemic ideas leads to products that are off-target in the Chinese real estate market is not unusual in contemporary China. In most cases, this results in demolition and new construction. This practice also points out the enormous discrepancy between property value and construction costs in the low-wage country of China, which makes this kind of reaction economically feasible. This is accompanied by thinking and acting in terms of comprehensive solutions: A neighborhood is seen as a singular commodity. If problems emerge that result in the withdrawal of building permits or in market failures such as customers' refusal of purchase, this does not lead to a differentiated reaction appropriate for real estate business. Instead, the entire settlement is simply regarded as one single commodity to be taken off the market completely. We therefore assume that no later than 2006 Holland Village had become a virtual speculative death valley – and will be some day torn down completely. Among city copies, this would be akin to the sinking of the Titanic.[78]

VIEW FROM THE EIFFEL TOWER TOWARDS ANGKOR WAT

— Let's now take a look at theme parks. Global template for all theme parks that employ elements of the city are the theme parks created by Walt Disney, more precisely Disneyland in the southwest and Disneyworld in the southeast of the United States. The urban fictions here are displayed firstly in the shape of a central, seemingly Baroque axis titled 'Main Street' and secondly a 'New Orleans Square' or also the city travesty 'Mickey's Toontown'. These are three of the altogether eight themed spaces based on myths and narratives of the United States, the others being Frontierland, Adventureland, Tomorrowland, Critter Country, and Fantasyland. The latter incorporates the central issue; fantasy, dreams, imagination – in one word: emotion. Visitors are supposed to feel like floating on clouds in the 'happiest place in the world'.

— Main Street is the embodiment of an inverted urban space in which the public domain is private or the private becomes public. Main Street is a reification of the dream of the good old days when the American city was still a quaint little town, easy to survey and with a clear allocation of functions, or more specifically, offering the 'common man' (Hardinghaus 2004) everything he needed for his hard struggle out there in the wilderness. Main Street U.S.A. is oriented towards the feudal-rural icon of Cinderella Castle.[79] Within this 'dreamland', a juxtaposition of this kind can be established without problem; it causes no headaches for North Americans, resistant to urban-rural dichotomies.[80]

— The 'Window of the World' in Shenzhen is a different case. It is not about 'dreamland'; no fantasy construct or built exaggerations are presented here. Instead, three-dimensional photographs of well-known buildings from almost all historic epochs and from every continent (with the exception of Antarctica) are on exhibit – seasoned with a water fountain (100 m tall!), imitations of Matterhorn and Fujiyama, and not to forget, 'The Hand of God'. It also targets emotions, yet in a balanced way. The counterbalance is supplied by content aimed specifically at knowledge-hungry children and grown-ups. 'Window of the World' is a popular destination for school groups.

Hyper-real assemblage, theme park 'Window of the World', Shenzhen

— The 'Window of the World' in Shenzhen, covering 480,000 square meters according to its own advertisement, features 130 reproductions of the world's most famous attractions. Among these is a copy of the Eiffel Tower, respectable 108 meters tall, visible as landmark from afar. The park is divided into nine segments (Asia, Oceania, Europe, Africa, Americas, other Regions Science and Technology Center, Sculpture Park, and importantly, International Boulevard). Among the sixty-seven most important copies there are, no less, seven from France, five from Great Britain, and one from Germany (the Cologne Cathedral in 1:15 scale).

— Even though equipped with a geographic-thematic structure and as such oriented on rational exhibition concepts used in galleries or museums, the park is full of arbitrary juxtapositions, which motivated an anonymous Wikipedia-author to speak of a "slightly kitsch appeal of this theme park". But beneath this 'kitsch' we find nothing less than a three-dimensional reflection of the ability to compile anyone and anything into a singular image in the age of digital imaging – and by doing so, to confidently transcend space and time. 'Window of the World' reflects this ability by juxtaposing lighthouses and other architectural and engineering wonders of the world as spatial copies in reduced scale before the astonished spectator.

— Even prior to passing the entrance, the theme park greets its visitors with a gable-ended row of houses that signal the 'European city' ('bella città') with its play of facades and its fictitious perimeter block construction. Right at the entrance, we find Michelangelo's David of Florence standing peacefully next to a Greek Helena in front of a backdrop consisting of the Eiffel Tower and framed by hybrids comprised of Roman arches and colonnades. It's just like a Chinese dinner: the composition of the whole is not most important, but instead the incrementalism of its components. Everything fits together, everything can coexist. Eating thus aims at sensations for the palate, and visiting a theme park like 'Window of the World' aims at sensations for the eye. The Sphinx of Giza and the Statue of Liberty? No problem! 'Window of the World', as the advertisement suggests, lets you eat Mexican food, view the Niagara Falls at the same time, and stroll along Angkor Wat after dinner, or go snowboarding in the Alpine ski paradise. One can let the evening wind down with bikini girls strutting on stage to the rhythm of Tom Jones' 'Sex Bomb'.

— Theme parks are exceptionally popular in China. They reflect a curiosity towards things, which in its intensity can only be interpreted as the radical negation of previous isolation; an isolation that was less total as portrayed many times in this country, but which is experienced as a collective trauma. There shall never be isolationism again! Thus, everything that the world has to offer in terms beautiful, sensational, strange, fairy-tale-like, impressive, or unmistakable is photographed, scanned, copied, transposed to China, built anew true to scale or miniaturized, and viewed with astonished eyes. According to estimates, there are about 1,000 theme parks in China (Sheng, Haitao 2007). Capital city of these is without a doubt the boomtown Shenzhen. Already in 1989 the first miniature landscape park, named 'Splendorous China', was opened here. The incomparable success of this park triggered the theme park boom, effectively turning China into the world champion of fictional worlds.

— Ever since Georg Simmel's observations on the behavior of the modern urban metropolitan or Theodor Adorno's, Max Horkheimer's, and Herbert Marcuse's critique of the culture industry, and most of all since Gerhard Schulze's sober study on the meaning of aesthetization in the late industrial age, we have been aware of the significance of experience consumption for the individualized human being (Schulze 1992).[81] Aesthetizations seem to close that gap between experience and sense, left behind by a thoroughly rationalized world of highly artificial urbanized spaces. Theme parks thus seem to be inextricably linked to urban life and the city.

— The particular situation of urban mimicry resulting from Fordist or functionalist Modernism has been pointed out repeatedly (Hassenpflug 2000). In this context, functionalism in architecture and urban planning and design – with the intention of designing the built environment more effectively by zoning and increase of velocity – caused a narrative impoverishment in the production of space that became decisive for the thunderous return of urban fictions. It was then possible to point out that the entertainment industry was first to identify the thus created scarcity of spatial aesthetization and translate it into a need that could be addressed commercially. As a result, the recognized market demand for citytainment space was satisfied preferably by fictions of the historic European city with its public spaces adorned with decorated facades. In China, this compensational effect of aestheticizing is combined with a tremendous interest for anything new, foreign, exotic, finally unleashed after the opening of a country that was introverted for so long.

— With the above reference to the historic framework of conditions for the popularity of theme parks in China we balance the claim for validity of a general theory of entertainment spaces (theme parks) according to which these generally need to be viewed as reaction to the functionalism of classic Modernism. The Chinese example teaches us that cultural factors and the particular developmental conditions of a country play a large role in the evaluation of urban aesthetizations. The simplified appropriation of citytainment by Postmodernism or Second Modernism ostensibly remains at an insufficient degree of complexity as singular explanatory approach.

'Citytainment' at 'Window of the World', Shenzhen

THE COMPACT CITY

7

GREAT STREET – VERTICAL BLOCK

— Europeans or Americans who approach a Chinese metropolis by car, after passing fields endlessly stretching before the eye, with the occasional village here and there, may suddenly encounter a solid wall of buildings. In front of it, bustling, vital activity. Chinese metropolises are unusually compact. Compared to most Western cities, the transition from surrounding agrarian countryside into the urban fabric is rather abrupt. Within a comparable area, they also house vastly higher numbers of people than Western cities.

— In Europe, compact urban growth took place in the nineteenth century. In the course of the twentieth century, the urban periphery, the area of transition between city and country, expanded ever further. As a result, a city-country continuum emerged, both urban and rural – but neither simply the one nor the other. Thomas Sieverts proposed the memorable term 'Zwischenstadt' ('the city inbetween': 'city web' or 'meta city') for characterizing this spatial phenomenon (Sieverts 2003; Christ, Bölling 2006).

— In contrast, Chinese cities seem capable of growing without blurring their borders. While expanding, they maintain their clearly visible borders, pushing them outward before them. A European type 'Zwischenstadt' with its disperse development clusters, low density housing estates, and transport routes intersecting the landscape doesn't seem to develop in China; and despite this country's millennia-old urban-rural identity neither can we find an 'urban sprawl' of North American type with its grotesque land consumption. Campanella points out: "The form and structure of the evolving Chinese suburban landscape is also markedly different from the American model. The archetypal suburb in the United States is low in density, with generous lot sizes and detached single-family homes." However, in China numerous settlements "are gated housing estates of clustered mid- to high-rise apartment buildings, which have become the basic unit of suburban sprawl in China. This is, of course, sprawl with Chinese characteristics – much denser and much more 'urban' than anything in suburban America" (Campanella 2008, 202).

— In general, the settlement density of the Chinese city doesn't decrease in suburban areas in a way familiar to us in the West. On the contrary: the settlements of the new middle and upper classes that push the city borders towards the outside, into the agrarian landscape, are generally – and in the time to come, probably even more so than today – high density neighborhoods. In their study of the Chinese metropolis in the transitional phase from state to market economy, Yan, Xiaopei et al. speak of a "pattern of making a pancake" or also "concentrated outward expansion" of urban development (Yan/Li/Jianping 2002). The neighborhoods mentioned are the 'swinging and dancing' vertical residential blocks of Zeilenbau and Punktbau-type in Postmodern design that we have already become familiar with. Residential buildings with twenty to thirty and even more stories are by no means rare. We call this settlement component characteristic of the new China's urban development a 'vertical block' (cf. "superblock", Campanella 2008), a basic element of today's Chinese city. We consider the scarcity of available land with simultaneously very high population pressure to be among the main reasons for this compact, high density urban growth (Lü Junhua, Shao Lei 2001, 204).

— In its verticality, this settlement type can also in no way be compared to European 'bedroom suburbs' of the 1960s and 1970s, where horizontal linear structures were mostly preferred to vertical nodal structures. But in China, the ratio of these two Modernist building types seems to be balanced. Yet, in inner city locations with small and narrow plots, nodal structures are preferred to linear structures, due to greater small-scale design freedom. In any case, buildings, whether Zeilenbau or Punktbau, generally feature a higher number of floors; the impression of verticality dominates.

— While Fordist settlements in Europe often struggle with ghettoization, social deprivation, vandalism, image problems, and vacancy, the vertical Chinese neighborhoods enjoy great popularity. This is not only due to advanced neo-Fordist spatial qualities, but also the willingness to rather naturally live in high-rise buildings and high-density residential environments – but only if certain paramount preconditions are met. The quarter needs to be closed and well secured, the apartments need to be large and oriented, and the introverted element needs to be represented in a neighborhood courtyard incorporating pleasant design and the promise of good luck. For this to happen, a (brand-) image is required that guarantees collective distinction gains.[82] Of course, a parking lot for a car as large as possible should also be included.

— We are now already talking about cars and streets. We know from European and North American urban history that automobilization is one of the most powerful forces behind urban sprawl; it is responsible to a decisive degree for the forms of rural and urban peripherization that emerged in the twentieth century. The 'Zwischenstadt' is to a significant degree a product of automobility.

Vertical block
at Suzhou He,
Shanghai

— The railroad as mass transport system connects cities, strengthens their centrality, and thus even supports their compact form. With railway terminals close to city centers, railroads contributed to the climax of centripetal dynamics of the nineteenth-century European city. Individual motorization on the other hand causes spaces of high density to disintegrate. Cities built in space are thus transformed into cities built in time, as Robert Fishman (1996/97) formulated succinctly.[83] The car is the vehicle of the urban periphery. It is the strongest power behind the expansion of the threshold between city and country, behind urban sprawl and its development.

— Does this finding, however, justify the assumption that Chinese cities – also along their periphery – are only built in such a compact way because motorization is relatively low?[84] The automobile is certainly just in its initial stage of influencing spatial production in China. But wherever this is the case, and this happens to be in the urban periphery, its influence seemingly doesn't lead, as one would usually expect, to the web-like small-scale landscapes intertwined by streets typical of the European and North American urban fringe. On the contrary: high-density structures expand further and density even increases, especially due to the objectives of urban planning authorities and recent planning and construction codes.

— How can we explain this development, which appears to be quite paradoxical from a Western point of view? In China, automobility seems to promote the construction of a new type of urban, or rather suburban road, the 'great street'. All signs indicate that the tremendous flow of cars that has been rolling into Chinese cities for a few years now is supposed to be funneled by this street type and thus led into an orderly direction.

— A 'great street' is primarily a higher-order access and tangential street in urban peripheral areas. Its width is often even wider than the width of city highways. While highways (mostly ring or radial streets, in inner city locations often elevated roads) are conceived as four to eight lane streets for cars, in the case of a 'great street' six to eight lane major thoroughfares are additionally equipped with bicycle and motorcycle lanes on both sides, broad pedestrian walkways (in Shanghai, with access for people with disabilities, e.g. directive systems for the blind and sidewalk ramps) and occasionally also parking lots including dedicated parking ramps. This creates enormous barriers, adorned only with green strips and so tremendously wide that they would marginalize every European city and actually make them disappear. But not so the Chinese metropolis. Here, the 'great street' is met with a vertical counterweight in adequate scale, the towering buildings of residential quarters.

Right:
'Great street – vertical block',
impression, Pudong, Shanghai

Left:
'Great street', Qingdao

— Where high-density middle class residential development takes place, we must also anticipate the increased presence of the status symbol most dear to the Chinese: the car. The development of new, high-density settlements doesn't take place without creating these excessively broad arterial, tangential, and access streets (Erschließungsstraßen). They are given priority and their construction takes place beforehand.

— The expansion of the city is therefore based on the significant dual structure of 'great street' and 'vertical block'. This urban design concept is aimed towards a balancing effect and has by now become a generally employed model. This is why it finds use in the redesign of urban cores as well. In these core areas, for about two to three decades, the old China – anything built prior to the opening in 1978 is already considered old – is extensively demolished, replaced by the new structure of 'great street' and 'vertical block', and complemented by primarily radial city highways.

— Representing the Chinese urban periphery, the dualism of 'great street and vertical block' takes possession of both, the surrounding landscape and the urban core, in equal terms. It is highly possible that the Chinese metropolis will make this dualism its future primary structure, characterizing its spatial rhythm. This doesn't necessarily have to result in spatial impoverishment – if we disregard for a moment the both mindless and unscrupulous destruction of the cultural heritage of small-scale, introverted residential quarters that offer potential for revitalization. There already is sufficient open urban space for commercial purposes where the city can dress itself up and make itself colorful, diverse, and thus also interesting for its inhabitants and its guests.

— In Europe for some time now there have been motions to adapt car use to inner city spaces through all kinds of deceleration measures and restrictions, i.e. residential streets, pedestrian areas, speed limits, speed bumps, shared space concepts. In China, similar traffic limitations are visible only in early stages. Also, a car-friendly city beyond the dense, historic city comparable to the North American situation has not yet become a planning subject. In China, it seems rather as if the path is ventured that resulted in the creation of inner city moonscapes in the course of rebuilding the urban cores of German cities destroyed in WW II, following the postwar paradigm of the car-friendly city. It is true that metropolises, including their centers, are made to fit car traffic, if necessary with elevated highways that entangle the urban fabric like cyclopean strings of spaghetti. Are these cities destined to become like the concrete Fordist deserts that have inflicted almost irreparable wounds on urban space in many German cities, still smoldering today and producing sustained image problems?

— Obviously not! On the contrary, Chinese cities seem vital, colorful, featuring mixed functions and steadily frequented, in short: downright urban. This finding is just as remarkable as the already observed compactness of the urban fringe. But this observation hints at more than just a comparison. The reasons for these surprising results (compactness of the periphery, vitality of urban cores) are the same; they are the balance of 'great street' and 'vertical block', the balance of width and height that holds the city together. The Chinese form of peripherization of urban cores makes the old, horizontal settlement structure of introverted neighborhoods and Fordist Zeilenbau-structures vanish and replaces them with a vital and balanced structure of open and closed urban space.

— That peripherization doesn't turn urban cores into 'moonscapes' as observed in some European city centers rebuilt according to Fordist paradigms is also due to typically Chinese vitality and mediality of commercialized open urban space in connection to vertical density of closed compounds. The vertical, compact city with its vital open spaces can, if not without problem, rather 'more or less', but sometimes very convincingly counteract the diluted city of the 'great street'. This often results in a cityscape of urban canyons with life bubbling between media facades. Just as we can assume a functional, aesthetic, and iconic relationship between the small street and the single family residential house, we can also assume a functional, aesthetic, and iconic relationship between the 'great street' and the 'vertical neighborhood'.

— The view rare in Europe of eight-lane arterial highways that terminate at bordering farmland is common on the outskirts of Chinese cities. Here, the transitional zone between city and country (between urbanized area and periphery) is rather small compared with the urban core. And even new developments and projects on the urban fringe such as commercial zones, tangential streets, logistics centers, recreation parks and similar built-spatial activities do not remain on the urban fringe for long. We can compare the speed of urban development to the effect of a tidal wave. Tangential roads situated within the urban orbit today are by tomorrow submerged by new commercial areas and neighborhoods. They thus become part of the expanding city and mutate from orbital streets to satellite streets, and from these to inner city radial streets.[85] A similar thing happens to the surrounding villages, integrated almost instantaneously into an urban body of high density.

SHENZHEN'S URBAN VILLAGES

— Some of the most exciting phenomena for urbanists in newer Chinese urban development are the so-called 'villages' of Shenzhen; high-density, closed, introverted habitats that clearly differ from the surrounding urban space (Ma 2006). Ipsen uses the term 'insularization' (Verinselung) in order to categorize them as one of five spatial principles or spatial-structural elements of Chinese high-speed urbanism (Ipsen 2004, 28).

— But first, Shenzhen. At the time of China's opening in 1978 about 30,000 people lived in what used to be a fishing commune named Bao'an. After being selected in 1980 by Deng Xiao Ping personally to become the first special economic zone of the new China and renamed Shenzhen, a tornado of development broke loose, one of its kind worldwide. Today the urban core (city and urban peripheral communes) comprises almost five million inhabitants and the incorporated area of Shenzhen (including rural districts, so-called counties) may have about twice the number of residents. The average number of inhabitants therefore has since Shenzhen's inception increased annually by about 200,000 to 250,000 people.

— This is a tremendous challenge for strategic and practical planning for urban development. However, the city masters its task so well with the urban planning instruments of open and closed city, great street and vertical block, swinging lines and dancing dots, noble places and introverted neighborhood courtyards, that the city became a serious competitor to neighboring Hong Kong in terms of urban image. For its success, the urban planning authority received national awards.

— A city with such a tremendous growth dynamic spills across the surrounding countryside like a storm flood and submerges everything in its path. Still, let us remember that the region was originally characterized by agriculture, most of all by rice harvest, but also by fishing. Fishermen and farmers lived in clans scattered in villages all across the countryside, sometimes sharing only one or two family names per village. The habitats of these family clans are now overrun by Shenzhen's turbo-urbanization. Did they succumb to it? No! The farmer families may have lost their rice fields, but they were allowed to keep the use rights for the area covered by their houses. Also, rural production associations or communist village collectives continued to exist and simply transformed themselves into market oriented commercial entities ('joint stock companies').

— While all around them the towering architecture of urbanization holds the little villages in its clench, their rather crafty inhabitants looked for new business opportunities, more or less as a replacement for their losses in rice and fish harvest. The first and best business opportunity that appeared was renting apartment space to labor migrants, flooding into golden Shenzhen from the western hinterland. The still operating village communes or better, firms rather professionally jumped to the task and began developing the properties that remained in village possession: for rent, to migrant after migrant, floor by floor, year after year. Labor migration was declared the new 'field crop'. It was sowed by expanding dwelling space, and profits were reaped in good hard Chinese currency.

— These 'villages', originating in the villages of the former farm hands and fishermen, should be clearly differentiated from those informal or ethnic 'villages' that developed in the course of labor migrants streaming into the metropolises of the east since the mid-1990s. Eduard Kögel writes: "These migrant villages in the city form their own social cores and developed without formal help from the city administration. In the grey area of legal and illegal, under bad framework conditions, on the basis of small family businesses, a vast variety of service and production enterprises emerged. Criminal organizations and so-called black societies operate here under the protection of shady conditions." (Kögel 2004a, 52)

— Even though they share the significance of family structures and partly also the informality with illegal migrant villages, the villages of Shenzhen in contrast prove to be socially highly effective urban integration machines for the disadvantaged rural population. They comprise a tolerated, partially informal structure that produces formality or legality through its integration activity. Many a registered city dweller of Shenzhen today has entered the space of city residency through the 'gate' provided by the 'villages'.

— In her seminal study on the *Villages in Shenzhen*, Ma Hang describes the management system of the villages she researched as a unit comprised of three institutions acting in different ways (in part more closely, in part more independently):

'Village', downtown Shenzhen

(1) SUB DISTRICT OFFICE. It represents the city administration on site, but depends on the cooperation of the other 'village' institutions.

(2) COMMUNITY COMMITTEE. It derived from the management of the former village collective and is directly connected to the local group of the Communist Party, the 'root party branch'.

(3) JOINT STOCK COMPANY. The joint stock or limited company (Ltd.) is the dominating management body of the 'villages'. It integrates social, economic, and administrative functions.

— The management functions of the limited village company are often held by individuals who also control the community committee (this is principally the case in small 'villages'). Liable partners are those who hold land use rights and are members of family clans: the original village dwellers. Thus, the village administration or village government is a kind of family business or an economized village collective (Ma 2006, 155ff).

— While the city of Shenzhen ascends to a metropolis of millions all around them, the former villages become entry gates; highly efficient spaces of transformation for the structural integration of labor migrants. Business is good – and is conducted, if possible, informally (Ma 2006, 166). The 'company' profits serve to create infrastructure,[86] install temples and statues at village squares (or should we say 'introverted village courtyards'?), provide loans for investments, open new branches of business: restaurants, drug stores, prostitution, often concealed under the name 'hairdressing', sports betting, golf courses, also countless little manufacturing businesses – people have plenty of opportunities today and also take advantage of them.[87]

— And actually, people still behave as they used to, back when the village was not yet surrounded by the city, but by the earth and water of the landscape. Yet today, they are wealthy and can move into new areas of business, thus creating those structures that we may call 'villages', but which are in fact among the most densely populated urban quarters worldwide (Ma 2006). Buildings can be ten and more stories tall and the access streets and pathways arranged in a grid pattern are often hardly more than one meter wide. The labyrinthine, dark tangle of streets only occasionally opens towards tiny squares flanked by little grocery shops and towards lively central places adorned with colorful statues of Buddha and Confucius, little temples, water fountains, light bands, neon advertisements, plastic plants and flowers.

'Village' life, Shenzhen

— Since there are about 240 of such 'villages'[88] embedded within the wildly sprawling metropolis, they deeply influence the character of Shenzhen's urban image; but planners and city leadership obviously don't consider them a benefit to the city's image. This is why the villages are supposed to vanish, without replacement. Carrying this plan out is, however, not that simple; the 'villages' are powerful, influential, and resourceful – and have been capable of resisting the city's cravings to this day.

— The 'villages' are remarkable in a number of ways, not only in how they contribute to the urban code of the city of Shenzhen. What is also remarkable is the persistence of their social family-based system. According to Ma Hang, the membership of the 'joint stock companies' consistently reflects the clan structure of the respective 'village'. Only in very few exceptions are non-residents active in 'village' joint stock companies (Ma 2006, 158). Basically, the village life of historic China is perpetuated within these organizations. The ease with which the transformation of labor type from farming and fishery to supplying dwelling space for rent to labor migrants and other business activities took place provides a good example for the generally low threshold between rural and urban culture in China, something we have already recognized in the section on 'rocks and plants' (Chapter 2).

— This phenomenon of an almost non-existent cultural gap between town and country is also perceivable in the fact that 'villages', due to their density and verticality, are devoid of any trace of village-like extensiveness and horizontality. In terms of semiotics we could define this 'village'-phenomenon as a negative or rather inverted iconic sign, because it denotes 'urban' but, regarding its content, should be interpreted as 'rural'. Although any spatial trace of the rural is missing, people still call these structures 'villages', in all seriousness and without a trace of irony. This is possible because villagers' lives, from their own point of view, have actually remained unchanged. OK, so they lost their rice fields. But, praised be Buddha, they were allowed to stay and were able to sow and reap new harvests. Also, the village collective has remained; the families are still the same.

So where are the existential differences? We could almost get the impression that the village dwellers intend to completely disprove the widely acknowledged theories on the urban metropolitan, from Simmel to Bourdieu!

— Indeed, China in general, and not only the urban villages of Shenzhen, seems to have much stronger reservations towards a pronounced individualization and, related to this process, a 'societization' ('Vergesellschaftung') of social integration mechanisms and infrastructures (e.g. labor, senior care/social security, child care) than the Western, and particularly the European world. The process of societization or modernization that is articulated in Europe rather as friction between society (Gesellschaft) and community (Gemeinschaft), i.e. in contrast to family and clan structures, is more or less placed into the custody of the community (family) in China. Thus, the cultural hegemony of community is maintained, and societal processes – from monetary transactions via institutionalization to individualization – are limited in status and scope. They remain the primacy of community. And this primacy both reifies and is reified spatially above all in the significance of exclusive, introverted neighborhoods and in its special forms, such as the urban villages. These can thus be interpreted as forms of the ruralization of the urban (and not as urbanization of the rural).

— The 'villages' of Shenzhen allow us to recognize more clearly that the closed, introverted neighborhoods that we encounter in Chinese metropolises and mega-cities are, in fact, villages that ingest the urban and assume control of it. Chinese urbanism is subject to the social and cultural hegemony of community ('Gemeinschaft'). No urban space denotes this more emphatically than the villages of Shenzhen.

THE BIG CITY

— The Chinese city has an ancient history. Urban settlements already existed 5,000 years ago. They were located in the vicinity of the Yellow River (Huang He) and the Yangzi Jiang. They must be interpreted as temple cities or superoikoi (oikos is the basic unit of the traditional rural society, i.e. characterized by priority of subsistence farming and strong family hierarchy, headed by the oldest male, see e.g. Weber 1923/1981 348f, 381ff, Childe 1942, 243f), as houses of god-kings presiding over 'hydraulic-bureaucratic' societies (Wittfogel 1932). Although the consolidated and developed Chinese empire cannot be attributed to the need for irrigation anymore, the Chinese Emperors ruled in the tradition of these former 'Pharaohs' of the Far East.

— Corresponding to the permanence of the Chinese city, their urban planning concept had basically remained unchanged until the early twentieth century. Chinese cities have always been palace cities, i.e. places representing the omnipotence and omnipresence of the Emperors and their central power apparatus. After Imperial unification by Emperor Qin, beginning with the Han dynasty, a semi-enlightened centralistic system of rule was established successively and persisted more or less for over 2,000 years, decisively preventing the emergence of a feudal system of European kind in China. This system of rule, being supported by the administrative activities of well-educated state officials, capable of reading, writing, and other artistic modes of expression (so-called 'literate officials', 'scholar officials', or mandarins), succeeded in suppressing the influence of the regional nobility with separatist mindset to a large extent.

— The literate officials (scholar-officials) weren't feudal lords, their status was not hereditary. They claimed their positions by successfully passing examinations that

**Confucian School at
Shenyang Jianzhu University**

concluded their particular level of education. In our view, Schmidt-Glintzer is completely correct in speaking of a semi-enlightened society in regard to the literate officials, thus rejecting the still common comparison of Chinese Empire with European feudalism (Schmidt-Glintzer 1997, 66ff). The scholar officials and the Imperial centralism they perpetuated contributed decisively to the permanence of Chinese culture and its urban system.

—   The entire country belonged to the Emperor in a way comparable to how today land and property belongs to the Chinese state. Each city with its walls, its bell tower, its ancestral worship and good harvest temples was considered a spatial representation of the Emperor and as such completely subject to his will. The Emperor supervised the markets held in cities and city peripheries. Market rights and all other city rights such as mint, jurisdiction, measurement units, tariffs, and taxation – in Europe, comprising the basis for the freedom of the city and thus its very existence – remained under the control of the Emperor (Hassenpflug 2004a, 27ff). At a time when there were no notable cities at all in Western Europe (from the seventh to the ninth century), the Imperial Tang city of Xi'an (formerly Cháng'ân) housed about one million inhabitants on an area covering 88 square kilometers, thus by far the biggest city in the world at that time. Life in large and very large cities also never ceased as in Western Europe after the fall of the Western Roman Empire. As a result, China not only comprises a very old, but also an uninterrupted and continuous tradition of metropolitan life – and as essential part of it, metropolitan urban planning. A case of a city of millions such as Rome ceasing its urban life almost completely over the course of a few centuries (at some stage in the Middle Ages the population number temporarily barely exceeded 20,000) never occurred in Chinese history. If a city was conquered and destroyed, it was rebuilt in the same place or immediately built anew somewhere else.

—   China is familiar with metropolitan life. A movement critical to or even opposed to metropolitan life such as in the United States, tracing back to Jefferson's reservations towards big cities (White, L. and White, M. 1962; König, R. 1977) or much more radical, in continental Europe in the nineteenth and twentieth century (Hassenpflug 2006d) is almost inconceivable here and has also never developed. This is also true before the background of Mao's seemingly anti-urban policies, e.g. the development of the hukou residency permit system beginning in the mid 1950s and the policy of the 'Great Leap Forward' (1957–1960).

— The hukou registration system, strictly employed even after the opening of China and until the mid 1980s, was directed against rural-urban migration and cut a strong line between urban and rural dwellers. It was therefore deeply anti-republican. Within this registration system, the rural population hardly had any prospect of attaining urban dweller status. They were factually exempt – even though the constitution of 1954 guaranteed certain liberties (Zhang, Minjie 2004). Whoever was born in a village remained a country dweller and had almost no chance of receiving permanent stay in the city. Rural dwellers required a permit in order to temporarily stay in the city.

— But this system has nothing to do with anti-urban sentiments, rather on the contrary, with anti-rural sentiments, even though its justification was based on the necessity of rural development. On the one hand, it is rooted in the tradition of hierarchical thought, where the city and urban life are considered to be of higher status than the agrarian countryside and rural life. On the other hand, it threatens to destroy this hierarchy's order precisely by excluding village life from its system. The hukou registration practice attributed Chinese rural life with a completely un-Chinese stigma that has persisted until today.

— Also, neglect of urban planning beginning with the 'Great Leap Forward' and continued after Mao's death in 1976, which included shutting down the corresponding authorities, should not be taken as an expression of an anti-urban mindset. This policy was not primarily directed against cities, but expressed the priority of developing the agrarian hinterland after ceasing the developmental cooperation with Russia in the mid 1950s (Friedmann 2005). Finally, neither can the 'Great Leap' be compared to an anti-urban stance of Western kind. This policy was rather based on the fundamentally Chinese assumption of (prior to this, symbolized in the Empire and now perpetuated by the Communist Party) consubstantiality of town and country. Only before the background of this concept of identity can we actually begin to understand the idea of transforming farmers into steel makers. Led by Sinicized visions of an egalitarian communist society, the 'Great Leap' was supposed to counteract a conceptual inferiority of rural life by transforming farmers into members of the proletariat and thus, rural life into urban life.

— Other than that, Mao preferred to think in military categories. He hoped that a ruralization of steel production would obviously provide better protection of heavy industries otherwise concentrated in cities as well as logistic and distributive advantages (Friedmann 2005, 20f). An idiosyncratic interpretation of industrializing the rural,

Portraits of graduates
inside Confucian school

brutally corrected by history, a real-time experiment that, as we know now, cost millions of people their lives. We can be sure that this campaign was unrelated to anti-urban sentiments. Concepts of the city as a wicked Babylon or a cancerous growth on Gaia's body are completely alien to Chinese culture. Equally alien as, incidentally, the myth of the city as a holy Jerusalem, also informed by anti-urban criticism.[89]

— China today has about 1.3 billion inhabitants. About 650 million (approximately fifty percent) currently live in cities. Of the remaining fifty percent, many millions are in the process of moving to the city, hoping to realize their dream of a better life there – if not for themselves, at least for their children. Every city in China holds such a promise, and as it becomes true day by day, people from the countryside keep on streaming into the cities. This tremendous redistribution from the country to the city is possible through easing the hukou residency permit laws. Since 1984 village dwellers have had the opportunity to purchase a non-countryside hukou-status, at least temporarily. Piece by piece, a further liberalization of migration practices took place, as a reaction to the conditions of a developing country (Zhang, Minjie 2004). Newest reports (2009) indicate that the hukou residency permit system will be completely discontinued in the near future.

— In contrast, the country is feeding its people better and better. Productivity is increasing, and the specter of unemployment is on the rise. That is why the countryside doesn't nourish hopes for a better future for the entire rural population. Many have to move to the city to make a living. From 1989 to 2000, more than 100 million men and women followed the call of the city – and this flow is increasing further. In early 2010, the number of the 'floating population' (rural labor migrants with temporal urban hukou residency permit) was estimated to be about 220 million. According to the *Shanghai Statistical Yearbook* of 2008 6.4 million rural labor migrants, 1.3 million of whom had a permit for less than half a year of residency, lived in Shanghai. In Beijing, Shenzhen, Chongqing, Guangzhou and many other mega-cities, the number of labor migrants is in the multi-million range as well.

— On a general level, we can compare this situation to Europe in the nineteenth century. There and then as well, a tremendous redistribution of people from the countryside to the city had taken place. The reasons seem equally comparable: the introduction of industrial capitalist and rationalist methods of labor and distribution resulted in a decrease of agrarian labor demand while industrial development, concentrating in the cities, required a cheap workforce.

Chinese mega-urban cityscape, Shenyang

— In regard to the sizes of cities, however, this migration process is taking place on a very different scale in China. In comparison to German cities, we can safely assume that Chinese cities comprise ten times as many inhabitants. While a German city reaches the fiscally relevant status of metropolis when it has 100,000 citizens, the corresponding number in China would be one million inhabitants. Already in 2009 the number of Chinese cities with more than one million inhabitants had exceeded 100 by far and today four cities have even more than ten million registered inhabitants: Chongqing, located at the central course of the Yangzi Jiang as biggest city of the world with more than thirty million, Shanghai with more than eighteen million, Beijing with more than fourteen million, and Guanzhou with about thirteen million. The expectation is that numerous cities, among them Tianjin, Shenyang, Wuhan, and Chengdu will exceed the ten million mark by 2015. However, we should take into account that the regional authorities or municipalities in China are composed differently as, for instance, in Germany. In China they often comprise or include 'counties', i.e. rural districts that are considered independent regional authorities in Germany and have official leadership in the form of an administrative head equal to a city mayor.[90]

— But Chinese cities are not only very big; they are also extraordinarily densely populated. The average population density of inner city and suburban areas (without rural counties) is 16,500 inhabitants per square kilometer, and of Shanghai approx. 16,950 people/sqkm (cf. Berlin with 3,800 people/sqkm).[91] The four urban districts of Shenyang, with more than seven million inhabitants forming the fifth-largest city of China, have an average population density of 23,700 inhabitants per square kilometer. Shenhe district with 34,070 people/sqkm ranks first, Heping district with 30,502 is second, and Tiexi with 20,600 is third (cf. Berlin-Kreuzberg, the district with highest urban density in Germany: 15,000 people/sqkm). The settlement density of peripheral urban areas in Shenyang is, in contrast, 1,420 people/sqkm and in rural districts about 210 people/sqkm. The large drop in population numbers between urban districts and rural 'counties' points out how intensely the spatial appearance differs between city and country. It also emphasizes the thesis on the compactness of the Chinese metropolis.[92] The city-country drop becomes even more pronounced the farther we move away from metropolitan regions, for instance towards the west, where we find cities like Wuhan, Zhengzhou, or the old Imperial city Xi'an.

— All Chinese experts we spoke to on this subject confirm that Chinese people like to frequent populated, vital and diverse places and consider calm, quiet, secluded spaces rather unattractive. Even extreme disarray and chaos do not convey any malaise or even horror as long as people can find their way and follow it within the confusion. A question of mentality? Most certainly there are culturally differently articulated modes of reacting and behavior in dealing with confusing, noisy, cacophonic, chaotic environments. In contrast to Northern Europeans, the Chinese seem – comparable to Italians or Spaniards – to be much more tolerant towards the challenges of high-density urban milieus. It could very well be that there are historical reasons for this. We can, of course, compare life in the neighborhoods and quarters of the old Chinese cities with life in a space of labyrinths. Metropolitan life and urban density seem to be an integral component of sinicity.

RIVER JUMPING

— From Hong Kong to Singapore, we recognize the importance of city images or urban guiding principles (Leitbilder). The potency of these images is also highlighted by the ostensible presence of investors and developers from these cities. Even better than the equally successful Americans, Canadians, and Australians, Eastern Asian developers understand how to interpret their Chinese customers' desires and transform these into corresponding spatial arrangements and images. But Hong Kong's, Singapore's, and Taipei's urban imagery serves merely as stepping stone for even more ambitious urban spatial images. In these, the historic visual treasures of art and architecture merge with spaces of power of Baroque impression and icons of modern universalism into a completely new world in which the million-fold poverty and filth of the western Chinese hinterland is blanked out. The new China, the utopia forged from Imperial palace, Baroque, Modernism, universalism, and Postmodernism is manifest and sustainably empowers the urban process of transformation.

— But urban guiding images (Leitbilder) also follow fashionable trends. One such urban design fashion in China is 'river jumping', and Shanghai is its pioneer. The urban planning 'jump' from Puxi (the western bank of the Huangpu Jiang) to Pudong (the eastern bank of the Huangpu Jiang) resulted in the creation of an inner city ensemble with unique power of imagery. On the one side of the river, the magnificent colonial architecture of the Bund, on the other side, the new skyscraper center Lujiazui in Pudong, growing within a bend of the Huangpu Jiang: the image of the old colonial town Shanghai superimposed by the new China, ascending towards status of world power; a breathtaking scenery especially after sunset, when the European facades of the Bund radiate in golden light and the skyscrapers of the new bank and business center across from it are illuminated in cool blue-green hues, interspersed with the multicolored coruscation of mediatized skyscraper facades. This is the symbol of the new China, and many Chinese cities feel obliged to follow the example of Shanghai and prepare for a 'river jump' of their own.

New city hall, pioneering 'river jump' building, Harbin

**View from the new
city hall to Harbin proper**

— The fact that geographic preconditions for 'river jumping' actually exist is due to historic reasons. Imperial city founding followed ancient cosmologically based rules. They prescribed that a city should preferably be built south of existing mountains or hills and north of a river. Mountains or hills represent protection from enemies and from cold weather, rivers symbolize fertility, nourishment, mobility, and trade. As a result of this geographic rule for founding cities in Imperial China, many Chinese cities to to this day are 'one bank cities', expanding between mountains or hills to the north and a river in the south.

— However, there are numerous exceptions, Shanghai being one of them. This metropolis originated in a fishing village and became a city during colonial settlement. There are no mountains or hills present here, neither does orientation follow the ancient rules. Still, Shanghai was until recently basically a 'one bank city'. A comparable situation exists in Harbin, northern Chinese metropolis with five million inhabitants and capital city of Heilongjiang Province. Harbin was founded by the Russians in the course of building the southern line of the Trans-Siberian Railway along the Songhua Jiang and significantly expanded on the southern bank, centered on the strategically important train station. The Songhua Jiang here flows from west to east; nearby mountains are missing for the most part.

— But the city has a 'one bank' site, allowing the city to prepare for the jump from south to north, following Shanghai's example. Landing on the opposite side of the Songhua Jiang was made possible by building a huge city hall complex in the middle of what used to be swamps; it is surrounded by garden areas of predominantly Baroque impression and accessed by an eight-lane 'great street' (for more details about this design see Chapter 5, 'Postmodern eclecticism in urban planning and design'). The city hall became a signal for a development in urban planning; in its course the city's area will eventually double.

'River jump' master plans. Left: Shenyang. Right: Harbin

— In the meantime, Shenyang, northern metropolis with seven million inhabitants, has also planned a 'river jump'. The 'Golden Corridor', its linear center featuring commercial, cultural, leisure and public functions, will bridge the gap between old and new city. The new southern bank of the Hun He represents – following the example of Pudong – success, good luck, and providence. If we consider that the cost of land use rights is comparatively low in the newly developed areas, we can very well imagine how desirable the new development will be. The 'customers' of the newly developed area not only include the regular residential construction investors and commercial park developers, but also the promoters of commercial, educational, sports, media and public facilities, and as the examples of Harbin or also Ningbo (Zhejiang Province) indicate, possibly even new governmental buildings. At present, however, the city government and the Liaoning provincial administration are still located in the very center of Shenyang city.

— In the attempt to profitably market their desirable inner city locations and at the same time improve their institutional image, almost all university administrations have decided to leave the inner cities and develop new, presumably more prestigious campuses out in the green on the urban fringe. As in many such cases, we can ultimately only understand the lack of objection to the urbanistic consequences of such site choices by taking the influence of Chinese traditions of higher education and in addition, the model employed e.g. in the United States, into account. Comparable to Anglo-Saxon universities, maintaining their ecclesiastical-monastic origins more clearly than their continental European counterparts, China can draw from a significant tradition of institutions of higher education, such as Confucian places of graduation or education facilities. However, they never functioned as an element of urbanity.

HYPER-GROWTH

— The process of catch-up development in China, directed by a centralistic power apparatus and orchestrated by a historically established 'Asian' tendency towards diversity and towards harmonization of opposites, offers the country the opportunity to synchronically retrace the Modernization process that had proceeded diachronically in Europe and, by doing so, pick up developmental speed.

— As European urbanists and adepts of a structuralistic perspective, we have become accustomed to base a culturally informed observation of history in an assumption on an evolutionary or revolutionary succession of eras/epochs and developmental steps (within an era/epoch). A common historic sequence of modernity draws from an advancement of the Marxian theory of surplus production. According to this theory, we can define three stages: extensive industrialization (also: early or incipient industrialization, where surplus production is mainly based on additional labor time consumption), intensive industrialization (Fordism or also 'etatistic' or rather 'social democratic' Modernism, where surplus production is mainly based on increasing productivity), and flexible industrialization (occasionally also 'post-industrial era' or 'second modernity', where surplus production is mainly based on a combination of innovation and computer-based intelligence).[93]

Phase of industrialization	extensive industrialization	intensive industrialization	flexible industrialization
Production type	manufacturing; artisanship	large series; 'blue collar'	small series; 'white collar'
State type	laissez-faire state	welfare state	activating state
Society type	polarized class society	balanced (mediated) middle class society	individualized knowledge society
City type	industrial city	social city	creative city
Infill structure	lot-based perimeter block	detached linear structures	perimeter block and detached linear structures
Spatial-functional concept	hierarchical; mixed	functionally divided; zoned	functional pluralism (mixed, mono-functional, functional blur)
Centrality	centralized city	decentralized city	polycentric urban-rural continuum
Urban paradigm	'Gründerzeit' city	Fordist city (dispersed and zoned)	narrative, themed city (Postmodern city)
Urban-rural relation	dualistic	integrated	continuous
Urban growth type	radial concentric	peripheral; dispersed	inverted (center and periphery change position)

— From a morphological point of view, each individual step can be interpreted as entity, i.e. as a system that, comparable to an organism, integrates all its parts or subsystems into a kind of 'time-personality' (Zeitpersönlichkeit). Following dogmas of philosophy of history, we can interpret the succession of these 'time-personalities' as process of completion or perfection (according to Hegel) or each step as a phase within a 'life cycle' of civilization (according to O. Spengler). However, the succession of industrial regimes or modern 'time-personalities' can also be used as mere heuristic model without particular ideological emphasis, appropriate for an intercultural comparison that we intend to employ here.

— In applying the succession model of Modernism to the city as spatialized form of each individual step of industrialization, we can formulate the following historic structure of urbanism: (1) industrial city, city of the 'Gründerzeit' or, according to Benevolo "liberal city" (Benevolo 1980); (2) 'social city' (the modern, Fordist city); and finally (3) the post-Fordist city, the city of reflexive Modernism, or also the 'themed city' as we can call it in reference to our observations in Chapter 6.

— In this context, the relationship of the three phases should be envisioned as a process in which each successive phase incorporates elements of each previous phase, absorbing them and transforming them into elements of their own new structure. Thus, the post-Fordist 'themed city' includes the Fordist social city, but gives it a minor role. While the first steps onstage, the latter has to make do with a place behind and beneath the stage. Fordist rationalism is thus not contradicted, but incorporated and decorated with traditional forms. We can compare this to the relationship of social and liberal city, i.e. the city of Fordism and the city of the 'Gründerzeit'. The answers that latter provides to the question of urban-rural redistribution (urbanization), e.g. garden city and sanitary infrastructure, are incorporated, but are subject to a fundamental revision in the terms of the "dispersed and zoned city in the park"[94] or the rational-egalitarian machine city, according to the principles of the Charter of Athens.

— Reflecting the European model of development, the following table correlates a number of urban spatial characteristics to the three periods mentioned above:

— If we apply the 'triadic developmental model' to the contemporary Chinese city, then we recognize that the three historic steps are rather completed synchronically than diachronically in the course of its catch-up development. We can observe a triadic developmental model that is based on the simultaneity of extensive, intensive, and flexible industrialization. China is currently in synchronicity with the developed tertiary societies – and is doing its historic 'homework' on extensive and intensive industrialization at the same time.

— We not only see the incorporation of elements of extensive into intensive and of intensive into flexible development, but beyond that, also an independent parallel development of all three phases. The Chinese developmental model is thus characterized by extraordinary complexity. The term 'hyper-growth' reflects this only to a limited degree. The complexity of the Chinese developmental model is amplified by the fact that there had already been a pronounced period of Fordist modernization of Sino-communist character towards the end of the 1970s, before the opening.

— China is undergoing, without a doubt – and not for the first time – a 'Gründerzeit'. Chinese capitalism today shares characteristics with extensive industrialization in Europe in the nineteenth century. Social polarization is enormous, and the state is still barely present as a force of social mediation.

— Not only the comparatively vastly important primary sector (agriculture), but also the enormous rural-urban migration and closely related hyper-growth of cities are indicators for defining the corresponding stage as 'early industrial'.

— The same plausibility that lets us identify elements and processes of extensive industrialization equally permits the identification of elements and processes of Fordist modernization. The application of scientific production methods and the systematic organization of knowledge transfer from the laboratory to market-oriented production are not only self-evident, they are also empowered by alliances with foreign partners, i.e. joint ventures, as well as by debatable practices of acquisition of intellectual property, copyrights, patents, etc. The rapid distribution of the automobile, especially the increase in number of mid-size and compact cars, also points out an equally rapidly growing middle class and the emergence of a consumer society. Further indicators include growing public transport systems and – yet still in an initial stage – beginnings of what may be called social housing. In general, more and more voices in a society that is rapidly shifting towards a state of economic polarization are being heard that call for stronger state intervention for social equity or social democratic measures endemic to Fordism, regardless which political subject executes them (Dahrendorf 1981).

— A bird's eye view of the Chinese city is particularly helpful to demonstrate the significance of Fordist spatial production. We see an ocean of oriented lines and dots, wave after wave of 'rank and file' monostructures bound together in former danwei quarters or contemporary residential compounds. Many of these structures were built before the opening; but the majority was built afterwards, as we can easily see in the form of swinging lines and dancing dots within organic settlement areas.

— No other era of industrial development has a comparable or similar aesthetic and iconic presence in China as post-Fordism with its diversity of aesthetizations, fictions, decorations, mediatizations; not only on the open urban theater stage, but also in the closed neighborhoods. China is the undisputed world champion of Disneyfication, of theme parks, of copycat cities, of urban fictions, and of eclecticism of style. The nation is dreaming the Western or rather American dream – and is realizing it instantaneously by decorating its Chinese creations with the bliss of Western dreams, viewed through rose-colored glasses. The ubiquity of Disneyfied signs and spaces here is unparalleled by its contemporaries, the industrially developed nations of the Western world and neighboring Asia.

— It therefore comes as no surprise that the urban visions of New Urbanism are vastly interesting to the Chinese. But only its picturesque character is important: the composition of the urban interior and the basic structure of the city is something the Chinese know best. China is dreaming the American dream in order to heal the trauma of backwardness – but not to achieve Americanization or Westernization. Or isn't it true that the occasionally still wallflower-like Chinese city looks much better in her Western outfit? From a Chinese point of view, the unequivocal answer is: Yes! But China is picking up speed, its lag is shrinking. The great spectacle of a nation stepping onto the global stage, clad in its urban dress made of materials from afar and from its own heritage, has already begun. It is already foreseeable that postmodern citytainment, i.e. the practice of equipping new towns and settlements with architectural narrations from the West, will be a temporal phenomenon. It will be followed by a specific Chinese image of the city, mirroring the country's hopes for the 'good life' in its height, size, density, and grandeur.

— The 'triadic developmental model', according to which China is synchronically completing the European development of the nineteenth, twentieth, and twenty-first century, comprises circumstances and preconditions of which a few can be related to particular aspects of Chinese history. One of these prerequisites is the nation's unusual openness towards development. The chain of dramatic societal changes that had already begun during the Qing dynasty in the nineteenth century, during the republican revolution, and continued in Mao's social experiments in the civil war via the 'Great Leap Forward' and the Cultural Revolution, have severely shaken the nation and distanced it from its historical memory, its natural course of traditions and customs so much that it now tends to look at its history in a reflexive way. Nothing seems to be self-evident anymore. Not only that: after all of these radical upheavals it obviously seems less difficult to the Chinese to open themselves to new influences, compared with other developing or emerging countries.

— According to the prerequisites of triadic high-speed development and related hyper-urbanization, technical aspects seemingly dominate. When Europe underwent the process of labor-based extensive industrialization, there was no Internet, no mobile phones, no GPS, no fax. Also, there were neither airplanes nor container ships nor other highly efficient transport and mobility technologies. In regard to these accomplishments we can thus, in comparison to the term 'hyper-growth', speak of a process of 'hyper-modernization' in China. Here, primitive labor exploitation typical for extensive industrialization occurs on the basis of Fordist mass production fueled and supervised by high-tech that characterizes flexible industrialization in the West. This can, for instance, mean the following: working long hours at low wages (period 1) with high productivity (period 2) on computer-controlled assembly lines with just-in-time supply (period 3) – an inconceivable combination from the viewpoint of so-called advanced (post)industrial societies.

— Something comparable could never have happened in Europe and America. When the control technology that enabled the flexibilization of labor was integrated into production, eight-hour workdays with comparatively high standard wages had already been in force. Thus, the mix of working regimes or industrialization regimes considered natural in China – and therefore not questioned – may in part explain the nation's enormous speed in development. China has had a sufficient amount of economic success to afford the technology for the nation's hyper-modernization; and since it can afford it, it is economically successful.

— This success informs urban planning and design in complex ways: in general, as "high-speed urbanism" as described e.g. by Ipsen (2004), where cities with millions of inhabitants grow into mega-cities with more than ten million people and urban agglomerations with more than 100 million people. Here, we see construction processes on the one hand accelerated by advanced technology, and on the other hand applied with inadequate materials and capabilities that not only produce tremendous cities, but at the same time enormous low-quality cityscapes.

Handmade
foundation
of high-rise
construction,
Changsha

— However, something else becomes apparent – and not only on the level of urban planning and design: an emerging process of overtaking modernization. In order to comprehend it, we have to cast aside the veil of imported styles and images and take a look at what is actually happening. Precisely here we find the germination points of a new urban culture of living: new introverted garden cities with ambitiously designed neighborhood courtyards surrounded by swinging lines and dancing dots. We see the twin structure of linear building arrangements in park-like spaces (Zeilenbau) and framing perimeter block strips, reflecting the fundamental dualism of closed residential compounds and open commerzcial spaces. While new extroverted urban theater stages are built within open spaces, thus meeting the increasing need for citytainment and distinction, closed neighborhoods perpetuate the desire for urban spaces that reify the strong role of the community, the desire for urban villages.

THE CHINESE CITY
AS A SEMIOTIC SYSTEM

8

— The task of this final chapter is to integrate the different observations within and on the Chinese city into a coherent, conclusive morphological understanding of this city type. For this purpose, it will be necessary to resort to our explanations on urban semiotics in Chapter 1.

— We posit that every city can be described as a complex socio-cultural system of spatial signs. From this point of view, the city is a 'landscape' of urban signifiers permanently transmitting signals that observers can process into sensible, meaningful messages. But urban signs only become 'real' carriers of meaning when they are assigned content. As shown in Chapter 1, this process of assignment is described as abduction, where the observer supplies an 'explanatory hypothesis' for determining the iconic, indicative, or also symbolic messages of the identified urban signs.

— This is precisely what we have offered in the preceding chapters. We have suggested these 'weak' proposals of meaning at risk of failure (of falsification); we have spoken of open and closed space; we have claimed the primacy of introversion, exclusion, southern orientation; and we have spoken of linear centrality, high degree of coverage, media facades, noble places, sutlers' settlements, great street, and vertical block. Each of these characterizations comprises an explanatory hypothesis through which we attempt to define and decode an element of the Chinese city as a sign. We can now ask the following question: how do we prove our claim (hypothesis), reinforce it, scientifically substantiate it, and thus achieve conclusive knowledge or 'denoted content'?

— Urban signs don't permit, as in Umberto Eco's example of the chair (as signifier) and sitting (as primary function), an easy assignment of convincing messages. In urban semiotics, we require particular knowledge in order to trigger the process of abduction and begin salvaging the supply of meaning incorporated in urban signs. This knowledge, as we have already noted in Chapter 1, is provided by the history and culture of Chinese society. With Walter Benjamin's technique of 'superposition', i.e. 'remembering the new', we find something akin to an epistemological 'key' that permits accessing the signifiers and the meanings hidden in their signals.

— A reading that focuses on the morphological dimension of the Chinese city and thus aims to break the socio-cultural code of the city only with a sporadic identification of urban signs and related meanings is, however, not satisfactory. Neither is the abductive identification of an individual element (such as the hypothesis of an introverted concept of space in residential compounds) as expression of Chinese traditions as such sufficient to serve as proof for the sinicity of urban spatial production in contemporary China. Dominant introverted spatial concepts exist in other cultures as well, e.g. in the Arabian practice of urban space production; and even in the 'Western world' we can nowadays observe an increase in interior courtyard architecture, especially in connection to commercial uses. Assigning 'sinicity' to urban elements thus requires that we assume the presence of a structural or syntactical interrelation between them. We need a framework that allows us to organize the particular elements according to their respective degree of affiliation or proximity to what we describe as 'sinicity'. Only when the urban signifieds are detected in this manner, as result of a 'cultural construction', can we consider the process of semiosis as completed. We are capable of reading the city because urban space offers, in the terminology of semiotics or rather, to borrow a semiological term from de Saussure (1986), a socio-cultural 'syntagma': a system that is, in principle, open towards the art of structural interpretation of meaning. The purpose of this type of hermeneutics, for which we employ the technique of superposition, is to reveal the immanent (wesensmässige) interior relationships between urban spatial signs and socio-cultural messages. The result for the Chinese city is as follows: only a structural hermeneutics of its idiosyncratic shapes and forms is capable of achieving a morphological integration of identified meanings that allows us to recognize their sinicity.[95] The following schematic illustration summarizes the phases and components of structural semiosis.

— The semiotically informed reading of the city has led us to many places (referents) that we can recognize as building blocks of the Chinese city, to residential compounds, streets, places of all kinds, city centers, suburban areas, to shopping streets and centers, to historic quarters and new developments. In all the places we visited, we found signs within and on urban objects that we could decode as carriers of meaning or transmitters of socio-cultural content. In order to identify relevant denotations (also: primary functions), we at first recurred to socio-cultural content in a rather unsystematic or arbitrary way: for instance, the interrelation of introversion and community, of linear centrality and social hierarchy, of Chinese gardens and philosophical concepts of harmony, or of 'river jumping' and, oscillating between desire, invocation, and fashion, the intention of copying Shanghai's economic success.

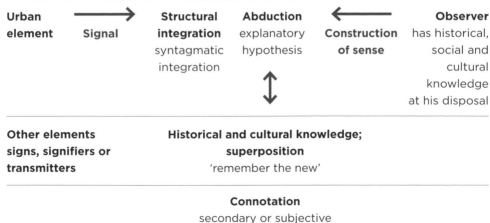

Denotation
primary or objective
functions or meanings

| Urban element | Signal → | Structural integration syntagmatic integration | Abduction explanatory hypothesis | ← Construction of sense | Observer has historical, social and cultural knowledge at his disposal |

Other elements signs, signifiers or transmitters   **Historical and cultural knowledge; superposition** 'remember the new'

The city as a system (syntagma)

Connotation
secondary or subjective
functions or meanings

— What is missing until now in our work is embedding our interpretations within a system of socio-cultural knowledge, as explained above, in a way that is coherent, rational, and transcends particularistic decodings. In other words: at this point, we have concluded abductively from signifiers (carriers of meaning) to signifieds (content, meaning, sense), but we intend to complement this with a syntagmatic explanation of the interrelation of the signifieds' content (the structure). The following will present a first schematic attempt in this direction.

— In order to formulate a rationale for the structural interrelation of the already recognized socio-cultural signifieds, we follow the logic of a dual or also dialectic terminological concept (Begrifflichkeit), which the structural method always and rightfully demands due to its ontological obviousness (Sinnfälligkeit). As a result, the socio-cultural spatial analysis can be conceived as a system of knowledge based on a specific 'binary code'. This code enables assigning a large part of the employed signifieds in a way that permits formulating their syntagmatical character constitutive of a spatial entity ('wholeness', orig. Ganzheit or Totalität), but also creating plausibility for considering urban space as syntagma. This substantiates the scientific nature of semiosis (the conclusion from signifiers to signifieds).

— The code that we consider appropriate to the task is the sociological dualism exemplified by Ferdinand Tönnies (but also discussed by Riehl, Marx, Weber, and many more) of community (Gemeinschaft) and society (Gesellschaft) (Tönnies 1979/1991). Community and society (or also, 'association') are the two possible social states (Verfasstheiten) or 'aggregate conditions' that apply to every human being simultaneously, at any time, and everywhere. Both terms or rather concepts constitute a context of reference (Verweisungszusammenhang) that is capable of maintaining the claimed socio-cultural system.

— Community (Gemeinschaft), the first of the two social states, refers to direct, immediate human relationships. These are based on family relations ('blood' or 'kin'), friendship ('emotions'), shared opinions ('interests'), ideologies ('convictions'), conventions, or also on direct forms of rule. The most ancient and most important form of community is the family and its derivate forms such as clan, tribe, kinship, nuclear family. Oikoi (geschlossene Hauswirtschaften), Christian or other religious congregations, 'brotherhoods', networks as well can be summed up under the term community. In our work, we posit that Chinese 'society'[96] is decisively more strongly centered on the community than Western or European 'societies' (centered on associations), and that this community orientation informs the production of urban space in numerous ways.

— In contrast, society (Gesellschaft), the second of the two social states, refers to mediated (vermittelte) human relationships and socially constitutive interactions of individuals. From the perspective of society, people are not related, not friends, not enemies, but exclusively contractual partners, buyers, sellers, occupational specialists (professionals, experts). On the theater stage of society, human beings interact with each other in an indirect, mediated way. The media of this mediation process are money, contracts, differentiated or specialized institutions.

— Money and contractual ties permit that human beings who are not acquainted with each other, have no opinion of each other, or do not care for each other, can relate to each other in a socially successful way. Society in this regard creates the foundation for a 'cold' rational social context of individuals based on reason and institutionalized in the division of labor. The origin of each form of societization (Vergesellschaftung) is the exchange of goods, the market, or the economic mode based on it. We describe the social individual also as an economic or contractual subject. The unfolding of trade, the evolution of products and capital separates community from society. The exchange of goods extracts the 'me' from the 'we'.

— The interrelation of society, individual, and market contains multiple references to the city. For one, the city as a cultural superstructure is dependent on exchange with the countryside, with agriculture and the peasantry (orig. Nährstand). From a purely material perspective, rural life is possible without urban life, but urban life unthinkable without rural life. Rural life is rooted in peasantry, but in contrast, the city's existence is based on the exchange of goods and the economic system it establishes. This is exactly the reason why it is no coincidence that, from a historic perspective, cities were always founded where the commodity character (Warenform) of goods became dominant, where trade and markets developed. The city and the market are indivisible, and all city types that don't meet this basic interrelation can, at most, be described as proto-cities.

— In real social life, depending on history and culture, the relation of community to society can vary strongly. In so-called traditional societies, the institutions of social interrelation are primarily based on the community (family, clan, tribe). Speaking of 'traditional societies' is contradictory insofar as these 'societies' are rather communities, yet can envelop proto-social and social institutions. In so-called developed societies, in contrast, the societal character of social interaction leads to an articulated individualization with simultaneous depreciation or weakening of community-related interaction, for instance in the societization of social security functions (social security, senior care, unemployment benefits, child care, education, etc.). But even within the social interrelations characterized by the highest degree of societization, the individual remains 'downward compatible' with community life, because community life surrounds and pervades social institutions. An example of this pervasiveness in modern societies is the contractual nature of marriage or also societization in the form of creating legal or juridical persons, common in the business world in various forms.

— Just like every social interaction, exchange activity also becomes spatialized. The form of the market place reflects this in an ideal-typical manner. Known in history as agora, it is the primordial locus (orig. Urort) of public space, and as such a 'total institution' (Habermas 1981 II, 235), still incorporating in an undifferentiated form later developed, differentiated social institutions.[97] But the market unfolds its social-systemic potential only in the course of urban history. If we consider the evolution of the market place as indivisibly connected to the evolution of the city, then this compels us to view it as the laboratory of individualization and societization. Already Max Weber has shown that the evolution of society occurs along the lines of an individualization process that is characterized by division of labor, institutionalization, bureaucratization, and scientification, for which the city is both theater stage and audience space. The city is the space in which the division of community and society takes place, a process that is also described as civilizing process (Zivilisierung). This is why many consider the city as a 'civilization machine'. This notion prompted Weber to formulate his famous phrase of the "disenchantment of the world."[98]

— Society is spatialized in extroverted spaces. In this regard, open public space, presenting itself in extroverted forms, is a genuinely societal place. In contrast, community is spatialized within spaces that are oriented towards the inside, private, introverted, for instance in interior courtyards. Introversion is a spatial language of a social context that is constituted by direct and immediate interaction, by proximity. Depending on which form of social nexus is dominant in a particular cultural context, in a region, or a state, the spatial context will be characterized rather by introverted or extroverted traits. Thus, in community-dominated cultures the courtyard house, demonstrating introversion, will play an exceptional role, whereas in society-dominated cultures the open or public space of the place or street will prevail.

— Orient and Occident are different precisely in regard to this differentiation of community and society or – in its spatial form – of introversion and extroversion, in a way that is clearly visible and persistent to this day. Extroverted European spatial culture is diametrically opposed to Chinese introverted spatial culture. A systematic preference for courtyard house architecture comparable to China or to interior courtyards was last seen in Europe in Roman culture and Moorish culture in the Muslim Apennines, in the sacred architectural culture of the cloister – as continuation of the Roman peristyle house typology – and naturally in the worldly architectural culture of the feudal Middle Ages, where castle courtyards and horti inclusi, for instance in the form of patrician Palazzi of the Renaissance, comprised elements of ascending early bourgeois (altbürgerliche) cities.

— In Europe – and only in Europe – approximately in the first millennium C.E. during the reconstruction of the urban culture that collapsed after the decline of the Western Roman Empire, a completely new, previously entirely unknown extroverted type of city emerged. We owe this to the specific synecism (Synoikismos) of traders and artisans, i.e. of market economy-oriented and in this regard genuinely urban actors that assembled in craftsmen associations and guilds, Hanseatic leagues, and city alliances of all kinds with the goal of city freedom and resistance against feudal dominance and paternalism.[99]

— If the bourgeois actors followed the example of the feudal lords, the emperors, the bishops, the kings, the princes and sovereigns or other feudal rulers and claimed representative spaces for themselves, then this permitted the gradual development of an open space of a special kind: the market place, denoting bourgeois pluralism. This space is special; its form no longer reflects the claim to power of 'Great Men' – according to the term introduced by Godelier (1986) –, but in principle a democratic constitution of an emerging or already mature early bourgeois society (altbürgerliche Gesellschaft).[100] The difference between hierarchical exceptionalism and bourgeois pluralism in design is immediately perceivable if we compare e.g. a Baroque place (Place Royal) with a market place (piazza). While the Baroque signifier presents itself iconologically as monolithic and dramatizes the power of rulers who demonstrate their claim within it by use of axes and geometric arrangement, the market place in contrast articulates the idea of bourgeois diversity through its frame composed of decorated facades in lot-based perimeter block construction.

— Early bourgeois society began the practice of dramatizing public spaces through gable-end facades. Similar to stage backdrops, facades here constitute a frame for places and streets and transform these into theatrical spaces, into theater stages of urban life. These 'theaters' with their pluralistically designed stage sets denote – if not the dominance – but nevertheless the growing influence of society opposed to community. The facade play of cities, typical for the medieval era and finally gaining dominance in the Renaissance as a general characteristic of the European city, became an equal counterpart to the architecture of cathedrals, city halls, and fortifications, thus pointing out the rise of a gradually individualizing society of citizens.

— Inclusion or openness is a key idea of the European city, even if it there indeed was once something akin to an early bourgeois (based on 'caste' or guild-oriented) practice of segregation and exclusion. Closed residential quarters, however, couldn't endure for long. They were abolished in the course of the political emancipation of the urban citizenry, just as traditional continental medieval land terms (Lehens- und Flurordnung) in the course of republican reforms. As a result, open space dominates closed space – and this dominance is the basis for the emancipation of open space and its resulting transformation into public space.

— In Imperial China, however, a strict division of community and society and therefore between country and city or also public and private never prevailed. Also, history doesn't indicate the presence of a culture of public urban space comparable to Europe, not even in generic terms. Streets in ancient China generally and exclusively functioned as means of access. Or, as higher-order streets, they can be symbolic spaces, reflecting within their orientation, width, spatial sequence, and existing buildings (bell tower, ancestral temple, buildings of urban government) the hierarchically structured allocations of meaning related to the Imperial court.

— Certainly, market places also existed. They were closed at first, but following the late Tang dynasty (seventh to tenth century) open types existed as well, over time accompanied by more and more open market streets. Already during the Song era (960–1279 C.E.), all urban places and streets dedicated to market exchange were open. However, market rights, market laws, and making sure that people followed them, remained at all times in the hands of the Imperial administration. Thus, synecistic activities for the purpose of creating independent civic governments, also of independent guilds and craftsman associations, could not develop in China.[101] An emancipation of representatives of market trade, of merchants and artisans, did not occur. Therefore, a bourgeois isonomy of economic subjects as in Europe also couldn't develop. Since trade remained a kind of 'palace economy', following the term of Polanyi (2001/1979), strictly supervised by Imperial officers, traders and artisans became arrested in a proto-bourgeois state.

— This is the reason why a public culture could never develop in Chinese cities. The Emperor remained the sovereign of all spaces, their representative, resulting in every single bit of the city becoming an element and an extension of the Imperial palace – and thus a carrier of meaning of Imperial power. In other words, even though something akin to citizen-based or societal (gesellschaftliche) elements developed in the expansion of trade and business, these always remained completely dominated by a community in which the Emperor was its be-all and end-all, its meaning, and its right to exist.

— Boundless capitalism in today's China is not all too different from the former palace economy. It is still a politically heavily controlled activity, a 'free economy' under strong restrictions of political centralism. However, the echoes of the former palace economy are now accompanied by another sound. It is the sound of (civil) society, developed in the footsteps of (capitalist) market economy, increasingly pervading the secluded world of communities, families, clans, and neighborhoods.

—   The open economy of the new China is doubly coded. By constituting a social nexus of individuals mediated through contracts and institutions, it unleashes forces of societization (Vergesellschaftung). The consequence could be – at least this is the hope – not only a strengthening of the today largely powerless democratic movement, but also a gradual emergence of a socially mediating regulation state. On the other hand, we can assume that in China market exchange, being constitutive of society, will be much more strongly than in the West subject to the hegemony of community, ranging from the family via strong guanxi-networks to the 'hyper-society' of the Chinese centralist state. Institutions informed by tradition inevitably lead to a 'collectivist' or a 'family-based' coinage of the capitalist model of economy. The term 'Confucian capitalism' precisely reflects this aspect of the Chinese developmental model, oscillating between community (Gemeinschaft) and society (Gesellschaft) (Souchou Yao 2002).

—   The expanding professionalized society of 'citizens', characterized by both division and differentiation of labor, offers less and less room for community-oriented aspirations of Chinese civic society. Balancing the resulting tension between community-oriented demands and societal reality is achieved by various forms of communitizing (Vergemeinschaftung) societal (business-oriented, institutional) interaction. For instance, a formal contract is, to this day, all the more stable the more tightly the social network that integrates business partners is maintained. Such connections are established preferably in a restaurant with food and drink. This is where everything is discussed and everything is decided. Only this form of familial accreditation can turn a contract into what it otherwise only can pretend to be: a societal institution. Joint eating and drinking serves to create and stabilize quasi-community-based social networks that are necessary to balance the persistent weakness of societal interaction. In China, you have to have the right guanxi or develop it in order to be successful in business and achieve social upward mobility. Whoever doesn't have access to this 'social capital' is a 'poor devil'; whoever

Small domestic altar, Shenzhen

Threshold altar,
Macao

doesn't respect the morals of family or community can also lose guanxi, for instance by underestimating the significance of personal ties or when questioning social hierarchy by criticizing persons higher up in the social order and making them 'lose their face' (Souchou Yao 2002, 101ff).

— It is the enormous demand for affirmation of societal interaction by community-based circumstances that has turned restaurant businesses into an important player in urban space. In Europe, we may have shopping centers, pedestrian streets, or places where a few or even many small restaurants are located. In China, however, we discover a type of 'shopping center' that almost exclusively consists of restaurants – and maybe a couple of stores catering to all the needs surrounding the ritual of eating. In this country, we find complete streetscapes, even quarters and actually entire villages that consist almost totally of restaurants, and often we encounter genuine food temples: multi-story, richly decorated buildings with Baroque driveways and ramps and a veritable army of service personnel.

— The continued existence of the oikistic spirit is also reflected in the vivid tradition of (Buddhist or also Confucian) domestic altars. It reminds us today that there were times in enlightened Europe as well when the family home was also regarded as a (small) temple, thus featuring a small altar or a 'Sunday room' (Sonntagszimmer). We can equally consider the occasional threshold altars as confirmation of the concept of the oikos, reminding us of the magic of these sphinx-like places that are simultaneously both inside and outside.

— China is on its way towards a culture of public space comparable to Europe. Open urban space will be transformed into public spaces to a degree that more or less corresponds to the proliferation of aspects of market economy. At the same time, however, this opening remains under the proviso of those institutions that are in possession of the nation's cultural hegemony – and these are the institutions of family and community, informed by Confucianism. This hegemony is responsible for the fact that open space can develop into public space only very slowly. But on the other hand, against the background of a continuously growing middle class, we can already foresee the strengthening of elements of civil society and the articulation of corresponding spatial demands. The future of a public urban space of Chinese type is pre-programmed within the present development.

— But the current 'gap' between open and public urban space cannot be filled by European urban copies of the like of 'Thames Town' or 'Luodian'. Even though these new towns transpose copies of built public spaces to China, these places and streets are instantly re-coded into open spaces of commerce. They remain fictions of public spaces. They become simple stage sets and thus merely sources for distinction capital and brand identity for the new Chinese middle and upper classes.

— The closed residential compounds, which have retained a kind of village-like flavor, only lose their rural connotations through the existence of commercial urban space; a neighborhood without a market is a village and not a city. The Chinese city, however, which connects closed neighborhoods and open commercial spaces, can be considered a landscape of urbanized villages. Here we encounter a phenomenon that was already noticed by none less than Walter Benjamin. Not even the modern European city had managed to completely detach city dwellers from the rural roots of their existence. In his Arcades Project (Passagenwerk) he shows us that typical Parisians don't actually even consider themselves as such. As the inhabitants of a quarter (Quartier) or an Arrondissement, they are actually dwellers of a village in the city: "The true Parisian shrugs his shoulders while rejecting the notion of living in Paris, even if never actually leaving the city. He lives in the treizième, or in the deuxième, or in the dixhuitième, not in Paris, but in his Arrondissement – in the third, or seventh, or twentieth – which is, in fact, provincial. Maybe this is where we find the secret of the city's gentle hegemony over France: that, in the heart of its Quartiers [...] it possesses more provinces than France in its entirety. [...] Paris has more than twenty Arrondissements and is filled with cities and villages," (Benjamin V2, 999). Already then, in the nineteenth century, the Arrondissements of Paris were spatially open administrative units, in complete contrast to the neighborhoods of the Chinese city, then as now closed towards their surroundings and governed with the support of neighborhood committees – which is the reason why, with even greater justification, we can describe them as urban villages.

— If we can easily identify the closed neighborhoods of urban districts as urban villages, as semi-urban structures, we can observe similar phenomena in rural areas or counties. Looking at villages allows us to recognize semi-urban settlements, village-like cities with densely cramped residential buildings, sprawling across the landscape in minimal intervals wedged between fields, crops, greenhouses, and fishing ponds. The population density of many rural regions identified as counties significantly exceeds the population density of suburban areas in the West (cf. Friedmann 2005, 40ff). In this regard, the rural is urban and the urban is rural in China. The message this form of urban-rural indifference transmits is the community-oriented nature of society (Gesellschaft) or the society-oriented nature of the community (Gemeinschaft). Both pervade each other with an intensity that enlightened civilizations of the West can neither imagine nor tolerate.

— The relationship of enclosure and openness structures urban space not only in China, but everywhere else where we encounter urban life. But this occurs in different ways, depending on the respective cultures. While in Europe closed space rather appears in the shape of individual privacy, closed space in China additionally takes on the form of a neighborhood as lifestyle community, as collective space. And while in Europe open urban space is capable of qualifying as public space (often barely, but on occasion spectacularly), this only succeeds in initial stages in China. Here, open space is liberated from its characterless state mostly by commercial interests, but also through the representation-desires of political actors at the top of a completely and entirely hierarchically formatted society.

— The dualism of closed and open urban space is substantially related to a number of further terminological pairings that have played a role in the course of our semiotically informed reading of the city. For one, we can name the dualism of introversion and extroversion, whereas introversion refers to closed space and extroversion to public urban space. As examples for introverted spatial configurations, we introduced and discussed courtyard houses and neighborhood courtyards. Both connote primarily a rural, community-centric residential typology. The example of the neighborhood courtyard shows us the following: in order to continue existing within cities, i.e. in a context foreign to its nature, rural space must seclude itself, shut itself off, encapsulate itself. In this regard, each neighborhood is an urbanized village, a village-like community restructured according to the demands of urban life. Thus, each urban courtyard house, each introverted neighborhood, each exclusive urban palace, whether small or large, is an urban heterotopia.[102]

— Extroversion, such as in the case of the urban market place, typically framed by gable-end facades or less often by facades with eaves facing the street, or by a mix of both, in contrast denotes public urban space and within it, urban space of civil society. Extroversion means that term ('concept') of the city and reality of the city are identical to each other, i.e. the term 'city' denotes extroversion. The places or the streets framed by dramatizing extroverted facades can therefore be defined as the 'isotopes' of urban space. If rural space is identical to itself (isotopic) as closed and introverted space, then urban space is, equally so, identical to itself as public and extroverted space. Mediated by its commercialization, open urban space – and within this openness, still unprogrammed – develops a tendency towards becoming public space, the space of an urban society or 'civil space'.

— This leads us to another pair of terms or concepts that we can also consider clearly related to closed and open urban space. We mean the terms 'exclusion' and 'inclusion', which have also emerged in the course of our study. Closed urban space is therefore not only generally introverted, but also exclusive. Enclosure is an important element of exclusion.

— Very often, enclosure is less related to physical defense than rather to stratification-based distinction behavior. In enclosure, the primary goal is symbolism, i.e. indicative or iconic exclusion. A Chinese neighborhood is usually accessible for strangers or non-residents (mostly under the supervision of guard personnel), but it is made clear to visitors that they don't belong, that the space they have entered is a foreign territory, and that they, if at all, will only be tolerated for a limited amount of time. Whoever intends to host a visitor in their apartment for a longer amount of time is well advised to introduce their guest to the neighborhood committee.

— As introverted and exclusive spaces, neighborhoods are rural elements in the body of the city. Everywhere, rural community-oriented life is on the retreat from urban-societal life. The adaptability of closed, introverted and exclusive neighborhoods in Chinese metropolises and mega-cities thus becomes all the more astonishing: a remarkable resistance of the 'rural/community' towards the disintegrative forces of the 'urban/society'.

— But we should be wary of an interpretation purely based on the developmental logic of the relationship between community and society in China. It is by no means sufficient to understand current urban spatial practice in China. What we have described here as the hegemony of the community-oriented is by no means only the expression of a certain 'lagging behind' we could consider typical for a developing nation. Even more so, it is also the expression of deeply rooted types of sustainable cultural practices, ensuring that Chinese urban planning will recognize the high importance of the community and the neighborhood with its closed, introverted and exclusive spaces for the foreseeable future. Chinese cities may be among the largest and comprise the highest densities worldwide – true asphalt jungles – yet they still remain village-like or rurally structured to a significant degree, a Chinese variation of town-country.

— An urban-rural dichotomy comparable to European history has never existed in the middle kingdom. Thus, an opposition between rural life and feudalism on the one hand and urban life and bourgeois society on the other is unthinkable here. The fact that city and country each represent independent cultural (social, political, economic) spheres is equally unimaginable. In China, town and country were always 'interwoven', as Friedmann says, an "urban-rural continuum" of a special kind (Friedmann 2005, 8). According to their definition as Imperial residencies, cities were never free in the sense of possessing their own legal domain, their own administration, their own government. The reason for this is something we have already addressed, the absence of a bourgeois synecism aimed at weakening royal or imperial central authority. Instead, after Imperial unification, following the Han dynasty (circa 200 B.C.E.), a semi-enlightened centralist system of rule emerged, resting on the two pillars of Empire and scholar-bureaucracy of literate officials.

Growing city approaches village, Shenyang

— Due to a missing socio-cultural differentiation of rural life (super-oikistic feudalism) and urban life (bourgeois society), the land extending outside the city walls, as long as it was still in China, was also described as 'suburban' (Wu, Weijia 1993, 90ff). However, the term 'suburban' here can't be compared to the European purlieu or municipal area (Weichbild). The Weichbild, not to be confused with the 'outskirts of town', was the legal domain controlled by free cities, yet located beyond the city walls, stretching like a buffer between independent or partly independent urban space and feudal fief or feu, composed of noble land (heredium), granted land in fief ('Salland' and 'Zinshufe') and common land (Allmende). The Chinese 'suburbs' in contrast comprise the country between city wall and Imperial wall or between city wall and mountain and river. China's urban spatial culture doesn't know any Weichbild.

— The relationship between city and country was never one of substantial cultural differences; if at all, a relationship of hierarchic status within a political and socio-cultural totality that was all-encompassing. Even though only about six percent of the Chinese population lived in agglomerations with more than 50,000 inhabitants at the beginning of the twentieth century, or even less than twenty percent lived in cities when the opening began in the early 1980s of the previous century, we can't conclude from these facts that China had been a purely agrarian nation at these points in time. Already in the middle of the nineteenth century the number of city dwellers had reached a remarkable twenty million people, i.e. five percent of about 400 million Chinese. And we equally can't conclude from this that the urban dwellers maintained a distinctly urban lifestyle that was significantly different from country life. The urban remained generally rural, while the rural had been forcibly urbanized by the political and cultural hegemony of the Imperial central authority for more than 2,000 years, turning the countryside into a kind of vestibule to the Imperial palace.

— The Chinese word for 'city' maintains the memory of the above-mentioned integration of centralist power and market under the integrating roof of the Empire. The word 'city' is comprised of the two elements 'wall' and 'market'. The wall – in contrast to Europe, where it developed into a symbol of city freedom and early bourgeois pride – is related to leadership, even the very presence of the Emperor as an, at most, proto-bourgeois institution. The element 'market' on the other hand represents what actually transforms a temple palace or a superoikos (the residence of the 'Great Man') into a city: the presence of trade and commerce.[103]

— The price that China had to pay for its centralistic integration culture, alleviating the difference between community and society, between country and city, between rural and urban, is the absence of an urban bourgeois emancipation – and resulting possible radical enlightenment (scientification and individualization), democratization (division of powers) and capitalization (advancement of trade into production capitalism). This fact informs space in a way that reveals the Chinese city (the referent) as composed of urbanized village-like structures (signifiers) that denote the primacy of community (signified).

城市

Chinese word for 'city'

SUMMARY

— Every city is unique, and the same is true for Chinese cities. They are cities with personalities of their own, socio-cultural sculptures of solitary and unmistakable composition. In this sense, every city can claim that it is a 'synthesis of the arts', a Gesamtkunstwerk. Justifiably so, as any good city or tourist guide can confirm.

— But our reading of the city does not primarily focus on Beijing, Shanghai, Xi'an, Shenzhen, Harbin, or other Chinese cities. Rather, we are interested in the genuinely Chinese nature of these cities, their generic characteristics. We deal with those characteristics that all Chinese cities, more or less, share. This book is therefore dedicated mostly to architects, urban planners and designers, urbanists, or urban scientists and researchers, such as urban sociologists, urban semioticians, urban geographers, i.e. everybody who has any kind of professional interest in the basic and infill structure of the Chinese city as a socio-cultural spatial phenomenon.

— For this admittedly wide target group, it is important to venture past the uniqueness of each individual urbanistic phenomenon, straight to the heart of the Chinese city, its syntax, its code. We thus consider it our objective to illustrate what is common to individual Chinese cities – and not what sets them apart. Only the decoding of these shared characteristics – what we describe as the sinicity of the Chinese city – opens the view towards its interior structure and allows us to understand it. Reaching this point enables us to evaluate and reasonably organize the diversity of empirical observations.

— How immensely important it is to precisely know what the Chinese city and the relevant structural elements it is composed of denote is something the case of the German city Anting has clearly shown us. Caught in the naïve belief that a European city can be substantially transposed into the Chinese socio-cultural sphere, the result was the implantation of an alien body in its suburban landscape. And now attempts are made to adapt it by all kinds of corrections, while every correction proves to be yet another questionable compromise further eroding the identity of the German city – without, in return, decisively improving the legibility of its structure for Chinese citizens and 'customers'.

— In its essence, the basic structure of the Chinese city today is comprised of the dualism of closed and open city. The entire orchestration of the city is obliged to reflect these two spatial types: dwelling is nearly without exception closed (that's why residential settlements are named 'compounds') just as places of private and public administration, places of production, education, culture, and leisure. Open, however, are mainly spaces of commercial use (especially retail and small scale services) and mobility, but also places of power and magnificence ('noble places'). Open space should not be confused with public space which refers to civil society, i.e. to an interpretation of 'the right to the city', which is still to a large extent alien to Chinese civic society, although on the advance, an advance strongly promoted by capitalist market economy that is insistently penetrating the community-based Chinese society.

— The dualism of closed and open space, of course, also applies to modern functional arrangements. The many new closed parks of manufacturing industry, located in the outskirts, follow the ideal of zoning most closely. Residential development may, at first glance, seem to be strongly monostructural as well. But at a closer look it proves to be mixed on a small scale – precisely along the separating line between closed space (dwelling) and open space (local supply such as retail, small scale services, parks, and so forth). Moving towards the urban core, open spaces cover larger areas and include buildings and installations with political-administrative, cultural, and commercial office functions. The degree of verticality increases and what is clearly recognizable as closed in the peripheral areas either hides behind an increasing number of perimeter block strips or wanders into the foyers of high-rise buildings and skyscrapers. The inversion of enclosure in urban cores helps to obscure the closed city and lets the open city gain prominence all the more clearly.

— This openness, as already mentioned, isn't simply the same as publicness. Public spaces may indeed belong to the open urban area, but are rather weakly developed, as e.g. indicated in the frugality or rather absence of public amenities and furniture of open spaces at shopping centers or community centers. Without a doubt, commercially utilized open space dominates strongly. Open urban space, from the outside to the inside, from periphery to center, is dominated by the 'great street', the commercial perimeter block strip, and the commercial center on different levels of integration – from neighborhood to community center, inner city shopping center and pedestrian area – as well as the 'noble place'. Closed space on the other hand is in the firm grip of the neighborhood, the urban village, in the form of gated, introverted, vertical, oriented, branded compounds – in a way that is characteristic of the image of the Chinese city. Of course, many other functions, most of all industrial businesses are closed, but they are not as visible, because they are either located at the urban periphery or in the core areas, where the closed city withdraws into individual buildings or behind perimeter block construction.

— China is currently experiencing its own 'Gründerzeit'. A tremendous redistribution of people from the countryside to the city is taking place. According to estimates, currently more than 200 million labor migrants are pushing into the metropolises. In order to relieve the pressure on the core cities, bursting at their seams, satellite cities are mushrooming everywhere around the country. This process employs in many ways new, Postmodern means that significantly differ from Western satellite city and new town planning in the nineteenth and twentieth century. We would like to emphasize the themed cities, representing the attempt to introduce urban planning cultures, lifestyles, or simply only spatialized images of foreign cultures to China.

— We could ask the question whether this transposition is in fact successful – and why it takes place at all. To answer the first part of this question, we analyzed three themed cities of Shanghai's 'One City, Nine Villages' plan: the 'German town' Anting, the 'British town' Taiwushi (as a part of the city of Songjiang), and the 'Swedish town' Luodian. The German city, this much becomes clear, demonstrates strong idealism, yet intercultural weakness – and is forced to struggle with enormous related marketing problems. The urban code of China was either misunderstood or ignored. On the other hand, the examples of Taiwushi and Luodian represent pragmatism and intercultural routine. The Chinese clients receive what they desire: a city comprised of closed neighborhoods with a commercialized, open urban theater stage including scanned or imitated European architectures and textures.

— Why these urban fictions? Because the presence of the other and the foreign is experienced as liberating – and not at all as threat. And because the symbolism of the exotic is employed as means to gain distinction – in this life environment, branding has long since become normal. The new Chinese middle and upper classes are now in conscious Postmodern simultaneity to their Western contemporaries. They enjoy aesthetizations of Postmodernism, however, not only as an answer to what Fordist Modernism (which is also Maoist) may have lacked, but also as a sign, as an iconic representation of the new China. Theming is a fashion in present China. On the other hand, a growing number of topical signs indicates that this Postmodern period of urban design will come to an end, sooner or later, and will be replaced by a consolidated, authentic strategy featuring Chinese codifications of urban mass, density, compactness, centrality, and grandeur; in one word: of 'Chinese modernity', to be seen as an exceptional contribution to 'reflexive urbanism', i.e. to a Chinese way of reconciling its tradition with modernity.

— As a result of our reading of the city, we formulate, among others, the following unique characteristics as constitutive elements of the urban code of the Chinese city:

a dualism of open and closed space that emphatically determines the basic structure of the Chinese city;

a preference for private or community-related spaces compared with public or also society-related spaces;

the common practice of designing residential space as exclusive, closed spaces or 'urban villages';

an equally clear and creative adherence to the introverted spatial traditions of China in the diverse forms of neighborhood courtyards;

the logical combination of linear and perimeter block structures in the type of the closed neighborhood with a commercial 'frame' ('bracket') structure;

the integration of commercial, retail and service related functions into orientation-free perimeter block structures, especially for provision on neighborhood level (Nahversorgung);

an adherence to the tradition of southern orientation in residential architecture, determined by climate, yet imbued with social status;

the creative advancement of modern linear structures into 'swinging lines and dancing dots', into tiered setback arrangements (cascades, grandstands) and picturesque residential landscapes;

a relatively high degree of coverage of neighborhood courtyards, private and public parks, continuing the tradition of the Chinese garden of harmonizing the artificial and the natural;

the social programming and thus valorization, through its commercialization and communitization (Vergemeinschaftung), of purely functionally determined, otherwise meaningless open space (residual space);

complementing noble and commercial urban open places with public community places, a type tending towards civic space with societal connotations;

the development of the both compact and car-friendly basic structure of 'great street and vertical block';

the utilization of roof symbols, light sculptures, auspicious names and numbers, facade decorations, and increasingly also architectural languages for the creation of distinct neighborhood brand identities;

a certain inability or unwillingness to recognize and utilize the aesthetic potential of facades, surprising from a European point of view, yet rooted in introverted traditions;

the creative transformation of urban sceneries comprising functionally determined building facades, bridges, streets, and sidewalks into urban media landscapes (media facades) transmitting messages in both a rich as well as redundant manner;

a combination of the luxurious and the serial in numerous neighborhoods of the upper class, hardly imaginable and generally unacceptable from the view of an enlightened Western individualism;

the excessive (though transient) use of urban and architectural fictions for the dramatization of open urban theater stages that can be interpreted as means for social distinction and iconic representation of the new China;

an urban development paradigm that is oriented on urban design utopias and fashions, lost in imagery, and unhampered by discussions on identity;

initial steps towards a reconstruction of linear urban centrality with hierarchically structured spatial sequences against the background of a currently still weakly developed conceptualization of centrality, oscillating between linear and nodal forms on the one hand, and formlessness on the other.

— We claim that these elements, characteristics, attributes, and messages comprise the most important, or at least adequately representative, elements of the urban code of the contemporary Chinese city. They serve to exemplify the sinicity of the nation's contemporary spatial production. China, and we see this as confirmation, is by no means Westernizing. It consumes Western ideas, concepts, and images just as much as the ideas, concepts, and images from its own history and traditions, using them as raw material for the creation of a new urban space of Chinese provenience: the future body of the Chinese dragon. Quod erat demonstrandum!

APPENDIX

ANNOTATIONS, BIBLIOGRAPHY,
ILLUSTRATION CREDITS

ANNOTATIONS

1 'Open' has a triple meaning in the original German 'aufgeschlossen' or 'aufschließen': to physically open something, to be open for e.g. new experiences, but also to catch up.

2 We can differentiate this position from the notion rather widely accepted in architectural-theoretical discourses that International Style, ex negativo connected to the concept of nation, is replaced on the global stage in the course of globalization by a general, transnational mix of regional architectural dialects.

3 The neologism 'sinicity' was created by Roland Barthes and in his usage characterizes a term composed of 'rickshaws, ringing bells, smoking opium' etc., at that time also reflecting the view that the 'French petty bourgeoisie' had of China (Barthes 1973).

4 In the current discourse on the developmental trajectory of the Chinese city, few involved individuals have seen this interrelation between cultural memory and recent urbanism so clearly as Barbara Münch, architect and planner living in Beijing (Münch 2004).

5 The term 'urban language' currently finds use in German language exclusively within so-called dialectology. Here, it appears in connection with the linguistic research of urban dialects. This use of the term is obviously unrelated to the way we employ it.

6 In international parlance, the term 'compound' is now commonly used for this form of Chinese settlement, a noun derived from 'fortification' or 'camp', which can also be associated with 'compilation', 'packaging'.

7 Li means something like 'neighborhood', and Long is the Chinese term for 'alley' (see Chapter 4, section 'Orient meets Occident – hybrid urban quarters').

8 This term, sounding strange to Europeans – since all of the new 'villages' are supposed to comprise more than 30,000 inhabitants (the 'ideal city' Lingang, designed by GMP from Germany, is even planned to eventually accommodate close to one million residents) – reflects the historic absence of a terminologically precise distinction between city and country (more on this subject in Chapter 2, section 'Rocks and plants' and especially Chapter 8).

9 Since this term hasn't yet played a role in urban semiotics, a short explanation seems appropriate. We speak of an 'urban travesty' if the unchangeable content (the Chinese city) is dramatized in a form alien to it (English city).

10 We speak of an urban 'parody' if the content (the Chinese city) is changed by a form alien to it (Dutch city) and, as result, loses its identity.

11 The assumption that every society spatializes in unique ways has already been introduced in Henri Lefèbvre's book *The Production of Space* (1991), first published in 1974 (*La production de l'espace*). Ever since, the decoding of the built urban environment constitutes an inherent part of good urban studies. Lefèbvre's hope for a semiotics applied to the city included nothing less than a reinvigoration of what the logos had once been for the Greek polis (cf. Lefèbvre 1995). For him, the activity of architects and urban planners is primarily a social praxis. The goal is the production of a spatial text that meets the demands of a socialist ethic. For this purpose, knowledge of the decoding and recoding of urban space is required. This book focuses on decoding, i.e. the perception and understanding of the urban 'gallery of signs' of China.

12   According to Mark Gottdiener, urban space is not a simple container of social processes, but the result of – sometimes controversial – signs or 'signifying practices' (Gottdiener 1986, 214). In consistent reference to Lefèbvre, his goal is to decode it in order to enable an emancipatory recoding. He develops his social semiotics from an acerbic criticism of semiotic reductionism within the social ecological liberal model of society. We think that his social-semiotic perspective on the signifying practices in social conflicts of stratified societies – for instance in regard to distinction strategies and ideologizations – should be complemented by a cultural semiotics of urban space transcending the spatial 'footprints' of class negotiations and quarrels. Its purpose would be the recognition of practices deeply anchored in the socio-cultural memory of societies from within the significant forms of their spatialization, since urban space is first produced as an ensemble of socio-cultural signs – prior to assignment of meaning in the course of social self-determination and struggle. The urban spatial categories developed by Kevin Lynch, i.e. paths, edges, districts, nodes, landmarks (Lynch 1960), refer to an appropriation and organization of spatial elements for the purpose of orientation. Due to their abstract-universal criteria, they are unsuitable for a hermeneutics of urban space aimed at sociocultural signs.

13   Regarding urban planning and design, Eco most of all has Lucio Costa's design for the Brazilian capital city Brasilia in mind, incorporating the outline of a condor in its master plan. Here, Costa's intention is to demonstrate that Modernism and figurativeness don't have to be contradictory in Brazil.

14   Culture, according to this holistic understanding, is the expression of adaptation strategies of social groups to a habitat (Cohen 1971, Vivelo 1978). The southern orientation of dwellings e.g. is, in this context, adaptation – and in locations where southern orientation becomes a scarce resource, it can become the object of privilege, determining the development of social hierarchies.

15   According to Lefèbvre, this interpretation problem is as follows: "Nowadays the most subtle of semiologists are saying that a code is a voice and a way: from the 'text' – the message – arise several possibilities, choices, various utterances, a plurality, a fabric rather than a line. [...] Each coding would be a proposed outline, taken up again, abandoned, always at the outline stage, engendering a meaning among many others" (Lefèbvre 1995, 192). The problem of meaning addressed here is equally valid for decoding, i.e. the opposite direction, as a problem of interpretation. Admitting that even with excellent sinological knowledge there may remain problems of reading and interpretation is something intellectual honesty demands. Regardless, we never veer off course so far as to say that "a white sheet of paper, the poorest of texts" is the one that can be read best (Lefèbvre 1995, 193).

16   What happens when we introduce ideologies superficially as interpretive schematics for decoding the city is detailed in our critical commentary on Umberto Eco's semiotic appreciation of Costa's and Niemeyer's design for the Brazilian capital city Brasilia (Hassenpflug 2004b, Hassenpflug 2006b).

17   Hans P. Bahrdt can be criticized for considering urban planning as an opportunity for compensation, i.e. social integration. He underestimates inasmuch the possibilities of information technology and automobile communication or integration. However, this critique doesn't disavow the theory of incomplete integration, which can be exclusively seen in reference to the integration performances of metropolitan urban space.

18   The objection could be made that the term 'city' is much too abstract in regard to the advanced differentiation of urban forms. In principle, however, this differentiation doesn't change anything; terms such as industrial city, global city, mega-city, edge city, Chinese city etc. don't claim to denote city, but instead industrial city, global city, mega-city, etc. Beyond that, however, it is interesting that semiotics, by distinguishing between denotation and connotation, perpetuates in its own terms the discourse on realism and nominalism that has inspired philosophy since Plato.

19   The term city connotes an infinite diversity of meanings, both from a diachronical as well as a synchronical perspective. The scope of association content here spans from holy Jerusalem to filthy Babylon, from 'cancerous growth' on the earth's body to civilization machine, from frightful Moloch to carrier of hope for a better world. This repertoire of more or less well-founded subjective interpretations is vast.

20   The use of the term 'non-place' here doesn't correspond to Marc Augé's use of the term. 'Non-places' in Augé's use (Augé 1995) primarily refer to a space without local characteristics or identity, a space that actually is meaningful because of its ubiquitous functionalism. We, however, speak of a space the identity of which is based on being considered a space weak in meaning – a space that is needed but not respected.

21   Xu notes that in historic China there had also been public space: introverted public spaces in closed places, in temple complexes, and Confucian or Taoist schools (cf. Zhang, Guangzeng 2004).

22   The only remaining county in Shanghai is Chong Ming Island in the Yangzi Jiang, where the attempt has been made in the context of EXPO 2010 to plan an ecological city (Dongtan).

23   In China, by the way, we were able to discover that mass ornamentation can not only be interpreted, as Kracauer (1995) assumed, as figuration of a societized body, but also as a symbol of communitized people. It refers to a 'we' without a 'me'.

24   Exchange transactions, as Hegel states, transcend the immediacy of 'eat or be eaten' towards an ethics of "production for others" (Hegel 1991). He thus valued the economic model based on this form of interaction, i.e. market economy, as a "system of morality". Unfortunately, he didn't comment on the ethical status of a state-driven planned economy of socialist provenience. Regardless of this omission, we should consider China's opening towards market economy, in accord with Hegel, as a positive development.

25   Communitization (Vergemeinschaftung) here means that profits benefit family members or networks, and not, as in the case of societization (Vergesellschaftung), the members of society or shareholders and, at least in part, the state. The pronounced unwillingness to report taxes or income data for public statistics also reflects the 'Confucian' character of Chinese market economy (cf. Souchou Yao 2002).

26   We could also use the term neighborhood place or park. In order to prevent confusion with the important term neighborhood courtyard (see Chapter 4), we focus on the use of the term community place or community park.

27   According to the teachings of Confucianism and Taoism, China still (or in other words, again) identifies itself with a culture in which natural and cultural opposites are rejoiced in harmonic, peaceful dualisms (Yin-Yang principle). In this interpretation of polarities, Chinese philosophy clearly differs from antagonist (continental) European interpretations, in which dialectic has never been capable of liberating itself from Manichean influences. While in China dialectics are aimed at a harmonically composed world order, dialectics in European thought are the ontological scene of action where things are born from their opposites, a both destructive and productive primordial ground of being. The reasons for this practice of interpretation may be identified within the partially intransigent doctrines of Christianity and, developed from it, in the medieval and early modern antagonism of parochial-feudal country life on the one hand, and city life tending towards the secular, enlightened and bourgeois on the other. Perhaps not coincidentally, the great German philosophers Schelling, Hegel, and Marx choreographed their dialectic systems in the manner of natural or historical teleological clashes of the titans.

28   A message comparable to that of the Chinese garden is, by the way, also denoted uniquely by classical Chinese music. Here as well, a world of sounds, songs, and noises conceived as completely natural is revealed simultaneously within the artificial nature of music.

29   For more on Goethe's relationship to classical Chinese culture see Zhang, Yushu (2007).

30   No other contemporary philosopher, in my opinion, has deliberated on the double embrace of culture and nature in such a comprehensive way as Wolfdietrich Schmied-Kowarzik, preferably in his reception of Schelling. Within the Chinese garden, he would surely find an architectural ally of high significance (cf. Schmied-Kowarzik 1996).

31   A programmatic statement attributed to American architect Louis Sullivan (1856–1924).

32   The language expert Chiang-Schreiber (Chiang-Schreiber 2007) notes on the didactics of teaching Chinese:

—   "The four 'tones' turn Chinese into a very 'musical' language that people can learn more easily not only through listening but also through kinaesthetic, visual, and emotionally affective learning strategies.

—   The seemingly simple grammar (no conjugations, no declinations, no articles) in general doesn't call for a logical, analytical mind, but a sensitivity for the intentions or emotional state of conversation partners and evaluation of conversation context.

—   Chinese writing is a sign system that maintains abstract visual notions. Dealing with these signs furthers cognitive abilities such as skills in interrelating meaning or associative thinking and thus visual cognition or reasoning"

33   It is possible that this Western antinomy is the deeper reason for the development of Rap/Hiphop in the ethnic-cultural 'melting pot' of North America – equally the result of "sublation and actualization" (Aufhebung und Verwirklichung, Hegel) of this contradiction.

34   As comparison: Berlin is located at approximately 52 degrees and Shanghai at approximately 31 degrees northern latitude.

35   The term 'Fordism' was made famous by Antonio Gramsci. He also coined the term 'cultural hegemony' used by us further in the text. Its analytical potential and the thus resulting frequent use have, however, resulted long since in detaching the terms from their original context. They have become sociological commonplaces.

36   We should actually speak of 'industrialized mass housing construction'. The very low wages for construction workers and construction trades, however, significantly reduce the pressure for rationalization in this line of business.

37   If many new low-rise, spread-out villa quarters are currently still under construction, then this is due to the fact that construction permits have already been issued.

38   The sixty percent as claimed by architect Jia Hu (Hu 2006) are to be doubted strongly, since neither the social comparison group nor comparison objects are indicated.

39   A house with the number 8 receives a significantly higher degree of appreciation than a house with the number 4, which may occasionally be difficult to market. Also, the rules of Feng Shui play a significant role. Chinese everyday culture is strongly pervaded by magical symbols, such as circles (referring to moon, money), fish-form etc.

40   Zeilenbau: a Zeile could be a 'row', but it is not as simple as that. The Fordist 'Zeile' is not a row house, nor a semi-detached house. But it is a 'linear structure' that is detached from block border construction, a line (see the term 'linear structure' in the superb English translation of Aldo Rossi's *The Architecture of the City*, where it is further differentiated into 'rectilinear' or 'curvilinear' structures (Rossi 1984). In the post-Fordist context, the linear forms become 'swinging lines'. Punktbau could be interpreted as a 'hairpin building', a vertical nodal structure. While in Fordist settlements these nodal buildings are placed in string formation (see Hansa-Quarter in Berlin), they start to 'dance' in the post-Fordist context, i.e. they are placed freely within the park-like environment. Take both, Fordist lines and dots, hence, as in this book, they become post-Fordist 'swinging lines and dancing dots' (for the purpose of clarity, accompanied by the German original 'Zeile' and 'Punkt').

41   In our opinion, there are very few other countries in which the development of residential compounds as a brand item has proceeded further than in today's China. We will discuss this aspect in detail further in the text (Chapter 4, section 'Branding compound lifestyles').

42   Hegel would have probably spoken of a "sublation and actualization" ("Aufhebung und Verwirklichung") of Fordism – and thus expressed that he had seen the restlessly innovative spirit of mankind, which he described as 'world spirit' (Weltgeist), at work in the evolution of urban planning and design as well. We not only could see it that way, we in fact should.

43   Halik and Küchler have noted that this form of enclosure has been subject to a particular change in recent history that we can consider significant in semiotical terms: "As symbol for the dissolution of the old cellular structure of Chinese society [...] we can consider the replacement of walls by so-called 'European fences'. It indicates a break with history if, since 1996, the perimeter walls of factories, residential compounds, schools, clinics, and administrative units are demolished and replaced with transparent, in general cast iron fences" (Halik, Küchler 2004, 50).

44   Münch refers to a typology used in planning and administration according to which residential areas in urban development are divided into three types: settlements with 30,000 to 50,000 inhabitants (j' zhù q'), 'micro-residential districts' or MRDs (xi'o q') with 7,000 to 15,000 inhabitants, and 'neighborhood clusters' (j'túan) with 1,000 to 3,000 inhabitants (cf. Münch 2004, 48). Since the distinction between MRDs and 'neighborhood clusters' hardly complies with my own accounts, I refrain from using the technical term MRD. The closed residential compounds that comprise the empirical basis for my explanations have population numbers that are in part significantly lower than in MRDs, but also in part significantly higher than in 'neighborhood clusters'. Münch's explications on both types, however, lead to the conclusion that she has in mind what I describe as 'closed neighborhoods' or 'residential compounds' (Münch 2004, 45ff).

45   The 'closed neighborhood' as spatial structural element receives no mention in the report on the research project 'High Speed Urbanismus' published in *archplus*. This 'non-consideration' is all the more surprising since closed neighborhoods or 'compounds' comprise an omnipresent phenomenon in Chinese metropolises – also in the observed Pearl River Delta, (Ipsen 2004).

46   "The public services included cleaning public spaces inside and outside of buildings; disposing of rubbish; planting trees, flowers and grass; handling residents' complaints; and maintaining public order" (Lü Junhua, Shao Lei 2001, 270). The word 'public' is, of course, used here mistakenly; actually it should read 'community-based', since the services described exclusively benefit the residents of the closed neighborhood.

47   The word 'open' (aufschliessen or aufgeschlossen) is given preference here, as market squares were closed and strictly supervised spaces in immediate proximity to the buildings of the Imperial residence or Imperial court officials until the beginning of the Song dynasty in the tenth century. This phase was followed by a partial opening of markets, resulting in the transformation of numerous city streets into market streets, still widely found today. At the same time, until the end of the Imperial era (and then again during the Mao era), markets remained factually under the supervision of the Imperial (later, the Communist) central government – very much in the vein of, as described and analyzed by Karl Polanyi, the proto-market economic 'palace trade' (Polanyi 1979, 387ff). The Imperial form of supervision explains why no free capital exchange and no independent bourgeois (urban) class could develop – with all related cultural implications as result (such as the absence of pushes towards individualization of Renaissance and Enlightenment …).

48   This dualism seems to be more appropriate to an analysis of its basic structure than the differentiation between private and public space. While this type of differentiation articulates itself spatially rather vaguely due to the hegemony of the private sphere, distinguishing between open and closed is comparatively obvious. In this regard it is interesting to point out that the Chinese word for 'city' (since the Song dynasty, 960–1279 C. E.) is a combination of the symbols for 'wall' and 'market' (cf. Wu, Weijia 1993, 90ff). We will return to this issue in Chapter 8.

49   By drawing parallels between danwei and closed quarters in the Imperial city Chang'an (today Xi'an) during the Tang dynasty era, he reveals himself as a proponent of a structuralistic approach in deciphering current urban phenomena (Friedmann 2005, XVIII).

50   "… the Chunyuan neighbourhood […] – a pilot project of the Ministry of Construction – put forth the idea of […] strengthening the concept of the courtyard, thus improving the area's living environment and public facilities" (Lü Junhua, Shao Lei 2001, 271).

51   Apartment construction, also social housing construction, plays a completely subordinate, even marginal role in the People's Republic of China. The general desire is to own residential property, if possible without paying mortgages – and people are willing to patiently save money (in many cases, also for family offspring) for this purpose. The percentage of private residential property in Chinese metropolises has by now exceeded eighty percent. Compare these figures to Germany with slightly above fifty percent.

52   The high turnaround in Chinese neighborhoods is, among others, based on the practice of profiting from speculation in a booming housing market. In order to limit housing speculation, Shanghai decreed a five-year-hold on housing sales. This resulted in numerous Chinese families moving exactly after 'five years and a day'.

53   Here it becomes clear that the difference between city and country in China is a matter of closeness and distance, centrality and periphery. Country life doesn't constitute an opposite to city life; it only orbits the Imperial central star at a distance (cf. also Wu, Weijia 1993, 202f).

54   Max Weber's expression for an emerging society characterized by increasing impact or relevance of contracts, individuals, and science.

55   Some places, pavilions, fountains, and garden complexes were created during the first half of the eighteenth century according to plans of M. Benoist from France and G. Castiglione from Italy, missionaries and artists who were active at the Imperial court.

56   We can distinguish three generations or basic forms (cf. www.lilong.de): early lilong (beginning in 1860), intermediary lilong (from 1900 onward), and newer lilong (from 1920 onward). Aside from these basic forms, two special types have developed in the twentieth century: garden house lilong (from 1900 onward) and apartment lilong (from 1920 onward).

57   The lilong are often also called shikumen. This reflects the old southern Chinese origin of this settlement type.

58   The sky mirrored in the fountain's water led to calling interior courtyards 'Heavenly Fountains'.

59   Japanese residential culture, closer to Chinese residential culture, has in some cases influenced Shanghai's lilong (e.g. in the lilong at Sichuan Lu, in the vicinity of Luxun Park).

60   Confucian capitalism on the one hand shares the status of the family or clan with patronistic capitalism (e.g. of Italian coinage), and on the other hand shares the work ethos with Calvinist capitalism or the 'Protestant ethic' of southwestern German, Swiss or Dutch origin. While these advanced in terms of an institutional ethic, Confucian capitalism still remains in the secure hold of the family (cf. Souchou Yao 2002).

61   Shenyang's Golden Corridor is considered one of the most renowned of its kind in China today. It "enjoys the reputation of 'a place of fortune'". The city uses it to improve its image and for self-advertisement: "Where to go at this year's Lantern Festival? [...] Golden Corridor may become a charming place to visit since Shenyang city government has launched a lighting project for the golden corridor on December 15. The project taken part in by many Chinese and overseas lighting designers will be completed around February 2. Citizens could go along the corridor at lantern festival which falls on February 12, being inspired by the wonders created by the experts. Golden corridor starts at Beiling park in the north and terminates at Taoxian airport in the south with a total length of 17 kilometers and an average width of 1-2 kilometers" (www.sybuy.net/bbs/dispbbs.asp?boardID=29&ID=7669&page=4). We will return to the significance of lighting sculptures for the image of the Chinese city at night in the section on media cities (Chapter 5, section 'Mediapolis').

62   In the context of reading the Chinese city, I prefer the term 'perimeter block strip', since it rather directly reflects the combination of linear structures and perimeter block structures. The character of these perimeter block strips is, of course, not indebted to actual land ownership (reflected in individual lots, original German Parzelle) or rather land use rights, but articulates on this level the neighborhood-related decentral and small-scale character of retail and services.

63   The brace-like framing of residential linear structures with retail stores and service buildings is also known to Fordist urban planning in Europe. Examples can be found mostly in the new federal states of reunified Germany, e.g. in Dresden's Seestrasse.

64   Detaching commercial strips and streets as in the famous Karl-Marx-Haus in Chemnitz, obviously in reference to the European tradition of the piazza or the market place, is something I have only discovered once in China. This case is described further in this chapter in the type of the 'neighborhood pedestrian street'.

65   Floor area ratio (FAR) describes the ratio of floor area (in square meter) to lot area (in square meter): building area = lot size x FAR. In newer Chinese compounds, the FAR is likely to be above 0.8.

66   In detail in Chapter 6: Urban fictions.

67   The fuzziness of the terminological difference between 'city' and 'village' can be compared to the absence of the pronouns 'he' and 'she' in Chinese language.

68   According to Olaf Boustedt's typology, satellite cities as 'Satellitenstadt' are located within the city fringe and satellite cities as 'Trabantenstadt' are located outside of the city fringe (Boustedt 1970, Tab. 2, 3207 ff). The 'One City, Nine Villages' plan features both types.

69   "All of these towns have a common point: emphasizing sustainable development, ecological protection and industrial support" (Dai 2007).

70   The incipient industrial "Werksiedlungsbau" in the Ruhr area has left its mark on this landscape. Beyond Krupp's workers housing in Germany, the settlements by Pullman (Pullman Town in Chicago, 1880), Cadbury (Bournville near Birmingham, 1880) and Lever (Port Sunlight near Liverpool, 1887) are noteworthy as international examples (Kiess 1991).

71   Settlements orbiting London such as Welwyn or Letchworth, the 'Siedlung Hellerau' near Dresden, or the 'Margarethenhöhe' in Essen trace their origins to this movement.

72   For 'New Urbanism' in general, see Bodenschatz 2000.

73   At www.designbuild-network.com we read that "Organised by the Urban Planning Institute, One City, Nine Towns involves the creation of a series of satellite communities around Shanghai, each inspired by a country that played a pivotal role in the colonial and commercial history of the city. The nine countries are the UK, the USA, Russia, Spain, Sweden, France, the Netherlands, Germany and Italy."

74   In 1990 Shanghai statistics indicated 13 'towns'. In 1998 the number had reached 117! There is a direct connection between the enormous increase in numbers of 'towns' and redefining rural counties as urban districts: not only the increase in urban districts, but especially the strong increase in the number of towns provides an index for the enormous process of urbanization (Wu/Li 2002).

75   We define 'mimesis' as the imitation of an ideal spatial reality, for instance the structurally homologous reproduction of an urban basic form.

76   We know since Humpert et al. that this structural characteristic is not only due to adaptation to topographic conditions, but simultaneously (or mostly) to aesthetic ideals (Humpert/Schenk 2001).

77   The maintenance of the central climate control system is rumored to be correspondingly expensive, regardless of the number of users.

78   As I wrote these words in 2007, there were already rumors regarding Holland Village's future, but demolition seemed hardly imaginable due to the immense scale of the project. We are smarter today. In the already mentioned *South China Morning Post* of 19 September 2009 we read that Holland Village had already been torn down five months before, in May 2009. "Yang's development, which includes a full-size replica of the Peace Palace in The Hague, windmills, castles, a Venice water park, a zoo and vacation villas, was bulldozed." I would like to take the opportunity here to extend my gratitude to Maja Linnemann of the editorial staff of the German-Chinese Culture Network for sending me a copy of the *Morning Post* and, most of all, for her thoughtfulness.

79   Cinderella Castle is a free replica of Castle Neuschwanstein commissioned by the Bavarian King Ludwig II. Neuschwanstein in return was inspired by the *Book of Hours* of the French Duke of Berry, a small book featuring illustrations of twelve miniature castles by the brothers Limburg for the pleasure of the high aristocracy: one Berry-Castle per month, each more beautiful and grandly staged than the previous one.

80   The absence of a city/country–dichotomy is represented by the absence of landscape (as opposed to the cityscape). One characteristic representation, for instance, is Frank Lloyd Wright's vision of Broadacre City. In the U.S.A., wilderness on the one hand and town and country on the other hand comprise a dualism. In Europe, in contrast, we find the differentiated trinity of landscape, cityscape, and wilderness, while wilderness is rather of a mythical character. It may very well be that landscape theory, originated in the U.S.A., has not given this fundamental difference appropriate attention or importance.

81   According to Mirjam Bürgi, Georg Simmel, by the use of his term of 'experiencing', anticipated modern metropolitans' event-orientedness (Erlebnisorientierung) (Bürgi 2003).

82   This important sociological term was coined by Pierre Bourdieu in his book *Distinction: A Social Critique of the Judgment of Taste* (Bourdieu 1986).

83   The phenomenon this neologism points out is as follows: while the size of a city built in time might be much bigger than that of a city built in space, the city built in time (the bigger one), however, can be crossed in only a fraction of the latter – of course, by car! (Fishman 1996/1997)

84   In the USA, approximately 1,000 people have 950 cars, in Germany 550, in China currently about fifteen. However, car ownership is increasing dramatically. In Shanghai, the number of cars rose by eighty percent from 2006 to 2007 and reached about two million cars in 2007. For each one of the 67,000 issued license plates in 2005, Shanghai residents paid on average more than 3,000 Euros (about 30,000 RMB).

85   We can see that the large degree of attention that concentric loop or bypass roads receive in mega-cities leads to a certain degree of neglect of radial streets.

86   Each company has a responsible manager for the village fire department in its community committee who runs a 'fireproofing office'. This unity reflects the particular challenge of protecting a built environment from fire if streets are impassable for regular fire trucks and vehicles.

87   In Xi'an in 2003 we observed urban villages specializing in Internet teahouses. Customers are mostly students from universities in the vicinity who are looking for efficient and open alternatives to chronically clogged Internet access terminals in their universities.

88   Ma Hang counts 241 'villages' in Shenzhen, 139 in Guangzhou, and 417 in Xi'an in central China (Ma 2006, 25). The average area covered by villages in Shenzhen's inner city districts is significantly higher than twenty percent (Ma 2006, 166).

89   For a slightly one-sided evaluation, in my opinion, of Jerusalem as guiding image in European urban history cf. Badde 1999. The urban-critical dimension in the case of the 'Leitbild Jerusalem' is posed by equaling the 'civitas' (Episcopal residency, alternatively temple or castle town) with the bourgeois city.

90   On general urban development in China cf. also Yusuf, Shahid, and Wu, Weiping 1997.

91   In order to understand the calculation of settlement density, the differentiation between inner city, suburban, and country districts (counties) is very important. In this regard, the Chinese district model differs e.g. from the German system, where counties or country districts (Landkreise) are regional bodies, i.e. municipalities independent from cities.

92   Following the example of Shanghai, Shenyang also plans the construction of satellite cities for urban relief. Since they are intended to be built within the urban periphery (urbanized zone and peripheral zone), we should consider them satellite cities. In analogy to Shanghai's plan, Shenyang's plan was named the 'One City, Four Towns Plan' (Shenyang Urban and Rural Construction Committee 2006).

93   This periodization was influenced by writings of French economist and politician Alain Lipietz, especially his explications on so-called 'regulation theory' (Lipietz 1992 and 1991).

94   This formulation cites a renowned book by Göderitz, Rainer, and Hoffmann on the dominating urban guiding image (Leitbild) in Germany immediately after the end of World War II (Göderitz et al. 1957; Whittick 2007).

95   It is no coincidence that the structuralistic perspective was, from the very beginning, inseparably connected to the semiotic method and actually originated from it (de Saussure 1986).

96   In German language, the term 'society' is used colloquially in such a general manner that it also includes 'community'. Tribal communities are thus also described as societies just as feudal or modern societies. This doesn't necessarily make the sociological use of the term society any easier.

97   We understand a social or socio-spatial system as a 'total institution' that is comprised of numerous subsystems that are not yet or only marginally differentiated in terms of division of labor and thus also marginally spatially differentiated. If the historic market place is also the locus of trade, of jurisdiction, of assembly, of information, of education or of spiritual cult, then it is a 'total institution'.

98   The entire echelon of great German sociologists of the nineteenth and twentieth century, from Marx to Tönnies, from Weber to Simmel, recognized this interrelation – but interpreted it differently. Marx intended to abolish the bourgeois society by revolution; the rather conservative Tönnies wanted to maintain community and strengthen it; the liberal Weber, who approved of bourgeois society, wanted to control it by use of an institutionalized ethics of responsibility (opposing an ethics of convictions); and Simmel discovered that urbanized, modern individuals were capable of choosing their own way of living in communities.

99   In Europe, two synecistic revolutions occurred that produced momentous results. From peasantry-based synecism emerged the Greek polis, which gained a decisive influence in the entire development of Greek and Roman antiquity. From urban bourgeois synecism emerged the urban culture of the High Middle Ages, the first urban cultural revolution of which we generally know as the 'Renaissance', the first great attempt at liberating individualistic, secular, scientific, enlightened thought. In interaction with centralistically organized politics and a liberally structured market, China currently attempts to venture a path of development without recurring to the urban bourgeois heritage of Europe.

100   In the medieval city, generally only a financially solvent, patrician faction of the urban bourgeoisie held the privilege of voting.

101   The term of a 'forced synecism' used by Weber (1978) in the context of his sinological studies is something we consider as a 'contradictio in adjecto'; reason being that the subject of synecism cannot be external to the synecistic result (the bourgeois city). A mandated 'settling together' (Zusammensiedlung) in the form of a so-called municipal reform should, in our opinion, not be identified as a form of synecism. In the genealogy of the medieval European city, the synecism based on trade and artisanship marks the transition from a feudal agricultural cooperative (Markgenossenschaft) to a bourgeois market cooperative (Marktgenossenschaft) (cf. also Maurer 1869/1962).

102   We understand as 'heterotopia', in loose reference to Foucault and Lefèbvre, places which have lost their genuine context or have not found it yet; places that are situated in a reality that is no longer or not yet their own. They refer to things past – or also things to come – within the present. The opposite of heterotopia is isotopia. We describe a place as isotopia that is situated within a context that it is related to. An isotopic place is identical to its spatial context.

103   This can be valid for Europe as well: A civitas (Episcopal residency) or castle (domain of a feudal lord) only becomes a city through the presence of 'citizens'. We can generalize this in historic terms inasmuch that only the presence of institutions of market economy transform a place (village) into a city. City denotes market economy. In principle, a city doesn't feature an autarkic or self-sufficient mode of economy.

BIBLIOGRAPHY

Augé, Marc. *Non-Places: Introduction to an Anthropology of Supermodernity.* Malden (USA), Oxford (UK): Blackwell Publishers,1995

Arkaraprasertkul, Non. *Shanghai Contemporary – The Politics of Built Form. How Divergent Planning Methods Transformed Shanghai's Urban Identity.* Saarbrücken: VDM Verlag Dr. Müller, 2009

Badde, Paul. *Die himmlische Stadt – Der abendländische Traum von der gerechten Gesellschaft.* Munich: Luchterhand Literaturverlag, 1999

Bahrdt, Hans Paul. *Die moderne Großstadt.* Reinbek: Rowohlt Verlag, 1961

Barthes, Roland. *Mythologies.* New York: Simon & Schuster, 1973

+ *The Pleasure of the Text.* New York (Hill and Wang), 1976

+ 'Semiology and the Urban.' In *The City and the Sign,* edited by Mark Gottdiener and Alexandros Lagopoulos. New York: Columbia University Press, 1986

Beck, Ulrich. *World at Risk.* New York: Wiley and Sons, 2008

+ *Die Erfindung des Politischen.* Frankfurt/Main: Suhrkamp, 1993

Bell, Daniel. *China's New Confucianism: Politics and Everyday Life in a Changing Society.* Princeton: Princeton University Press, 2008

Benevolo, Leonardo. *The History of the City.* Cambridge: MIT Press, 1980

Benjamin, Walter. *Das Passagenwerk. In Gesammelte Schriften V, I und II.* Frankfurt/Main: Suhrkamp, 1991

+ *The Arcades Project,* translated by Howard Eiland and Kevin McLaughlin. Cambridge: Harvard University Press, 1999

Bodenschatz, Harald. 'New Urbanism. Die Neuerfindung der amerikanischen Stadt' In *Stadtbauwelt* 145, 2000

Bourdieu, Pierre. *Distinction: A Social Critique of the Judgment of Taste.* New York: Routledge, 1986

Boustedt, Olaf. *Stadtregionen. In Handwörterbuch der Raumforschung und Raumordnung.* Hanover: Akademie für Raumordnung und Landesplanung, 1970

Bürgi, Mirjam. *Die Moderne im Verständnis von Georg Simmel.* Zurich: Internet-Publication, 2003

Busch, Joachim and Angelika Ebrecht. 'Die Intimisierung der Öffentlichkeit. Zur Psychologie und Politik eines Strukturwandels.' In *Psychosozial* 28 (2005). Vol. 1, No. 99

Cai, Jonjie and Hongtao, Bo. 'Anting Neustadt – Die Transposition europäischer Raumformen nach China.' In *Die aufgeschlossene Stadt – Öffentlicher Raum in China von Anting bis Zhuhai,* edited by Dieter Hassenpflug. Weimar: VDG, 2004

Campanella, Thomas J. *The Concrete Dragon. China's Urban Revolution and what it Means for the World.* New York: Princeton Architectural Press, 2008

Chiang-Schreiber, Uei. *Chinesisches Multivitamin.* www.chinesisch-training.de, 20 October 2007

Chiang, Shiao-Yun. 'Interformative Meaning of Signs: Brand Naming and Globalization in China.' In *Social Semiotics,* Vol. 19, Issue 3, September 2009: 329–344

Childe, V. Gordon. *What happened in History.* Harmondsworth: Penguin, 1942

+ *Stufen der Kultur. Von der Urzeit zur Antike.* Stuttgart: Kohlhammer, 1952

Christ, Wolfgang and Lars Bölling. *Bilder einer Zwischenstadt. Ikonographie und Szenographie eines Urbanisierungsprozesses.* Wuppertal: Müller und Busmann), 2006

Cohen, Yehudi A. *Man in Adaption – The Institutional Framework.* Chicago: Aldine Atherton, 1971

Dahrendorf, Lord Ralf. *Life Chances: Approaches to Social and Political Theory.* Chicago: University of Chicago Press, 1981

Dai, Qian. *Living in a Small Town.* In www.expo2010china.com/expo/expoenglish/wem/0502/userobject1 ai36247.html, 27 August 2007

Dong, Nan Nan and Stefanie Ruff. 'Managing Urban Growth in Shanghai.' In *City Strategies* 58 (2007): 32–35

Eco, Umberto. *A Theory of Semiotics.*
Bloomington: Indiana University Press, 1979
+ *Einführung in die Semiotik.*
Munich: duv, 1972/94

Elias, Norbert. *The Civilizing Process.*
Malden (USA), Oxford (UK): Blackwell
Publishers, 2000

Fingerhuth, Carl. *Learning from China.*
The Tao of the City.
Basel: Birkhäuser Verlag, 2004

Fishman, Robert. 'Bourgeois Utopias – Visions of
Suburbia.' In *Readings in Urban Theory,* edited by
Fainstein, Susan S. and Campbell Scott. Malden
(USA), Oxford (UK): Blackwell Publishers, 1996/97

Friedmann, John. *China's Urban Transition.*
Minneapolis: University of Minnesota Press,
2005

Gehlen, Arnold. *Moral und Hypermoral –*
Eine pluralistische Ethik.
Frankfurt/Main: Klostermann Verlag, 2004
+ *Man: His Nature and Place in the World.* New York:
Columbia University Press, 1988

Godelier, Maurice. *The Making of Great Men.*
Male Domination and Power among the New Guinea
Baruya.
Cambridge: Cambridge University Press, 1986

Göderitz, Johannes, Roland Rainer and
Hubert Hoffmann. *Die gegliederte und aufgelocker-*
te Stadt. Tübingen: Wasmuth Verlag, 1957. Some
information about the subject of this book in
English: Whittick, Arnold. *European Architecture*
in the Twentieth Century, Vol. 1.
Goodridge: Dodo Press, 2007

Gottdiener, Marc and Ray Hutchison. *The New*
Urban Sociology. Boulder: Westview Press, 2005

Gottdiener, Marc. 'Culture, Ideology, and the
Sign of the City.' In *The City and the Sign.*
An Introduction to Urban Semiotics, edited by
Mark Gottdiener and Alexandros Lagopoulos.
New York: Columbia University Press, 1986
+ *Postmodern Semiotics: Material Culture*
and the Forms of Postmodern Life.
Oxford, Cambridge: Blackwell Publishers, 1995
+ 'Urban Culture.' In *Encyclopedia of Semiotics.*
Berlin: Monton de Gruyter, 1994

Habermas, Jürgen. *The Theory of Communicative*
Action. Cambridge: Polity Press, 1986 (German:
Theorie des kommunikativen Handelns, I and II.
Frankfurt/Main: Suhrkamp 1981)

Halik, Ümut and Johannes Küchler. 'Es grünt so
grün – Chinas Stadtgrün.' In *archplus* 168,
Berlin 2004

Hall, Edward T. *Beyond Culture.* New York:
Anchor Books, 1976

Hardinghaus, Matthias. *Zur amerikanischen*
Entwicklung der Stadt. Frankfurt/Main:
Peter Lang Verlag, 2004

Harten, Hans-Christian and Elke Harten.
Die Versöhnung mit der Natur – Gärten, Freiheits-
bäume, republikanische Wälder, heilige Berge
und Tugendparks in der Französischen Revolution.
Reinbek: Rowohlt, 1989

Hassenpflug, Dieter. 'Citytainment oder die
Zukunft des öffentlichen Raums.' In *Metropolen,*
Laboratorien der Moderne, edited by
Dirk Matejovski. Frankfurt/Main, New York:
Campus, 2000
+ 'Walter Benjamin – Looking at the Dream-Side
of the City.' In *Cities in Transition,* edited
by Arie Graafland and Deborah Hauptmann.
Rotterdam: 010 Publishers, 2001
+ 'Die Produktion des öffentlichen Raums in
China.' In *Die aufgeschlossene Stadt,* edited by
Dieter Hassenpflug. Weimar: VDG, 2004a
+ 'Some Remarks on Urban Signs and Symbols in
History.' In *City Images and Urban Regeneration,*
edited by Frank Eckardt and Peter Kreisl.
Frankfurt/Main, New York: Peter Lang
Publishing Group, 2004b
+ Sobre centralidade urbana. In www.vitruvius.
com.br/arquitextos/arq085/arq 085—00.asp,
20 March 2006a
+ 'Stadtbilder.' In *Reflexive Urbanistik – Reden*
und Aufsätze zur europäischen Stadt, edited
by Dieter Hassenpflug. Weimar: Verlag der
Bauhaus-Universität Weimar, 2006b
+ 'Reflexive Urbanistik.' In *Reflexive Urbanistik –*
Reden und Aufsätze zur europäischen Stadt,
edited by Dieter Hassenpflug. Weimar: Verlag
der Bauhaus-Universität Weimar, 2006c

+ 'Die Lärmverletzlichkeit der leisen Stadt.' In *Die leise Stadt,* edited by Alexander Schmidt and Reinhard Jammers. Essen: red dot edition, 2006d

Hegel, Georg W. F. *Elements of the Philosophy of Right.* Cambridge: Cambridge University Press, 1991

Hu, Jia. *Chinesisch Planen – Deutsch Planen.* In www.stadtkultur-international.de/doks/nadst. June 15, 2006

Humpert, Klaus and Martin Schenk. *Entdeckung der mittelalterlichen Stadtplanung –Das Ende vom Mythos der gewachsenen Stadt.* Stuttgart: DTV, 2001

Ipsen, Detlev. 'High Speed-Urbanismus.' In *archplus* 168. Berlin 2004

Kiess, Walter. *Urbanismus im Industriezeitalter – Von der klassizistischen Stadt zur Garden City.* Berlin: Ernst & Sohn, 1991

Kögel, Eduard. *Zwei Poelzigschüler in der Emigration: Rudolf Hamburger und Richard Paulick zwischen Shanghai und Ost-Berlin (1930–1955).* Diss. Bauhaus-University Weimar, 2007

+ 'Informeller Urbanismus.' In *archplus* 168, 2004a

+ 'Von der Nachbarschaft zur Gated Community? Planungsprinzipien der Stadt in der V.R. China.' In TRIALOG Nr. 81, Darmstadt 2004b

+ 'Stadtöffentlichkeit und leerer Raum.' In *Stadtbauwelt* 12, Berlin 2005

König, René. 'Großstadt.' In *Handbuch der empirischen Sozialforschung,* Vol. 10. F. Stuttgart: Enke Verlag, 1977

Kracauer, Siegfried. 'The Mass Ornament.' In *Weimar Essays,* edited by Levin T.Y. Boston: Harvard University Press, 1995

Lefèbvre, Henri. *Writings on Cities.* Malden (USA), Oxford (UK): Blackwell Publishers, 1995

+ *The Production of Space.* New York: Wiley & Sons, 1991

Li, Sandy. 'Dream City Falls into Ruin with Builder.' In *South China Morning Post.* 19 September 2009

Lichtenberger, Elisabeth. *Die Stadt – Von der Polis zur Metropolis.* Darmstadt: Wissenschaftliche Buchgesellschaft, 2002

Lipietz, Alain. *Towards a New Economic Order: Postfordism, Ecology and Democracy.* Oxford: Oxford University Press, 1992

+ 'Zur Zukunft der städtischen Ökologie – ein regulationstheoretischer Beitrag.' In *StadtRäume,* edited by Martin Wentz. Frankfurt/Main, New York: Campus, 1991

Logan, John, R. (ed). *Urban China in Transition.* New York: Wiley & Sons, 2008

Lü, Junhua and Shao Lei. 'Housing Development from 1978 to 2000 after China Adopted Reform and Opening-up Policies.' In *Modern Urban Housing in China, 1840–2000,* edited by Lü Junhua, Peter G. Rowe and Zhang Jie. Munich, London, New York: Prestel Verlag, 2001

Lu, Duanfang. *Remaking Chinese Urban Form: Modernity, Scarcity and Space, 1949–2005.* New York: Routledge, 2005

Lu, Xin. *China, China – Western Architects and City Planners in China.* Berlin: Hatje Cantz Verlag, 2008

Lynch, Kevin. *The Image of the City.* Cambridge: Harvard University Press, 1960

Ma, Hang. *'Villages' in Shenzhen – Persistence and Transformation of an Old Social System in an Emerging Mega City.* Diss. Bauhaus-University Weimar, 2006

Maurer, Georg L. v. *Geschichte der Städteverfassung in Deutschland.* 2. Vols. Erlangen /Aalen: F. Enke Verlag, 1869/1962

Münch, Barbara. 'Verborgene Kontinuitäten des chinesischen Urbanismus.' In *archplus* 168, Berlin 2004

Oldiges, Victor. 'Ideal und Gemuetlich: Two more Satellites Tested.' In *Sinocities blog,* 16 Mai 2007

Peirce, Charles S. 'Peirce on Signs.' In *Writings on Semiotics,* edited by Charles Peirce and James Hoopes. Chapel Hill: University of North Carolina Press, 1991

Polanyi, Karl. *Trade and Market in the Early Empires.* New York: The Free Press, 1957

Polanyi, Karl. *Ökonomie und Gesellschaft.* Frankfurt/Main: Suhrkamp, 1979

Rossi, Aldo. *The Architecture of the City.* Cambridge: The MIT Press, 1984

Rowe, Peter. *East Asia Modern. Shaping the Contemporary City.* London: Reaktion Books, 2005

Ruff, Stefanie. *Between Walls – Reprogramming Residual Urban Space in Beijing.* Master thesis, Bauhaus-University Weimar, 2007

Saussure, Ferdinand de. *Course in General Linguistics.* Chicago: Open Court Publishing Company, 1986

Schmied-Kowarzik, Wolfdietrich. *Das dialektische Verhältnis des Menschen zur Natur.* Freiburg/Munich: Verlag Karl Alber, 1984

+ 'Von der wirklichen, von der seyenden Natur, Schellings Ringen um eine Naturphilosophie in Auseinandersetzung mit Kant, Fichte und Hegel.' In *Schellingiana* 8. Frommann-Holzboog, 1996

Schmidt-Glintzer, Helwig. *China – Vielvölkerreich und Einheitsstaat.* Munich: Beck, 1997

Schulze, Gerhard. *The Experience Society.* London: Sage, 2007

Shanghai Municipal Statistics Bureau. *Shanghai Statistical Yearbook.* Shanghai: China Statistics Press, 2009

Sheng, Haitao. *Chinesische Themenparks – Kulturimbiss für das Volk.* In www. stadtkulturinternational. de /pubshen/099—SHENG—HAITAO 1004.PDF, 10 May 2007

Shenyang Urban and Rural Construction Committee. *New Century New Shenyang,* edited by Xing Kai, Hou Bowei, Qin Wenjun et al. Shenyang, 2006

Sieverts, Thomas. *Cities Without Cities: Between Place and World, Space and Time, Town and Country.* Abingdon, Florence: Routledge Chapman & Hall, 2003

Simmel, Georg. *Soziologie. Untersuchungen über die Formen der Vergesellschaftung.* GA Vol. 2. Frankfurt/Main: Suhrkamp, 1992

Song, Yan and Chengri Ding (eds.). *Urbanization in China: Critical Issues in an Era of Rapid Growth.* Cambridge: Lincoln Institute of Land Policy, 2007

Sorkin, Michael. 'See You in Disneyland.' In *Variations on a Theme Park,* edited by Michael Sorkin. New York: Macmillan, 1992

Souchou, Yao. *Confucian Capitalism – Discourse, Practice ant the Myth of Chinese Enterprise.* London, New York: Routledge Curzon, 2002

Stockman, Norman. *Understanding Chinese Society.* Cambridge: Polity Press, 2000

Tönnies, Ferdinand. *Community and Society: Gemeinschaft and Gesellschaft.* New Jersey: Aldine Transaction Publishers, 1988

Ulman, G. L. *The Science of Society. Toward an Understanding of the Life and Work of Karl August Wittfogel.* Berlin: Walter de Gruyter, 1978

Vivelo, Frank Robert. *Cultural Anthropology Handbook.* New York: McGraw-Hill Inc., 1978

Volli, Ugo. *Semiotik. Eine Einführung in ihre Grundbegriffe.* Tübingen/Basle: A. Francke Verlag, 2002

Weber, Max. *Economy and Society. An Outline of Interpretive Sociology* (edited by G. Roth and C. Wittich). Berkeley, Los Angeles: University of California Press, 1978

White, Morton and Lucia. *The Intellectual versus the City: from Thomas Jefferson to Frank Lloyd Wright.* Cambridge: Harvard University Press, 1962

Wittfogel, Karl August. *Oriental Despotism. A Comparative Study of Total Power.* New Haven: Yale University Press, 1957

Wu, Duo and Taibin Li. 'The Present Situation and Prospective Development of the Shanghai Urban Community.' In *The New Chinese City – Globalization and Market Reform.* Oxford: Blackwell, 2002

Wu, Fulong. *Packaging a New Way of (Sub-)Urban Life: Gated Communities and Chinese New Urbanism.* Cardiff: Cardiff University Paper, 2006

+ *China's Emerging Cities: The Making of New Urbanism.* Abingdon, New York: Routledge, 2007

Wu, Weijia. *Stadtgestalt und Stadtgestaltbedeutung.* Diss. TU München, Munich 1993

Xu, Yinong. *The Chinese City in Space and Time – The Development of Urban Form in Suzhou.* Honolulu: University of Hawai'i Press, 2000

Yan, Xiaopei, Jia Li, Jianping Li, and Jizhuan Weng. 'The Development of the Chinese Metropolis in the Period of Transition.' In *The New Chinese City – Globalization and Market Reform,* edited by John R. Malden Logan (USA), Oxford (UK): Blackwell, 2002

Yusuf, Shahid and Weiping Wu. *The Dynamics of Urban Growth in Three Chinese Cities.* New York: Oxford University Press, Washington (World Bank), 1997

Zhang, Lingling. 'Ein öffentlicher Raum für eine nord-ost-chinesische Stadt.' In *Die aufgeschlossene Stadt,* edited by Dieter Hassenpflug. Weimar: VDG, 2004

Zhang, Guangzeng. 'Struktur und Wandel des öffentlichen Raums in Shanghai.' In *Die aufgeschlossene Stadt,* edited by Dieter Hassenpflug. Weimar: VDG, 2004

Zhang, Minjie. 'Arbeitsmigration in China.' In *Utopie kreativ,* No. 164, 2004

Zhang, Yushu. *Goethe und die chinesische Klassik.* In www.info.sophia.ac.jp/g-areas/DE-Goethe-SymZhang.htm, 7 July 2007

Ziegler, Edward. *China's New Towns, Housing, Sprawl, the Automobile and Sustainable Development.* In ENHR Conference-Papers Ljubljana, 2006

ILLUSTRATION CREDITS

Page 45: Model, Sìhéyuàn (Exhibition ABB I, Luo Li, Che Fei 2006)

Page 70: Strategic Plan of Beijing (2004–2010): Municipal Institute of City Planning & Design (BICP), Beijing

Page 72: Shenyang Urban and Rural Construction Committee (2006): New Century – New Shenyang (eds.: Xing Kai, Hou Bowei, Qin Wenjun et al.), Shenyang

Page 89: Municipality of Harbin (2004): Planning Exhibition of Harbin

Page 89: Municipality of Shenzhen (2002), City Planning Exhibition

Page 134: Shenyang Urban and Rural Construction Committee (2006): New Century – New Shenyang (eds.: Xing Kai, Hou Bowei, Qin Wenjun et al.), Shenyang

Page 134: Municipality of Harbin (2004): Planning Exhibition of Harbin

Page 146: Ma Hang (2006)

All photos, illustrations, graphics, tables by the author unless otherwise noted

IMPRINT

This book was originally published in a
German edition (*Der urbane Code Chinas*) as
volume 142 of the series Bauwelt Fundamente.
The translation of this work was supported
by a grant from the Goethe-Institut which
is funded by the German Ministry of Foreign
Affairs and by the University Duisburg-Essen,
Main Research Area 'Urban Systems'.

Translation from German into English:
Mark Kammerbauer
Proof reading: Julia Dawson
Graphic design: Andreas Hidber, Actar Pro
Paper: PlanoPlus 120 g/m², Mirricad Gold 270 g/m²
Printed on acid-free paper produced from
chlorine-free pulp. TCF ∞
Printing: fgb. freiburger graphische betriebe

A CIP catalogue record for this book is available from
the Library of Congress, Washington D.C., USA.

Bibliographic information published by the
German National Library. The German National
Library lists this publication in the Deutsche
Nationalbibliografie; detailed bibliographic data
are available on the Internet at http://dnb.d-nb.de.

© 2010 Birkhäuser GmbH, Basel
P.O. Box, CH-4002 Basel, Switzerland

ISBN 978-3-0346-0572-4

9 8 7 6 5 4 3 2 1
www.birkhauser.ch